WORLD MAKING IN NEPANTLA

WORLD MAKING IN NEPANTLA

Feminists of Color Navigating Life
and Work in the Pandemic

*Edited by Gloria González-López, Sharmila
Rudrappa, and Christen A. Smith*

University of Texas Press   *Austin*

Requests for permission to reproduce material from this work should be sent to permissions@utpress.utexas.edu.

♾ The paper used in this book meets the minimum requirements of ANSI/NISO Z39.48–1992 (R1997) (Permanence of Paper).

Library of Congress Cataloging-in-Publication Data

Names: González-López, Gloria, editor | Rudrappa, Sharmila, editor | Smith, Christen A., editor
Title: World making in nepantla : feminists of color navigating life and work in the pandemic / edited by Gloria González-López, Sharmila Rudrappa, and Christen Smith.
Description: First edition. | Austin : University of Texas Press, 2025. | Includes bibliographical references
Identifiers: LCCN 2025013871 (print) | LCCN 2025013872 (ebook)
   ISBN 978-1-4773-3299-3 (hardcover)
   ISBN 978-1-4773-3338-9 (paperback)
   ISBN 978-1-4773-3300-6 (pdf)
   ISBN 978-1-4773-3301-3 (epub)
Subjects: LCSH: Minority women—Social conditions | COVID-19 Pandemic, 2020-2023—Social aspects
Classification: LCC HQ1161 .W676 2025 (print) | LCC HQ1161 (ebook)
LC record available at https://lccn.loc.gov/2025013871
LC ebook record available at https://lccn.loc.gov/2025013872

doi:10.7560/332993

The University of Texas Press gratefully acknowledges the Louann Atkins Temple Women & Culture Endowment for its support of this publication.

We honor the memory of the millions of lives lost during the COVID-19 pandemic

and the inspirational human beings who gave their hearts and souls

to take care of them

and our world in pain.

With love and gratitude.

CONTENTS

PART VII. UTOPIA
"The Language of Love . . . Will You Speak It with Me?"

WORLD MAKING IN NEPANTLA

INTRODUCTION

*Sharmila Rudrappa, Gloria González-López, and
Christen A. Smith*

AS THE COVID-19 LOCKDOWNS ROLLED in, on March 15, 2020, Christen A. Smith sent an email out as the director of the Center for Women's
and Gender Studies (CWGS) at the University of Texas at Austin. "Dear
CWGS Community," she began,

> We hope this email finds you well despite all of the tension and
> chaos of the moment. At the risk of over-filling your inboxes, we
> wanted to send a message of feminist and queer solidarity as the
> University (and the world) faces the coronavirus pandemic. First,
> we want to clearly acknowledge the privilege that we have work-
> ing in academia, where it is possible for many of us to work from
> home with flexible schedules. That means we have a large role to
> play in "flattening the curve" so that health care resources can go
> to those who must work or are especially vulnerable to a conta-
> gious disease.

Different versions of this kind of message circulated in many institutions of
higher education in the United States and around the world. What seemed
at the time like a momentary blip in our lives, the pandemic continued
to have devastating effects on us, our loved ones, and our communities
around the world. Millions did not survive.

As feminist ethnographers, all cisgender women of color, the three of
us felt compelled to document the collective experience of fear, apprehension, despair, and death we experienced individually and collectively within
the US academe. We wanted to hear from other feminists of color: those in
the working space of US academia, some students, and others in far more
tenuous positions as untenured faculty or adjunct colleagues. Our official
invitation for contributions very early in the pandemic lockdown, titled

"World Making in Nepantla: Feminist Ideals for Pandemic Times," invited US-based feminists of color to share their engagements with the pandemic and the subsequent quarantine. We asked how the pandemic shaped their personal lives, families, and communities. What were their greatest fears, and how were they coping? What interventions did they propose, given the realities of national boundaries and a flatlining economy? How did they imagine an alternative post-pandemic future? We were not disappointed; our contributors offered possibilities for radical hope and love, and richly imaginative alternative futures for families and communities of color.

In this anthology we turn to the concept of *nepantla*, a term used by the Nahuas peoples and adopted by Gloria E. Anzaldúa to mean *en medio*, or a space in between, neither here nor there, a point that is simultaneously alarming and promising but always charged with possibilities for safer, more beautiful worlds.[1] The pandemic found us suspended in time and space, not working/working, in isolation yet not, as we all collectively withdrew into our homes. We were in limbo, wondering when we would resume our older lives, whether that was even possible, given the crises we ourselves were in, as were our families and our communities. What would life look like on the other side of the pandemic, or at the very least, on the other side of quarantine lockdowns? The essays and poems presented here are testimonies to floating in ambiguity, a place of being in transition, a potential for reinvention of the personal and the political. The many variants of SARS-CoV-2 led to mass death. We lost our own loved ones, but we were also flooded with images on our screens of patients on gurneys in hospital corridors, refrigerated trucks still holding hundreds of bodies of COVID-19 victims, funeral homes overflowing, so many mass cremations in India that city parks and trees were denuded of branches. We were not there when our loved ones passed on, and there was no space or time for the rituals of death to bring closure and peace to their souls and ours.

With so much death and suffering, our worlds came to a screeching halt. Not being at work, in those early months before we got pulled into the busyness of Zoom, we had time to pause. We breathed, as Faith Deckard reminds us in her essay. We had time to listen to ourselves and to our loved ones, and abide by our/their boredoms, anxieties, fears, and hopes. The forced interlude of the quarantine led to new ways of being simply because we were not doing the same old thing, again and again. We had to learn to discard old habits and attempt to learn new ones. Gardening. Baking. Sewing. For those of us who had the space, walking in parks and woods, wandering aimlessly to clear the mind. We were forced to learn to be at peace with the beasts that screamed inside our heads and inside our hearts. What did these beasts want to be fed? And how could one tend to them so they would not consume us slowly, limb after limb? We needed to learn not to eradicate the monsters that raged within us but to make space for them, and to live with them. The sickness that we were feeling might have been felt deep within, but its sources were all external. We needed to learn resilience to make that peace. Pandemic lockdowns restructured time and relationships, which provided some space to attempt inner quietude.

We also need to note that those early pandemic days that brought mass death and heartbreak and so much horror also ushered in strange beauty. The virus affected the upper respiratory tracts of those afflicted, but many of us who were uninfected, from Los Angeles to Delhi, breathed easier for a few months. The unprecedented reduction in global economic activity and transportation—business as usual—meant fewer emissions and fewer pollutants in the air.[2] Air quality improved. Air pollution is a major issue with critical toxicological effects on human health. A World Health Organization report states that about 7 million people die worldwide, every year, due to air pollution.[3] Why did it take this awful pandemic for us to collectively slow down so we could all breathe easier?

Waterways also cleared up. During the pandemic lockdown period, industrial sources of pollution shrank as factories and workshops slowed down operations or completely stopped, which reduced water pollution.[4] People recorded dolphin appearances where they had not been sighted in decades.[5] Fish diversity improved in the seas because previously timid fish that had hidden because of human activity appeared once again.[6] Like the air, the waters became cleaner and quieter for a few months.

Coyotes, deer, and pumas became braver, wandering into neighborhoods and now-quiet streets. Birds responded to less human activity. Some species like pigeons suffered population losses because there was far less food waste. Other species flocked to cities during lockdown—or perhaps human urban dwellers were now noticing birds in ways they never had before. Sea birds began expanding their nesting sites. But without human activity, raptors, too, arrived and stressed nesting endangered birds.

Just as earthquakes and volcanoes cause the Earth's crust to move, so do the vibrations caused by cars, trucks, trains, and industrial machinery. With the pandemic lockdowns, our incessant human movement and our pounding of the earth's surface was suspended. Seismometers measuring the earth's movement now recorded an eerie quiet. Poignantly, a geophysicist noted that it was "now easier to hear Earth's voice above the anthropogenic noise."[7] Because of all we had learned, would we now begin to listen to this other voice that had been shouted down and drowned out?

Scientists have proposed the word *anthropause* to describe the unparalleled reduction in human economic and social activity, as well as mobility on land, in the air, and at sea.[8] Amid all this devastating loss, what beautiful things could we as humans have learned during the anthropause? One way to think about the pandemic is to not focus only on despair, because it has not simply been all death, death, and death. Accompanying all this death are other kinds of possibilities, other ways to understand the worlds we inhabit. The pandemic is that collective nepantla, that transition, ambiguity, place of despair but also place of endless possibilities.

The impetus for this book was to document our lives, our individual and collective experiences, as we made sense of a world dominated by a virus while socially isolated but simultaneously deeply interconnected by chaos, death, and radical hope. All three of us, too, were affected. We were unable to go home, halfway across the world, to see parents and loved ones who seemed to be aging faster and faster with each passing day. It would be unreal for us to maintain that all three of us learned new ways of being through the pandemic, and that we somehow persisted in spite of all the odds and emerged better feminists and better people by the end of it all. We need to recognize that suffering does not always lead to deeper knowledge; often, suffering is just that. It is simply enduring grief, anguish, and misery, and hoping that the pain shall be dulled eventually. Our experiences over the course of suffering are multivalent: Sometimes there is the effervescence of hope, but the next day it evaporates and throws us in the absolute depths of despair. Even the ways by which we cope with despair can vary—some days we're curled up into tight balls of human flesh under blankets. And other times we might lie in the grass and watch the clouds drift by. Still other times, seeking the simple pleasures of childhood, we might play in the mud.

Sharmila

Not knowing what to do with this endless death, of burning funeral pyres up and down the Ganga, of lockdowns and migrant worker deaths, I planted an imperfect garden. I learned to not kill all the bugs but to leave some greens for the caterpillars. It was not the end of the world (yes, it is true!) to have deformed fruit. I learned to share the fig tree with the squirrels that perhaps needed those figs more than I did. Through the labor of growing okra that summer of 2020, I learned the perfection of seeds, of something that might look so inert and dead but carries the potential of growth, life, and more life. Plants are a lesson in resilience; they stand there uncomplaining in one single spot, unmoved, under blessed showers and the scorching sun, knowing that regardless of what is rained down on them, or perhaps *because of* it, they will continue to grow until they, too, must let go. But in the meantime, they flower and feed the bees and the butterflies. They go to seed and feed bugs, beetles, and birds. The end of their life is a transcendence because many things live because of them. A small lesson to learn through gardening is this: The end of life lies not in death but in hopelessness.

I also spent endless time with my cat, who would climb up to the roof and insist I follow her up. On random days and evenings over the course of 2020–2021, you might have found me and my cat up on the roof either at noon or at 9:00 p.m. We would sit together, the cat on my lap, looking at the world around and hearing the sounds that drifted up. Soon I began to realize that the cat was taking care of me; each time I despaired, the cat meowed and called me out to sit on the roof under the pecan trees. In caring for my cat, I learned that there are other ways of being in this world, that it is okay to sit and while away time under the clouds and the stars, thinking of just the here and the now, simply focusing on the leaves that tremble on the trees. The lesson in focusing on the garden and the cat is that human time is just one way to understand time. Plants and animals have their own rhythms, and trying to understand these other nonhuman life tempos can potentially hold lessons in other ways of being.

Gloria

"You will not be able to visit your mother for the time being. I am sorry." I remember the words of the social worker at my mother's nursing home. It was early March 2020, right after the COVID-19 pandemic hit Austin. Shortly after, I called the nursing home and asked the nurse to put my ninety-four-year-old mother on the phone. Using my humor in a poor attempt to keep it light, I told her playfully about a *virus loco* running around the city and the need to stop my visits to protect her and the residents at her nursing home. She did not say much. I hung up, crying, wondering whether I would ever see her again.

Day after day, week after week, I looked forward to reading the letters sent via email by an administrator representing the nursing home, announcing the number of people who tested positive along with detailed CDC-informed health protocols. Soon I learned about the residents who had died. Apprehension and fear became my normal state of mind. In the meantime, hardworking and caring nurses and assistants were being identified as "essential workers." Many of them were people of color, mostly women, wearing face masks that could not hide their teary and exhausted eyes. Overworked yet tireless, they successfully navigated the crisis; the deep respect and admiration I had already developed for them years earlier only increased exponentially. Some of them contacted me periodically to schedule weekly Zoom visits with my mother.

Mother's Day 2020: I walked all the way to the nursing home and waved to the somber building from a distance, two blocks away or so, crying to a mother who did not know I was out there, feeling deeply afraid I would not see her again. How do you prepare for the worst-case scenario? Should I look at the funeral home papers she asked me to arrange many years back? How are my best friends who have a parent living in a nursing home coping? I talked to one of them only to learn about his mother testing positive and dying a few days later. Sobbing, lost in my fear, I wondered, *Is my mother next?*

Loneliness plus solitude redefined. The virus became my best teacher, and the pandemic became an unexpected retreat on humility. My poor attempts to meditate every day to cope were supported by a generous online Buddhist community; Tibetan Buddhist pujas of monks reciting Green Tara, Medicine Buddha, or other rituals available online eventually became the background of my working-from-home routine. My daily life revolved around my teaching, office hours, meetings via Zoom, disinfecting food after shopping, my few supportive friends in the United States and beyond borders, and the Feminist Writing Salon, my beloved campus-based online community, the space that gave me so much hope and strength. My daily walks while wearing a face mask became part of my routine as well. Strangers engaged in the same routine soon became familiar faces, also wearing face masks, frequently crossing over to the other side of the street whenever they saw anyone getting closer, honoring the new social distance mandate.

Time collapsed and slowed down dramatically but also went by fast. After the longest months of my life, my mother was vaccinated in December 2020. Eventually, I got vaccinated after overcoming my own skepticism and fear of the vaccine. More doses followed at some point, and eventually the nursing home's restrictions were lifted for family members. After learning new protocols and a rigorous process to enter the facilities, I was authorized to visit my mother again. No hugs, no kisses—keep your distance, wear your mask, be mindful—always. It is still surreal.

Writing these modest lines during my recent visits to the nursing home, while my mother sleeps so peacefully or prays her rosary with so much faith, does not do justice to a journey that cannot be captured with words. She survived the worst (hopefully) of the pandemic, and I am still alive to share the highlights of a more complex story. *Gracias a la vida que me ha dado tanto*—thanks to life, which has given me so much—Violeta Parra taught us to sing. Her lyrics came true for me during these pandemic times, and my heart overflows with gratitude. May my gratitude become healing energy for the many on Earth who were less fortunate and who are still in pain.

Christen

One night, toward the beginning of the shutdown—I don't remember the day or the year (Does it even matter?)—my husband's cousin called from Brazil just to talk. The last time we had seen each other was just before the pandemic, when he and his wife invited us and our kids to their house for pizza and laughs. They wanted to show off their apartment, which they had worked very hard to afford on a daycare teacher and a law student's salary, and which "shared a garden" with their grandmother's house.[9] After dinner we got the chance to meet Grandma, who was quite elderly and confined to the house at that time but still moving around a bit. It was great to see her, and I was delighted that they were able to live there next to her to help take care of her. At that time, my own grandmother was nearing ninety, and I knew how much it meant to be able to take care of an elder in that way. This time, our conversation was much less jovial, however. He called to say that his grandmother had fallen ill and they had called the paramedics to check on her. When the paramedics arrived, however, they said that her condition was dire and she would probably die. The paramedics, exhausted I'm sure, advised that it would be better to keep her at home and care for her there. Despite the fact that she could have received pain-easing medicine and some form of comforting care at the hospital, they noted that if they took her to the hospital, the family would most likely never see her again or be able to bury her because those who were dying in hospitals had to be buried in designated graves without funerals, according to new COVID procedures. So, for several painful days, they tried to make her as comfortable as possible, although she was still in pain, while they waited for her to die.

The pandemic felt like holding on to a tree branch in a flooded river of death. One, two, three, four, five, six, seven, eight, nine . . . of my husband's family members died of COVID. Friends calling, crying, frantic and ashamed, asking for money to bribe IML[10] officials to release a loved-one's body ahead of the line so they could be buried. Remittances for funeral costs. Remittances to buy food and pay for water because life went on during the pandemic despite the death, despite the disease (or didn't you notice?). Remittances to those who lost jobs. Remittances to those who lost Grandma's monthly retirement check when she died. Oh, yes . . . and the disasters . . . the disasters did not stop or shelter in place either. Remittances for fathers and mothers that lost everything in landslides, floods, fires. Remittances, remittances, remittances, death, death, death. At some point, the body simply shuts down and refuses; tears back up in the chest and throat, refusing to come out any longer. Those tears turn into headaches and memory loss. Loss loss loss loss . . .

My own struggles with the pandemic were not as grave as those of my husband's family. In many ways my family was fortunate. While my husband was dealing with death after death after death, my family was thankfully well, although we also experienced death. My ninety-one-year-old grandmother's dementia became acute in March 2020, and my mother moved her into my parent's house. Shortly thereafter, amid our collective mourning in the wake of the police killing of George Floyd, my mother called me to say that my grandmother's condition was worsening. In June 2020, my husband, my two kids, and I packed up our things and went to Washington, DC, where my parents live, quarantined, and then moved in with my parents to help take care of my grandmother. From July to October 2020, my mother and I provided hospice care for my grandmother at home. In August, my two sons went back to school online full-time while we were in DC. I, like many people who identify as women and who are caretakers, began the journey of taking care of both the young and the old amid the global pandemic—juggling logging children on to classes on time on two devices, homework assignments, my grandmother's medicine schedule, medical appointments, personal care, and my own work schedule. My days ranged from navigating math worksheets and plastic bottle terraform experiments to spoon-feeding my grandmother her favorite thickened liquids so that she could have some comfort as her dementia took hold. Eventually, the weight of the routine was too much, however. My husband went to Brazil. A week before my grandmother died in October, my children and I returned to Austin to try to put our lives back together again, if that was even possible after such chaos.

What does it mean to have death constantly at your doorstep? As a Black woman living in the United States with familial ties in Brazil, very much caught between Brazil and the United States, I am aware that the pandemic also had its diasporic dimensions. Our collective condition in the Americas—well before the COVID-19 pandemic—was one of death, dying, and yes, being killed. As Christina Sharpe reminds us, ours is the condition of the wake (Sharpe 2019). We need only remember the tragic murder of George Floyd in May 2020 to recall that our conditions of living in the wake were not suspended by the pandemic's lockdown. Our stories repeat themselves through time and space and resonate across borders in ways that we ignore and/or refuse to see because we have been taught to think about time and space in only a linear fashion, by longitude and latitude, according to the ancient rules of geopolitical mapping. Yet I cannot help but notice the disorienting slippage between worlds here and there and the ways that they interconnect and ricochet between one another.

This book is intersectional in nature. We cannot understand the impact of the pandemic without first recognizing the unique ways that interlocking forms of oppression shaped the experiences of those around the world. Women of color were particularly affected by the pandemic precisely because our everyday lives before it (and now after it) are shaped by the legacies of conquest, slavery, and colonialism. Just as we as feminists cannot understand sexism without first recognizing that gender is always raced and classed, we cannot understand the pandemic without recognizing that those gendered, raced, and classed realities continued to shape our realities during the global crisis. It is no accident that the first person to die of COVID-19 in Brazil, for example, was a fifty-seven-year-old Black woman and domestic worker, Rosana Aparecida Urbano. She contracted the disease after her white employer returned from vacation in the United States, carrying the disease back with her. Who got sick, how sick they got, how they died, and the existence that people were able to carve out for themselves while the crisis was happening had everything to do with race, gender, and class, as the essays in this volume and my own story demonstrate. Even as a middle-class Black woman with the considerable privilege of being employed as a university professor who could keep working during the pandemic, my experience working from home was quite different from that of my non-Black woman counterparts. Indeed, because of my privilege and my commitment to family, I invisibly and silently carried many on my back throughout this time, unbeknownst to my colleagues. As an administrator as well as a professor, I (ironically) sat on university committees tasked with finding ways to create leave and special dispensation for faculty and students most impacted by the pandemic while I navigated the heavy burden of the pandemic as well. (In)visible labors of care created racialized and gendered fault lines of difference across our society during this time in curious ways.

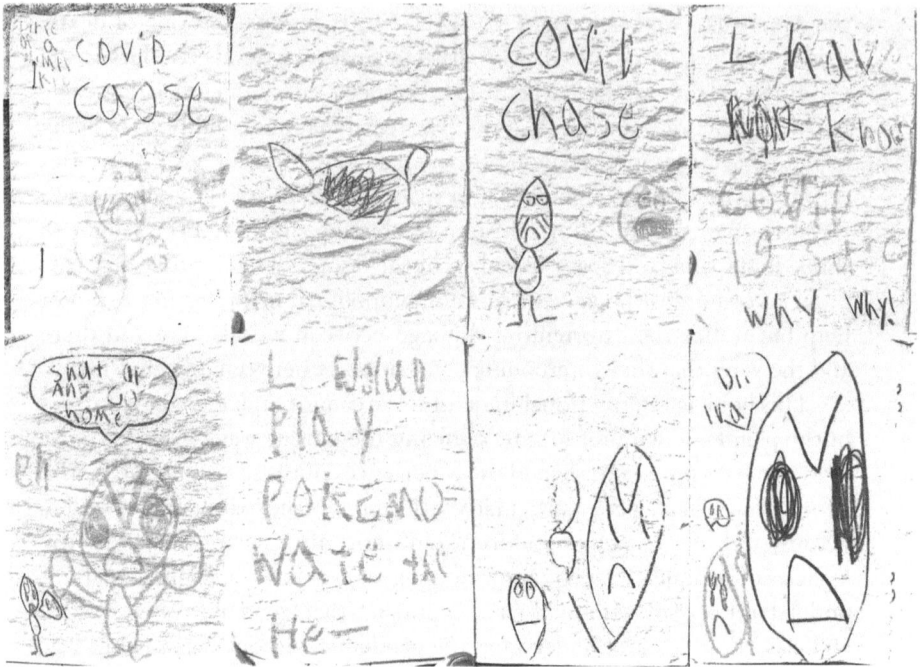

Covid Case, *by Hoji Smith Souza, March 2021.*

As I began to write this brief reflection, I combed back through my scribbled notes and scraps of thoughts from the pandemic time. Many of these bits and pieces were thoughts that I had already begun to forget—it's amazing how the mind heals itself with forgetting. One night, a few weeks ago, I found one of the comic books my youngest son drew during the pandemic. He was six when the pandemic began and is ten at the time of this writing—much of his childhood was spent under lockdown.

My son's generation will forever be marked by this time, as will we all. Our children's stories are our own. What will these memories tell us years from now? Where will we be then, and will we truly appreciate the full dimension of where we have been?

In Community: Embracing Feminism During Uncertain Times

We were living through extraordinarily difficult, and extraordinarily creative, times. We were not alone, and the three of us knew we wanted to reach out to, hear from, and learn from others who were dealing with the pandemic and the quarantine in their own ways. They, too, were making their own lives meaningful under extraordinary conditions. The essays we sought were a way to explore our individual and collective sufferings along with the potential opportunities to emerge on the other end beaten down and somewhat intact, but with a whole new sense of knowledge and wonder about the world. We wanted to document our ordinary lives, to commemorate and to make visible the everyday that somehow remains invisible and thus is so utterly forgettable, and ultimately erased, because it is so mundane. This anthology, then, is an effort toward keeping a feminist archive of personal stories by academic feminists of color in their journeys during the COVID-19 pandemic.

This anthology is also inspired by the *aesthetics of resilience*. We understand the aesthetics of resilience to be the individual effort of transforming a challenging life experience into something inordinately beautiful that can help cope with the moment and open paths toward personal and political truths. We use the metaphor of the lotus, *Nelumbo nucifera*, which remains rooted deep in the mud up to eight feet underwater while the flowers float gently above the water's surface. The lotus needs that mud, that muck, to produce blossoms. Some species are known to have up to five thousand petals per blossom. Lotuses standing in murky ponds, lakes, and slow-moving rivers drop thousands of seeds every year; some grow into more lotus plants, but most others are eaten by wildlife. Still others sink to the ground and remain dormant as the water dries out. When it rains again and the muddy ponds form, the seeds can rehydrate and begin a whole new colony of plants. Lotus seeds can remain dormant, only to be reborn again after hundreds of years.

A second tenet we offer in this anthology, along with the aesthetics of resilience, is that suffering does not make us better people. There is no deeper meaning to suffering. Yet we also recognize that hope exists only because there is despair. Despondence is not necessarily disabling; it also enables particular acts of caring, particular kinds of connections, and particular ways of moving forward. This brings us to the *notion of practice*—that is, for us as feminists, meaning comes through practice. Practice refers to the acts of caring, of doing the everyday work to sustain ourselves, our beloveds, and our communities. Here we strive (and very often fail) to include the nonhuman world into our notion of communities: the quadrupeds, avians, reptiles, and insects that share our homes and the plants, trees, and fungi that grow all around us. We need to recognize that some of our acts, of doing, may be classified as completely useless, counterproductive to writing that one more article, getting that one more book read, and building yet another argument. We focus so much on productivity that we forget the real harm such productivity does to our souls and to our worlds. Here is a question we hope this collection leads the reader to ask: Why does everything *have* to have a use? Might there be tremendous joy in pursuing what is deemed completely useless? The quarantines of 2020–2021 froze us; we were unable to follow the routines we always followed. Appointments were cancelled. Travel came to a screeching halt. To pass the time—endless time where we met no one—we made bread, embroidered, learned to ineptly play a musical instrument. There was so much joy in that imperfection, in the pursuit of nothing of value, simply doing, moving fingers, hands, lips, and bodies through space and time.

What Does It Contribute to the Field?

The essays in this anthology are written by feminists of color in academia. We chose to focus on academia because this is the realm of economic activity that we are most familiar with. But also, the university reflects much of what is happening in the global economy. As state resources shrink, university administrators increase tuition and turn to not-for-profit funding agencies such as Mellon or Ford, and to private donors who hold exorbitant wealth to sustain these "temples" of higher learning, these spaces of "academic freedom." Some scholars rightfully name these spaces the "imperial university."[11] Students are increasingly treated as clients who are rendered a service, where entertainment and client satisfaction are primary. Faculty are pushed to produce, produce, and produce, competing relentlessly against each other so that departmental rankings are buoyed and they themselves are much sought after in the job market. Yet others circle in and out as contingent faculty who are dependent for their "academic freedom" upon the vagaries of balanced budgets and student interest. The staff who make the university happen are low paid and undervalued.

The essays presented here validate what many in academia have identified all along: The university is a neoliberal institution. Yet, it is within these neoliberal institutions that we practice an ethos of caring through our teaching, reaching out to colleagues and to students. What did this practice of work, and of care, in this neoliberal space look like under pandemic lockdown? Care work, especially that of healthcare personnel and teachers, was deemed essential work, even as the workers themselves were, in reality, treated as discardable and replaceable. Teachers in universities were not essential workers in the same political or socioeconomic sense, but they engage in deep caring every single day. As care workers, especially persons of color care workers, the contributors to this anthology rethink what it means to continue to care within the strictures of the structures imposed on us, especially during the global crisis wrought by the pandemic. The pathways they provide within the belly of the neoliberal university also matter in other neoliberal spaces, especially those centered around the labor of caring.

In a multitude of ways, the essays and poems in this anthology are dealing with the afterlives of settler colonialism. We understand settler colonialism as the historical, political, cultural, and socioeconomic processes that have systematically displaced Indigenous populations, communities, and nations with migrants, who over time have developed a distinctive racial ethos and ideals of sovereignty built around white nationhood. By *afterlives* we do not mean that the era of settler colonialism is over, but that it persists in the organization of everyday life, in privileging particular kinds of being(s), closure, private property, privatization, productivity, and profits. We are meant to declare our fealty to things as they are, in order to be successful. But as the contributors to this anthology ask us: As immigrants, persons of color, queer and marginalized workers, what does it take out of us to be successful in this world we are asked to inhabit? What are we supposed to give, and what in our lives is going to give in, under these conditions?

The pandemic revealed that much of the paid work we did was not valued. The essayists in this anthology reimagine where that value lies, somewhere in the interstices of our lives as paid workers and the unpaid work we do outside the academe. The coeditors and contributors of this anthology have family histories rooted in Argentina, the Bahamas, Bolivia, Brazil, China, Colombia, Costa Rica, the Dominican Republic, El Salvador, Ghana, Guatemala, India, Korea, Lebanon, Mexico, Nicaragua, Pakistan, Palestine, Panama, Puerto Rico, Spain, Syria, Taiwan, Turkey, the United States, and other countries and cultures. Our call for papers was inspired by the Anzaldúan invitation to "risk the personal" as part of the process of documenting a challenging experience. Personal narratives, *testimonios*, are placed at the center of the stories. We invited contributors to share their stories beyond what could be perceived as narcissistic, but only as a vehicle to produce knowledge. As we received, read, and organized the moving contributions, we identified the common themes uniting all the pieces. Soon, very specific themes emerged and common threads selectively united these pieces of creative writing. The contributors to this anthology, who established that human connection of intellectual intimacy with us, the editors, through their creative writings, revealed the themes that would give life to the anthology. This project took on a life of its own, and as we organized them, we identified a progression, a sequence, and a common thread that held the essays together.

Unmaking Our World: Anzaldúan Epistemologies for Pandemic Times

The anthology is purposefully unconventional in nature, and we encouraged all expressions of creative writing. We attempted to create a space for the kind of writing that is not always welcome in the social sciences, our disciplinary spaces, but one that we thought was urgently needed, especially in times of despair and fear but also hope and opportunity to reinvent ourselves individually and collectively. Creativity is essential during times of crisis and chaos, and we encouraged that possibility. Poetry, personal journal entries, essays, and other forms of creative writing are included in this anthology to validate our collective efforts and honor all forms of knowledge production.

As we explored ways to arrange these moving expressions of creative writing, we read and reread each contribution, identified main themes, and created groups to start working on the organization of the volume. We witnessed an interesting pattern as seven groupings emerged: Each one of these seven groups had common themes that united them, giving life to seven sections that mirrored the seven stages of *conocimiento*—knowledge—that Anzaldúa proposed in her celebrated publication "Now let us shift . . . the path of conocimiento . . . inner works, public acts."[12] Like the seven stages of conocimiento, the contributions of each section had a common spirit, which was not always linear or unidimensional, but the coincidence was moving and revealing.

Anzaldúa identifies the **first stage** of conocimiento as "el arrebato . . . rupture, fragmentation . . . an ending, a beginning," which is accurately represented in a moving way by one specific reflection on that particular stage:

> Cada arrebatada (snatching) turns your world upside down and cracks the walls of your reality, resulting in a great sense of loss, grief, and emptiness, leaving behind dreams, hopes, and goals. You are no longer who you used to be. As you move from past presuppositions and frames of reference, letting go of former positions, you feel like an orphan, abandoned by all that's familiar. Exposed, naked, disoriented, wounded, uncertain, confused, and conflicted,

you're forced to live en la orilla—a razor-sharp edge that frag-
ments you. (546–547)

This first stage of this consciousness or knowledge engendered through
the pandemic was rupture, a shattering that announced the state of shock,
disbelief, and disruption. Ada Cheng opens this section through discussing
the overt racism, in the form of anti-Chinese prejudice and violence, that
came with the pandemic.

Anzaldúa identified the **second stage** of conocimiento as "nepantla
. . . torn between ways." An iconic concept, she identifies nepantla as the
following:

According to Jung, if you hold opposites long enough without taking sides a new identity emerges. As you make your way
through life, nepantla itself becomes the place you live in most of
the time—home. Nepantla is the site of transformation, the place
where different perspectives come into conflict and where you
question the basic ideas, tenets, and identities inherited from your
family, your education, and your different cultures. Nepantla is
the zone between changes where you struggle to find equilibrium
between the outer expression of change and your inner relationship to it. (548–549)

This passage resonated with the spirit of the second part of this volume,
"Academia Exposed: Resistance and Inner Reinventions," where contributors—all scholars at different stages of their professional careers and across
disciplines—generously shared their keen awareness of the contradictions
and tensions they encountered in the academic world. The pandemic
exposed the university as a neoliberal space, a space where academic capitalism is consistently reproduced, but also a space where women have experienced caring. Hard work and labor by persons of color remains invisible
and unpaid in academia. But tensions and discomfort existing within the
ivory tower are also opportunities for growth; being torn, being always
in transition, being always in progress, means always reinventing oneself.
Recognizing and sharing our collective vulnerabilities can become a source
of strength.

Anzaldúa calls the **third stage** of conocimiento "the Coatlicue state . . .
desconocimiento and the cost of knowing," where the suffering of knowing
is unveiled. Anzaldúa explains this stage as:

A paradox: the knowledge that exposes your fears can also remove them. Seeing through these cracks makes you uncomfortable because it reveals aspects of yourself (shadow-beasts) you don't want to own. Admitting your darker aspects allows you to break out of your self-imposed prison. But it will cost you. When you woo el oscuro, digging into it, sooner or later you pay the consequences—the pain of personal growth. Conocimiento will not let you forget the shadow self, greedy, gluttonous, and indifferent, will not let you lock the cold "bitch" in the basement anymore. (553)

The third section, "Beyond Virtual Classrooms: Education Reimagined," reveals that even in the neoliberal space of the university, caring happens: In the classroom, we are care workers engaging in compassionate pedagogies that emerged in the rituals of the quarantine. In the end, the pandemic not only exposed the paradoxes and contradictions of academia but also offered opportunities for resistance and personal and collective reimagination, re-creation, and transformation.

The **fourth stage** of conocimiento is called "the call . . . el compromiso . . . the crossing and conversion." Echoing the spirit of her now-classic *Borderlands/La Frontera*, Anzaldúa asserts:

The bridge (boundary between the world you've just left and the one ahead) is both a barrier and point of transformation. By crossing, you invite a turning point, initiate a change. And change is never comfortable, easy, or neat. It'll overturn all your relationships, leave behind lover, parent, friend, who, not wanting to disturb the status quo nor lose you, try to keep you from changing. Okay, so cambio is hard. Tough it out, you tell yourself. Doesn't life consist of crossing a series of thresholds? (557)

The fourth section of this anthology, "Immigrant Hearts: 'Stay Home' . . . but Where Is Home?" is a collection of essays that reveal the lives of the intellectual care workers who navigate the complex world of US academia: immigrant women with family roots across the world. Deciphering life as immigrants in a country that may not always feel like home exposes the borderlands of the diasporic heart when pandemic protocol exhorts us to "stay home." This section explores what it meant for us to remain home, and the caring tasks that come with every home.

The **fifth stage** of knowledge is represented by Coyolxauhqui (*coh-yohl-shau-kee*), the goddess of the moon, or *la diosa de la luna*, who is a key figure in Aztec mythology and frequently referred to as "the dismembered woman." The Coyolxauhqui monolith was found in the heart of Mexico City in 1978, stimulating prolific research across disciplines. Coyolxauhqui became a keystone for Anzaldúa in her reflections on self-healing through writing as a part of that journey. Anzaldúa offers a powerful reflection:

> Coyolxauhqui personifies the wish to repair and heal, as well as rewrite the stories of loss and recovery, exile and homecoming, disinheritance and recuperation, stories that lead out of passivity and into agency, out of devalued into valued lives. Coyolxauhqui represents the search for new metaphors to tell you what you need to know, how to connect and use the information gained, and, with intelligence, imagination, and grace, solve your problems and create intercultural communities. (563)

In this anthology, specific contributions capture the wisdom of what was there for us after being immersed in our individual and collective suffering during the pandemic. They help us reimagine and assemble our inner Coyolxauhqui—"putting her together"—as we try to resolve our unresolved stories and heal old wounds while also giving birth to and loving a new generation during difficult times.

Thus, our understanding of Coyolxauhqui is inspired by the possibility to see her far beyond a passive role, beyond the victim as dismembered woman, "but rather as an empowered woman warrior that is in process of labor and birth."[13] The fifth part of this anthology was organized and catalyzed by this possibility, giving life to "Motherhood Is Radical Love: On Being a Mother During COVID-19." This part of the anthology offers a moving lesson: Being a mother who is also a scholar during the pandemic became a form of radical love. And radical love exposes, among other things, the revolutionary nature of the human bond emerging out of motherhood and its reinventions in a wide variety of family arrangements, and across cultures and generations.

The **sixth stage** of conocimiento is "the blow up . . . a clash of realities." The stage identifies some of the emotionally exhausting and unresolved tensions, conflict, and pain that have been present in feminist spaces and other communities, promoting social justice and change. However, Anzaldúa suggests, a distinctive intermediary can make a difference: *las nepantleras*. They "live within and among multiple worlds and, often through painful negotiations, develop what Anzaldúa describes as a 'perspective from the cracks'; they use these transformed perspectives to invent holistic, relational theories and tactics, enabling them to reconceive or in other ways transform the various worlds in which they exist."[14] The nepantleras rely on the wisdom of their painful experiences, as Anzaldúa explains:

> Where before we saw only separateness, differences, and polarities, our connectionist sense of spirit recognizes nurturance and reciprocity and encourages alliances among groups working to transform communities. (568)

This sixth section, titled "The Wisdom of Our Wounds: Inner Transformation Through Community," highlights resilience, collective healing, and the sacred love in our immediate communities.

Finally, the **seventh stage** compels us to undertake collective transformation. Anzaldúa's reflections on this closing stage of knowledge production reflect the heartfelt urgency that motivated us as coeditors of this anthology. She writes, "Through the act of writing you call, like the ancient chamana, the scattered pieces of your soul back to your body." She continues:

> You commence the arduous task of rebuilding yourself, composing a story that more accurately expresses your new identity. You seek out allies and, together, begin building spiritual/political communities that struggle for personal growth and social justice. By compartiendo historias, ideas, las nepantleras forge bonds across race, gender, and other lines, thus creating a new tribalism. Este quehacer—internal work coupled with commitment to struggle for social transformation—changes your relationship to your body, and, in turn, to other bodies and to the world. And when that happens, you change the world. (573–574)

We can change the world. The last section of this anthology is titled "Utopia: 'The Language of Love . . . Will You Speak It with Me?'" and offers closure through reflections of scholars of color who weave words of hope: Children of color carry in their hearts a map highlighting promising futures; a survivor's breath offers moving lessons about our humanity; queer experiences of collective care teach us more than one lesson about life; and abolition becomes a possibility to transform our society. Ultimately, as humankind we have the potential to become immeasurable and to eventually embrace ascendance in our collectively shared humanity. These last reflections are inspired by the creative words of Kiana Murphy and Sara Rezvi, respectively.

Arundhati Roy writes in her essay "The Pandemic Is a Portal" that "historically, pandemics have forced humans to break with the past and imagine their world anew. This one is no different. It is a portal, a gateway between one world and the next." Published on April 4, 2020, right as the COVID-19 pandemic shook up our world, Roy's words invited us to think about the pandemic as a doorway through which we walked, without knowing what we were going to find on the other side. At the doorway, Roy writes, "We can choose to walk through it, dragging the carcasses of our prejudice and hatred, our avarice, our data banks and dead ideas, our dead rivers and smoky skies behind us. Or we can walk through lightly, with little luggage, ready to imagine another world. And ready to fight for it."[15]

Thresholds, those spaces at doorways, demarcate the inside from the outside, zones between the sacred, inviolable home and the profane dirt of the streets. But thresholds also hold other meanings: The word *threshold* is also used in phrases such as "threshold of pain." The *Merriam-Webster Dictionary* defines *threshold* as "the point at which a physiological or psychological effect begins to be produced."[16] That is, we move from the point of no pain to the point of knowing pain. The pandemic was precisely that threshold, the juncture at which we individually and collectively moved from not-knowing/not-feeling to knowledge and feeling.

The word *threshold* is also used to signify the potential emergence of something new that is laden with uncertainty and, because of that, is potentially dangerous. It is reaching that threshold of pain that opens doors to enable the advent of maybe something different. But something different does not always mean something good.

The pandemic opened possibilities; we were at the threshold of seeing the world we live in differently. Less noise meant we could hear the rhythms of the world, our stillness meant other cohabitants of our world could now move, and we did not have to endlessly produce, chasing some imaginary goal that always moved out of reach. Yet what we saw on the other side of the pandemic was a very quick reorganizing that became far more socially, politically, and economically punitive. In spite of halting production, workloads in academia actually increased. Because the economy was ostensibly fragile, contingency in the workplace deepened. We imagined the neoliberal university would change post-pandemic. It did. Neoliberal pressures deepened.

Under these circumstances, it is easy to give up hope. We had survived the pandemic in some form and fashion, and having emerged on the other side, we were faced with a far more disciplinary workplace. But one of the things that we know, especially as persons of color, transgender individuals,

Indigenous scholars, women in Black communities, those from Dalit communities, and survivors of violence, is this: As awful as this pandemic has been, some of our communities and some of us have been through worse. If we were to roll over and give up, we would be dead. So there is always hope. Despair is the ground on which hope grows. And it is from that space of radical hope that these essays emerge.

Notes

1. In *Bridging: How Gloria Anzaldúa's Life and Work Transformed Our Own* (University of Texas Press, 2011), AnaLouise Keating and Gloria González-López explain, "Anzaldúa used this term [nepantla] to develop her post-*Borderlands* theory of process, liminality, and potential change that builds on her theories of the Borderlands and the Coatlicue state. For Anzaldúa, nepantla represents temporal, spatial, psychic, and/or intellectual point(s) of crisis. Nepantla occurs during the many transitional stages of life and describes both identity-related issues and epistemological concerns" (243–244). Anzaldúa offers insightful reflections on nepantla as a paradigm in her celebrated article "Now let us shift . . . the path of conocimiento . . . inner works, public acts" and the book *Interviews/Entrevistas.*

2. Zander S. Venter et al., "COVID-19 Lockdowns Cause Global Air Pollution Declines," *Proceedings of the National Academy of Sciences* 117, no. 32 (2020): 18984–18990, https://www.pnas.org/doi/full/10.1073/pnas.2006853117.

3. "Air Pollution," World Health Organization, https://www.who.int/health -topics/air-pollution#tab=tab_1.

4. Ali P. Yunus et al., "COVID-19 and Surface Water Quality: Improved Lake Water Quality During the Lockdown," *Science of The Total Environment* 731 (2020): 139012, https://www.sciencedirect.com/science/article/pii /S0048969720325298.

5. "RARE DOLPHIN SIGHTING as Cox's Bazaar locks down under COVID-19 Coronavirus!!!," posted March 24, 2020, by Mahboob Rahman, You-Tube, https://www.youtube.com/watch?v=gjw8ZlIIbQ.

6. Sarah J. L. Severino et al., *Hanauma Bay Biological Carrying Capacity Survey, 2020/21 Annual Report* (Hawai'i Institute of Marine Biology, 2021), https://www .honolulu.gov/rep/site/dpr/hanaumabay_docs/Hanauma_Bay_Carrying_Capacity _Study_Year_3_2020_to_2021-compressed.pdf.

7. Geophysicist Jeroen Ritsema, cited in "Michigan Stadium Seismometer Captures Eerie Quiet During Pandemic," Michigan News, April 15, 2020, https:// news.umich.edu/michigan-stadium-seismometer-captures-eerie-quiet-during -pandemic/.

8. Christian Rutz et al., "COVID-19 Lockdown Allows Researchers to Quantify the Effects of Human Activity on Wildlife," *Nature Ecology & Evolution*, no. 4 (2020): 1156–1159, https://www.nature.com/articles/s41559-020-1237-z.

9. The expression translated as *sharing a garden* in Brazil refers to houses split into multifamily units that are usually split up between families to divvy up expenses but also are sometimes rented to outsiders.

10. Instituto Médico Legal is the government agency responsible for handling deaths at the state level in Brazil.

11. Piya Chatterjee and Sunaina Maira, eds., *The Imperial University: Academic Repression and Scholarly Dissent* (University of Minnesota Press, 2014).

12. Gloria E. Anzaldúa, "Now let us shift . . . the path of conocimiento . . . inner works, public acts," in *This Bridge We Call Home*, ed. Gloria E. Anzaldúa and AnaLouise Keating (Routledge, 2002), 540–578.

13. Jennie Luna and Martha Galeana, "Remembering Coyolxauhqui as a Birthing Text," *Regeneración Tlacuilolli: UCLA Raza Studies Journal* 2, no. 1 (2016): 8.

14. Keating and González-López, *Bridging*, 244.

15. Arundhati Roy, "Arundhati Roy: 'The Pandemic Is a Portal,'" *Financial Times*, April 3, 2020, https://www.ft.com/content/10d8f5e8-74eb-11ea-95fe-fcd274e920ca.

16. *Merriam-Webster Dictionary*, "threshold," accessed January 24, 2025, https://www.merriam-webster.com/dictionary/threshold.

PART I · 2020 UNMADE OUR WORLD

Arrebato . . . Days Running Together, Death, Fear, Isolation

1. el arrebato . . . rupture, fragmentation . . . an ending, a beginning

With each arrebatamiento you suffer un "susto," a shock that knocks one of your souls out of your body, causing estrangement. With the loss of the familiar and the unknown ahead, you struggle to regain your balance, reintegrate yourself (put Coyolxauhqui together), and repair the damage. You must, like the shaman, find a way to call your spirit home. Every paroxysm has the potential of initiating you to something new, giving you a chance to reconstruct yourself, forcing you to rework your description of self, world, and your place in it (reality). Every morning in ritual you turn on the gas stove, watch the flame, and, as you wait for the teapot to boil, ask Spirit for increased awareness. You honor what has ended, say good-bye to the old way of being, commit yourself to look for the "something new," and picture yourself embracing this new life. But before that can happen you plunge into the ambiguity of the transition phase, undergo another rite of passage, and negotiate another identity crisis.

GLORIA ANZALDÚA, "NOW LET US SHIFT," 547

1 • A LETTER TO MY YOUNGER SELF

Ada Cheng

Characters

Student: An international student from China. Any gender.
Ada: A middle-aged woman from Taiwan, a university staff member conducting training and outreach on gender-based violence.

Setting

There are two chairs onstage. The student and Ada are sitting slightly facing each other and reading email exchanges. They have never met and will never meet in person.

Time

The first email was sent by the student in mid-February 2020.

Dear university staff: Hello. I want to report an insulting incident that happened to us today. My friends and I were at this building trying to grab some coffee. We were waiting in line, and finally, when it was our turn to order, we stepped forward. During that short time, we heard an absurd racist joke that people at the cashier made, saying, "Watch out for the Corona virus."

As everybody knows, the Corona virus is a global issue that has taken away more than 500 innocent lives. Treating us as that virus is both humiliating and insulting to the people who are suffering and fighting for that contagious disease.

It is very unfortunate that this occurred during the Black History Month, the month that we all believe everybody should not be discriminated by the color of their skin.

I hope you examine this issue. We sincerely want an apology for this inconvenience.
Sincerely,
Student

Dear student: Thank you for the message. I am very sorry this happened to you. I would like to meet in person to discuss the situation further. Let me know when you can stop by.
—Ada

Dear Ada, Thank you for your kindness.

We were all furious about the incident. However, after knowing that there are people who care for minorities like us, it gives us pride, knowing that we chose to come to this school.

Again, thank you for offering us options to deal with this matter, but we have decided not to make a scene.
—Student

Dear student: I don't think you will ever read this message. I do hope at some point you will tell this story on your own.

I haven't been able to sleep for days since I received your email. That last sentence, "we have decided not to make a scene," hit me hard.

That sentence has filled me with sadness. It feels like someone has driven a knife slowly into my heart. I am not going to die from it, but my heart aches and bleeds with each gentle cut and push.

Your message was the first complaint I received, but it was not the first one I have heard. Since the outbreak of the coronavirus, we have seen an increase of hatred toward Chinese people, people of Asian descent, or Asian Americans in general. Physical assaults have taken place, racial slurs hurled, suspicious looks cast, masks put on specifically when Asian people are present; otherwise socially conscious people have made jokes and references about the virus and Chinese people; businesses in Chinatown have plummeted due to misinformation, xenophobia, and racism.

In a world where racism is often seen between Blacks and whites, discrimination, prejudice, racism, and xenophobia toward and against Asians are often so taken for granted and normalized that even UC at Berkeley briefly posted something online along the lines of: Xenophobia is a normal response after the outbreak. Our own president insisted on calling the virus the Chinese or Wuhan virus, knowing full well that the pandemic would bring out preexisting hatred, xenophobic sentiments, and racist assaults against people of Asian descent. Different universities sent warning emails to students about the virus, yet very few made public statements denouncing anti-Asian racism.

We didn't label any germ, disease, illness, or virus "white" when it wiped out Native American tribes; why do we label coronavirus "Asian"? This pandemic shows how easily we, as Asian Americans, can go from being Model Minority to Yellow Peril in this country within seconds.

But what I want to write here is not about the virus. It is about that last sentence of yours: "We have decided not to make a scene." I truly see you because you remind me of my younger self, when I used to believe that people would understand where I was coming from and empathize with my position if I were polite enough, respectful enough, articulate enough, or liked enough.

And then it dawned on me one day: My degree of politeness, respectfulness, or likability has little to do with whether people can grasp the complexity of issues. For many, they understood them all along.

In my/our culture, I was taught since I was young to be quiet, to not speak up, to not challenge authorities, and to keep peace and maintain harmony. I had to work very hard to develop my own voice and to have one.

When I was younger, I tried hard to balance having a voice and wanting to be liked, having ideas/opinions and being seen as too opinionated/loud, and telling people how I really felt/what I really thought and not wanting to alienate anyone with my truths.

I still struggle with that. And I am in my fifties.

The reality is: There is no balance. It is a lose-lose situation. For me, as a woman.

I do have the benefit of racial perception: I am hardly seen as militant or aggressive as an Asian woman even when I am, compared to a Black woman, who can easily be seen as aggressive even when she is simply being assertive. My body, as much as it may be sexually objectified, exoticized, or violated, is not seen as threatening, thus allowing me to "freely" navigate the world without anyone calling the police on me.

And we know the ways our bodies are perceived can have life and death consequences.

But the worst part is this: When you don't practice speaking up for yourself, you end up losing the only voice you have.

Your own.

I want you to remember this:

Silence can be a strength, but it isn't always a virtue.

Being quiet doesn't always bring you peace.

Being polite doesn't always keep you out of trouble.
Being respectful doesn't always get you the respect in return.
Please learn to tell your own story, as I can't always tell stories for others.
Learn to shout. At the top of your lungs.
Make a scene.
Be the troublemaker.
Be the trouble.
For yourself and others.
It's time.
It's time.
—Ada

Note from the playwright: These were email exchanges between the playwright and the student, except the last email to the student. The last email from Ada was written but was never sent. The playwright did not change the student's writing.

"A Letter to My Younger Self" was made into a short film by Collaboraction Theatre Company. Ada Cheng owns the right to this piece. The short film premiered on October 21, 2020, and it is available at https://www.youtube.com/watch?v=FfSw4XPMXII&t=48s.

2 • THE IN-BETWEEN

Transitional-Pandemic Times

Judy Cervantes

Just like the good times don't last forever, neither do the difficult times.

I'M USED TO THE IN-BETWEEN. Growing up in East Los Angeles then Montebello, California, the in-between was a constant navigation between English and Spanish, between the rules at school and those of survival in your hood and in your home. It was in the duality of feeling American but not fully. Being proud to be Mexican *American* but needing to quiet it down in certain environments and around certain people so that you could appear and feel to others more American than Mexican. Of working as hard as you could to do well in school because "an education was your ticket out of the hood" and in the process subconsciously training yourself to get rid of every hint and trace of where you grew up so that when you did get out, no one would know where you came from. I'm used to the in-between, but in 2020, the in-between doubled up, and things got real, quickly!

I was in year two of a contentious divorce when COVID-19 officially became a pandemic in the States. I had been following the news closely but never quite preparing myself for a shutdown of active life as I knew it. (First-world privilege.) I was in the middle of a shitty divorce, for goodness' sake, which on its own felt like a full-time job. I didn't have the mental energy to consider a pandemic. For all the trauma I had endured as a child, nothing, and I mean nothing, prepared me for divorce, and most certainly not for a f*cking pandemic to be happening in the middle of it! I was learning how to be on my own again: a single mother and daughter, balancing returning to school and working while caring for everyone in my household as the tangible and emotional fallouts of living through a global pandemic and through a divorce challenged my daughter, my mother, and myself. We were in a state of transition. A state of in-between. A state of figuring out who we were in those moments of deep challenge and how these moments would help us grow as females.

I cannot separate, at least not in this moment, my divorce from the pandemic shutdown because the shutdown greatly affected the outcome of the divorce in all regards: custody, support, and property. In a time when I most needed fairness and equity, I received the opposite—much like the communities most affected by COVID-19. Managing the life changes brought on by a global pandemic while navigating a difficult divorce was the straw that nearly broke this woman's back. Moving to a new home, doing online learning for both my girl and me, teaching from home while my girl was doing schooling from home, preparing meals, keeping a home tidy, shopping for provisions, keeping us all emotionally healthy and our bodies moving, the daunting task of keeping us safe from catching COVID (I swear walking into the supermarket was the most anxiety-riddled experience for months) . . . something had to give. For me that something was the "fight" to get all of what was rightfully mine. And what a weight that lifted even in the middle of global pandemic.

When the ping-pong of being in-between is mastered, what can one fear? Even death is an in-between between this world and the next.

By the fall of 2020, my mother went to stay with my cousin, who had recently delivered a set of twins. My mother is wonderful with babies, and my cousin welcomed the extra set of hands. It was a welcome change for all. My mother felt a deep need to be among other people. To see other walls besides the ones in our home. I felt the respite of having one less person to worry about getting sick, even though the worry of my mother potentially catching COVID never truly went away. My girl was happy to have me all to herself. She and I were once again on our own managing life and its continued responsibilities together from home. It was a time reminiscent of when my girl was a baby and I a new mom working from home and learning to balance a family and a career. We were back at it with a shared knowledge that we had practice in doing hard things. We developed a nice system that worked and where we both thrived. I will not pretend it was easy. I got very little sleep. During the day I worked and helped my girl with schoolwork. I attended online courses in the evening, using late nights and early mornings to complete assignments. And always present was the labor of mothering my girl and myself.

Our daily work and schooling, together, sustained us. In many ways this intense togetherness offered healing from the effects of being a family now divorced. The adjustments we had to make to each other's roles strengthened our bond and connection. We were each a witness to one another's growth, physically, mentally, emotionally, and spiritually. There was the visible relief in her body when she was able to get immediate help with schoolwork. Or the happy rush of showing me what she just completed during art class. There were the Wednesday afternoons when it was her responsibility to make us lunch because I had a class to teach during her lunch break. There were the Thursday evenings when she would prep dinner while I attended class so that all I had to do was cook or bake the meal once my class was over. Then there were the powerful moments when she'd listen to a course lecture with me and later ask questions about what she heard, which led to discussions of social awareness of racism and classism and the disproportionately negative effects of COVID-19 on communities of color.

We were together, making it work. Some days without a hitch and other days by the hair on our chinny-chin-chins. Always together and doing our best and looking toward the next day when the current day was not a great one. I was, as a newly single mother, able to work, attend school, and tend to my child because I was able to do all of this from home. I was fortunate and privileged in many ways. I didn't have a commute, which in Los Angeles can be multiple hours per weekday. I didn't have to worry about finding or paying for childcare in order to earn a living or receive an education to better myself. The COVID-19 pandemic highlighted a host of inequities in our nation and throughout the world. In addition, it highlighted something I believe gets lost in the reporting: our ability as a people to continue to produce and function with nontraditional methods of contributing to society. For women, employing various modalities for survival is not uncommon. It's the act of functioning and ultimately thriving in the in-between. Of mastering the ping-pong of going between our various identities and responsibilities and needs. This is where the magic happens, and where the power within us is realized.

It should not require a global pandemic to sustain this power, this flexibility in the ping-ponging of life. What we all did to remain safe, to follow protocols, to proceed with life and living through a global pandemic was incredible. It should be celebrated, and it should continue for those who need it. Online learning did work for lots of students and teachers; it should remain an option. Working from home could remain a solid option for folks because it, too, worked for many, both employees and employers. Imagine what working from home could do for new parents to fully bond with their babies. Or how helpful it would be for adult children needing to care for aging parents. Or for the purposes of maintaining mental health.

We don't yet live in a world that makes space for grief and healing. When bad or sad things happen, we are expected to get it together and move on as soon as possible; industry has no time for sadness or pain, nor does it for a pandemic. But the pandemic happened, and industry insisted that the work must go on, and so it did and much of it from home. Perhaps now is the time for those of us who sustain industry—the mothers, the women who care-give, who educate, love, and labor—to insist on options to better sustain ourselves and those we love.

3 • THE PANDEMIC LET US BREATHE

Faith M. Deckard

AS I SAT IN THE back seat shifting my gaze from Papa, who intently focused on the road, to my brother, who had the latest mixtape blasting through his headphones, I let out what seemed to be months of pent-up breath. They had embarked on a 480-mile roundabout trip to bring me home for the summer so that we could collectively social distance now that the semester had ended. Any other time, it would have been much more difficult for them both to secure time off from work, let alone sacrifice an entire day's wages to make the trip. However, my brother's boss at Jack in the Box was more forgiving, and Papa was on his alternating paid off-week, both conditions courtesy of COVID.

The weeks leading up to my return home were marked by mixed feelings of both anticipatory excitement and looming fear. Excitement because I had spent the past month and a half social distancing on my own. As a result, I craved the company of my rambunctious, personality-plus family. Fear because although we always made do with what we had, what would "making do" look like in a pandemic? What would it mean to "make do" with even more precarity than one was accustomed to?

Previous phone calls had given me a preview of the landscape back home: My mother and grandmother had indefinitely lost their service jobs along with others in our extended family network; anticipated "extra cash" from tax returns had not yet surfaced, contributing to short tempers and exacerbated anxiety; our small town had the highest number of COVID cases in the county, and very quickly the best and worst of humanity was seeping out as people grappled with confusion, uncertainty, shortages, and loss.

In light of this knowledge, I had prepared myself for the aroma of my grandmother's cooking, the humming of the familiar, too-loud air conditioner, and the jokes and laughter of my siblings reverberating off the thin walls. But I had also doubly prepared for pervasive stress, for the frustration that stems from feeling powerless, and for the "making do" in an unprecedented time.

However, when I stepped through the door of our double-wide trailer, I was overwhelmed by an unexpected and indescribable peace. While it was welcoming and a pleasant surprise for my socially deprived soul, I was also suspicious. In the back of my head I wrote off the peace as "first night" charm . . . surely the onset of "making do" would hit in the upcoming days.

But as I perched with one eye open—half-expecting the other shoe to drop while simultaneously praying that it wouldn't—chaos did not come.

Instead, I was met with the release of multiple held breaths.

My mother was tired and had been tired for a long time. She was tired of working long hours for little pay in a hostile environment that extracted her labor but devalued her person. When she was let go, she was surprised to find out that unemployment enriched by the stimulus plan would pay her more than any job she had had in years. Melting into the couch with the knowledge that she wouldn't be degraded at work the following day and the promise of financial support, she let out a full-body's-worth stream of air.

My nanna was both sick and tired. Having recently had neck surgery, and contending with diabetes, employment in the kitchen of the local high school was not gentle on her body. Not only did the repetitive long hours on her feet leave her seeking Epsom salts and a heating pad each night, but the compensation wasn't enough to cover the price of the medication that could help her feel better. When schools across the country closed due to COVID, my grandmother let out a long train of breath. Though she loved her job and her daily interactions with students, coworkers, and teachers, she was grateful for the luxury of being able to stay in bed when her body ached, and she was grateful for the stimulus check that allowed her to prioritize buying the on-brand, doctor-recommended medications. Truth be told, it had been a while since I've seen her move and breathe so well.

My aunt's well had run dry. The primary breadwinner of her own family, as well as an indispensable part of ours, I've always looked upon her ability to keep the many pieces afloat in awe. However, it is no secret that raising two girls quickly approaching their teenage years *on top of* working in a physician's office *on top of* incrementally working toward a bachelor's degree left her in a nonstop game of tug-of-war. When COVID transformed the primary medium of doctor appointments to a virtual platform, my aunt was temporarily taken off the payroll. As she kicked off her shoes and hung up her scrubs, the fatigue and exhaustion of years spent running kicked in. Looking inward, deep inside to her internal well, she realized that it had run dry—although she could not pinpoint exactly when her reserves had been depleted. What she did know, however, is that as of late, she had been going on nothing but her daughters' dreams and a prayer. When she allowed herself to exhale, she almost immediately felt pounds lighter.

My brother, along with millions of other low-income minorities, is currently in between cases for low-level criminal charges. Having already had his court date pushed back twice, he lives each day with uncertainty and apprehension around which day he could be convicted in court and potentially sent to jail. Such uncertainty discouraged him from his plan to enroll in a local junior college—because what's the point of starting a new life when there's a chance it could be snatched away? And, more practically, with what money, when sizable portions of each check went to paying off a bail bond, probation fees, and court fees? However, since the onset of COVID, my brother has dared to smile, to temporarily suspend worry, and breathe deeply. Ironically, he breathes because with COVID he has certainty, certainty that his court date will not be scheduled and then postponed. He's off the hook until distancing bans are lifted and court activity returns to full pace. Though he will likely resume holding his breath when the injustice wheels turn once again, for the time being, my baby brother breathes.

And me, well . . . I breathe knowing that they breathe.

That a pandemic has bought us time, has bought us rest, has bought us more financial security than usual, and has bought us breath is a condemnation of the time and circumstances of before. Why did it take ubiquitous, nondiscriminatory (though uneven in its effects) uncertainty for a society to seriously acknowledge financial insecurity, lack of access to affordable healthcare and insurance, and arbitrary justice operations as dire dilemmas? Why is it that in the midst of a pandemic some folks find air to breathe? Air that wasn't accessible to them before?

We are always in a pandemic of sorts, facing conditions that unevenly wear on people, increasing risk, susceptibility, disease, and even death. The call, then, should be for continued outpouring from social safety nets, recalibration and development of collective consciousness, and unremitting care for each other to make breathing a more frequent and consistent affair.

4 • RESISTING THE HORROR

Hope as an End in Itself During COVID-19

Nohely Guzmán

May 21, 2020

Today I woke up agitated by a call from my mom. It was almost 8:00 a.m. and it was her fourth attempt to contact me. By the tone of her whispers, I sensed that something bad had happened, and within seconds I knew it was about my grandfather. In silence, I felt my heart race. In the distance, the knots in my throat were more difficult to decipher. Words failed us because the pain overflowed, but also because we lacked the contact of the embrace that weaves the senses that cannot be named. Miles from home, I write these lines while my grandfather struggles between life and death in Cochabamba, Bolivia. Yet I hold on to the hope that all the pain, rage, exhaustion, and uncertainty of this time are the germ of the regeneration of the world we want to build. Today more than ever, with the tangibility of death around us, expressions of life shake the system, its agents, and its apparatuses of annihilation and pain. It is true that the virus has confined us, terrified us, and atomized us, but not stripped us of our imaginations for a better world. This world is not the same after all we have lost, but new horizons are being envisioned as we walk. Nothing can prevent the healing of a new world coming.

In my grandfather's hospital, emergency patients are given a mattress, one without sheets, blankets, or pillows. Just a mattress. Those who are lucky have the resources to cope with the freezing nights of the coming winter, a fleeting visit that helps with cleanliness and food, and a nurse or volunteer who eventually monitors the small rooms shared by four, five, perhaps six people. Hearing the desperate crying of my aunts using doubled-up masks to try to protect themselves as they walk between people dying on the ground, the official speeches fell apart. "The virus does not discriminate," the authorities said, and yet in the stories and photographs, we see the opposite. Once again, the most underprivileged bodies predominate death rates. This reality, for many, is not new and is hardly surprising. In the end, the virus has operated as a magnifying glass—one that has made it clear that those in power enjoy immunities at different scales, where calculations of power and privilege afford some people life and others death. While more than 20 million people lost their jobs, and more than 580,000 lost their lives, the world's top billionaires became 15 percent richer.[1]

That we are all equal, then, is a falsehood. There is tyranny in the blindness that denies difference and hides under the label of "humanity" against the virus. If we are equal, why is the virus mainly destroying the most impoverished populations? Black,[2] migrant, Latino,[3] peri-urban, Indigenous, and/or rural communities are dying at the highest, and fastest, rates.[4] Brutal domestic violence and *feminicidio* (intentional killing of girls and women) are exacerbated.[5] Police harass Black people on the streets for wearing masks.[6] People with disabilities and special needs suffer more than able-bodied individuals in the absence of social contact that in many cases determines their access to basic and essential care. Why has the pandemic been used as an essentializing excuse to negate, repudiate, and denigrate LGBTQIA+ people and identities?[7] Why does militarization rest on specific bodies and spaces, and why does justice never target those who have profited from the crisis and our pain? The questions roam in confinement, and it is difficult not to look with disappointment even at those who promised us a transformation but then postponed it. The pandemic has amplified, armored, and justified all violence in the name of contagion prevention and has made quarantine a pressure cooker. These have been months of unmasking the grotesque rot not only of state institutions, but of the system itself. The falling of public life's veil has forced us to see upfront the day-to-day horrors that brought us to this sort of rehearsal of apocalypse—one whose cruelty is overtaxing, again, the same as always. COVID-19 is, in the end, a portrait made in the image and likeness of the system: racist, classist, ableist, and patriarchal.

May 22, 2020

It seems incredible to think that two months ago all this seemed distant and unreal. I remember waking up on March 11, my last day of school before spring break, with messages from my family after the WHO declared

COVID-19 a global pandemic. Joking about the coffee we never had, later, I hugged my friend Karla one last time. At times I felt naked, not knowing what to believe. The only general prompt was to wait. Soon after, however, time dissolved into the uncertainty of stillness. How do you deal with the incalculable and excessive effects of stoicism? On this side of the world, the days passed by as distressing photographic sequences for me. My window, however, did not look the same as my grandmother's in Ecuador. "Scavenging birds go round and round in the city. If you look up, you see big black spots in the sky of the birds that seem to wait for the bodies of the dead to eat them," she said. In her words, the horror of this unveiled collapse resonated with the despair of my Indigenous friends in the Amazon. Today they are threatened by the virus, loggers, settlers, and the redoubling of extractivism in their territories as the "only" (post-)pandemic economic solution. For fascism that rules—as in Bolivia or Brazil—with one hand on the Bible and the other on a gun, COVID-19 is an opportunity to strip life and territories with impunity. Capital, it is clear once again, is worth more than life to them; they never tire of affirming it.

Day after day, from this half of the world, I cross long distances on bridges woven with the words of the other women in my life. In Beni, Bolivia, where I do my research, Indigenous leaders tell me with a broken voice the tragedy that is walking through the streets of nearby towns. Among the bodies of the people lying on the streets, the weeping of the families that accompany them, and the crosses that have turned the margins into cemeteries, the landscape itself is composed of grief. Although most territories are still safe, fear spreads rapidly, infiltrating provisions, canoes, roads, and images. There, however, the technification surrounding the virus's language, which hyper-hygienizes and endorses social atomization, hardly makes sense. Memory pushes toward the commons and is stronger than the unapproachable sciences that have betrayed marginalized peoples a thousand and one times in the name of "development."

May 24, 2020

Today, in Bolivia, almost ninety days of strict lockdown have ended. In the voices of my cousins, aunts, mother, sister, and friends, I hear fierce exhaustion. Listening to them, it is clear that the quarantine rebuilt and legitimized the traditional gender roles in which fear was established. At this point it is no secret that the quarantine can produce a sensation of being held hostage. This is particularly true for women, and it has put a huge weight on the domestic tasks that seem to never end. The physical and emotional exhaustion of both paid and unpaid work without pause signals an oversaturated recapture of women in the domestic sphere. In the kitchens, among the exchange of recipes, a series of questions are asked both aloud and silently: What do the care tasks we do tell us? What of this serves as a compass to rethink life? What is the political grammar of intimate and collective healing in confinement? No one can deny it anymore. The system is falling apart, and every table in every house is somehow a place of contention for the common, the just, and the essential.

May 28, 2020

It has been a week since I started writing this, and three days ago the police killed George Floyd.[8] Their brutality and ruthlessness seemed to send a message to Black and other people of color—one that has inflamed cities in anger and outrage in response. "May the things we burn light the way" was graffitied in one of the streets near where I live in San Francisco. The intense clarity of these words shakes every fiber of my body. What can be cultivated from pain? How can we coexist with the world as we know it and simultaneously poison the rancid rationalities that brought us here? How can we reconstruct the language of smiles, the power of reaching out, and the silent codes in which the deepest empathy dwells in spite of hyper-individualization? Perhaps now that the quarantine has forced us to "pause," it is time to listen in order to redefine our directions. There is radicalism in opening our eyes, remaining silent to listen, and naming what we thought was impossible. Resisting the horror of this time depends, to a large extent, on spreading hope in our communities. For those in power, this is the most feared contagion: the spread of hope and solidarity. Now, living in the clinging ruins of what we knew as normal, we can not only visualize why it led us here, but also draw the lines of the nonnegotiables of the world we want to build. The hope of transformation in these times is an end in itself. In it lies a form of healing.

July 7, 2020

After several weeks, I return to this text today seeking some solace. Amid many turbulences, I find firmness in embracing the body I inhabit. In the COVID-19 propagation charts, racism, classism, sexism, and its lethality are omitted. Yesterday, the US Immigration and Customs Enforcement (ICE) agency announced that we, international students, must register for in-person classes in order to maintain our visas and remain in the United

States.[9] In their official announcement, ICE stated that students who plan to remain in the US taking online-only courses may face "immigration consequences including, but not limited to, the initiation of removal proceedings." That is, we must choose between our health and safety and that of our communities, and deportation. In many cases, our genealogies have carried that weight for years, and history repeating itself on the same bodies causes incalculable harm.[10] We, however, are stubborn. Our fear, anger, loss, and pain have no place in the official pandemic data, but neither do our dreams end in the horror of real-time body counts or state policy. Today, it is important to remember that we were already in an emergency when COVID-19 hit. In moments of serenity, now more than ever, I find comfort and hope in Arundhati Roy's words: "Another world is not only possible, she is on her way. On a quiet day, I can hear her breathing."[11] We have lost a lot. Let's take a moment and catch our breath. Vast utopias have sprouted from deep pain. Let's redesign ours.

Notes

1. See "Tale of Two Crises: Billionaires Gain as Workers Feel Pandemic Pain," Americans for Tax Fairness, May 21, 2020, https://americansfortaxfairness.org /issue/tale-two-crises-billionaires-gain-workers-feel-pandemic-pain/.

2. See Ibram X. Kendi, "Stop Blaming Black People for Dying of the Coronavirus," *The Atlantic*, April 14, 2020, https://www.theatlantic.com/ideas/archive /2020/04/race-and-blame/609946/.

3. See Rakesh Kochhar, "Hispanic Women, Immigrants, Young Adults, Those with Less Education Hit Hardest by COVID-19 Job Losses," Pew Research Center, June 9, 2020, https://www.pewresearch.org/fact-tank/2020/06/09/hispanic -women-immigrants-young-adults-those-with-less-education-hit-hardest-by -covid-19-job-losses/.

4. See "COVID-19 Is Affecting Black, Indigenous, Latinx, and Other People of Color the Most," COVID Tracking Project, last updated March 7, 2021, https:// covidtracking.com/race.

5. See Zhang Wanqing, "Domestic Violence Cases Surge During COVID-19 Epidemic," Sixth Tone, March 2, 2020, https://www.sixthtone.com/news/1005253 /domestic-violence-cases-surge-during-covid-19-epidemic.

6. See Derrick Bryson Taylor, "For Black Men, Fear That Masks Will Invite Racial Profiling," *New York Times*, April 14, 2020, https://www.nytimes.com/2020 /04/14/us/coronavirus-masks-racism-african-americans.html.

7. Approaches such as Peru, Panama, and Colombia's "pico y género," which aim to regulate people's transit during quarantine, have turned into explosions of violence against the already precarized trans and non-binary community.

8. Roxane Gay, "Remember, No One Is Coming to Save Us," *New York Times*, May 30, 2020, https://www.nytimes.com/2020/05/30/opinion/sunday/trump -george-floyd-coronavirus.html.

9. See "SEVP Modifies Temporary Exemptions for Nonimmigrant Students Taking Online Courses During Fall 2020 Semester," US Immigration and Customs Enforcement, July 6, 2020, https://www.ice.gov/news/releases/sevp-modifies -temporary-exemptions-nonimmigrant-students-taking-online-courses-during.

10. See Chantal Da Silva, "ICE Offering 'Citizens Academy' Course with Training on Arresting Immigrants," *Newsweek*, July 9, 2020, https://www .newsweek.com/ice-launching-citizens-academy-course-how-agency-arrests -immigrants-1516656.

11. Visit Arundhati Roy's website, https://www.weroy.org/arudhati_quotes .shtml.

5 • TOWARD A SLOWNESS-CENTERED LIFE IN A POST-PANDEMIC WORLD

Meztli Yoalli Rodríguez Aguilera

BEFORE THE PANDEMIC HAPPENED, WE already lived in a world where the heteropatriarchy, racism, and a colonial system imposed on us a time. TIME, with capital letters. This colonial time is the time of modernity, the time of production, the time of consumption, which has also been a time of exploitation, of spectacularization of violence, and of normalized racialized and gendered violence. When COVID-19 appeared, the world didn't change its core structure: The people and communities dying kept dying; the people sustaining life are still doing it. These are people of color and/or immigrants: Black, Latines, and other racialized and/or working-class people. It's important to mention that, as a non-binary queer person of Mexican origin, I use *Latines* as a political stance, one that I embrace as a future where gender binaries are abolished and one that will become part of an archival memory of the times I am living in. COVID-19 makes even more visible the interrelated violence: anti-Blackness, anti-indigeneity, transphobia, homophobia, classism, and sexism. This imposed colonial time has conditioned us to believe our value is quantified by productivity. We are conditioned to feel guilty if we are not producing something, if we are not laboring. *Labor* not only in the sense of what one does to receive a salary, but also emotional labor and housework, which in many cases is done by women, especially women of color.

What I have learned during this pandemic is the need to imagine another kind of TIME, the need to center slowness in our life. Slowness has been stigmatized in our everyday lives as a synonym for laziness and lack of productivity. People even mock others for being too slow—people who walk slowly on the streets, people who eat slowly, people who answer questions slowly, create anxiety in a world where speed and quickness are perceived as ideal qualities. We have devoured the idea that "time is money," even in symbolic forms of money or capital.

In this pandemic, I have recognized that I was too used to a speedy, quick life. I was running around the city every day, doing multiple things, and even when I got home, activities would continue. The burnout feeling was normalized. After some weeks of this pandemic, I realized it was the first time in my whole life that I was not in a rush. I realized that for the first time I had time to let myself slow down, as there was nowhere to go outside. I realized that for the first time I could embrace slowness in my life.

The year 2020 is a historic moment, or at least that is what it feels like, and I believe this is a time to potentialize our imagination, a time to radicalize our imagination and name it for manifestation. I imagine a world where people have time to embrace slowness to rest, to feel, to think, to eat, to feel joy, to feel sadness, time to slowly grieve our different losses; we need time for rituals of healing and mourning, time to pray and connect to the sacred. I imagine a world where we have time to slow down, to slowly cook, slowly think, slowly love, slowly feel, slowly touch, slowly smell, slowly taste, slowly hear, slowly navigate the world. During this pandemic I had more time to pay attention to details around me, to be affected by my immediate surroundings, like the plants in the house, the smell of the food cooking, the music in the background. I imagine a world where racialized and gendered bodies are not exploited emotionally or physically in their everyday lives. I imagine a world where Black and Indigenous people are not constantly dispossessed. I imagine a world where ancestral territories are protected. I imagine a world where communities can produce transformative justice without the state and carceral system. I imagine a world where the actual state does not exist anymore. I imagine a world where we stop policing our bodies and the world. A world where borders and nationalism do not exist. I imagine a world where the people who materially sustain life—farmworkers, service workers, care workers—can rest and have fair conditions of work and life. I imagine a world where more-than-humans, nature, are not exploited and even feel joy and time to grow slowly, without the pesticides and agrochemicals people use on them. I imagine a world where gender binaries are not imposed, where transphobia does not exist, and where bodies can feel pleasure without guilt. I imagine a place where pleasure is centered (Brown 2019). I imagine a place where we can eroticize our existence, in the broadest meaning of the erotic, as Audre Lorde (2007) taught us. To center slowness is to live in intimate relation with the world, with others, with ourselves, with the more-than-human.

During the pandemic, we created other ways of staying connected to different geographies of the world through technology; we imagined other ways of keeping our loved ones close. But we also have to be careful not to let the capitalist colonial time take over this new possibility; we have to make sure that even in isolation, even during a pandemic, we defend our slowness, defend our time to disconnect, and defend our time to feel grounded in the world.

COVID-19 and the isolation it brought have made me observe carefully how plants grow. I have learned lessons from them: I have learned that even in stillness they grow, but they take their time. In slowness they bloom, they live; they just need care. I believe that even in this weird time of apparent stillness but where time and life are still happening, we can find ways of living a livable life and not just surviving. We need community, reciprocal care, and joy. We just need to keep planting more seeds for another time, and, as the Zapatista Movement says, to keep imagining other worlds that are possible.

Bibliography

brown, adrienne marie. *Pleasure Activism: The Politics of Feeling Good*. AK Press, 2019.

Lorde, Audre. *Sister Outsider: Essays and Speeches*. Crossing Press, 2007.

6 · AN INVITATION TO PIVOT

Briana Barner

IN THE EARLY DAYS OF the pandemic, a podcast I listen to, *Fare of the Free Child*, invited us to view the unknown as a chance to pivot and to not fall into our normal, everyday routines. There was no way to define what normal looked like or how it would look in the future. The idea of pivoting, in (what I hope to be) the final year of my PhD program, while also caring for a still-brand-new baby and a six-year-old, was overwhelming but also intriguing.

I am at the very beginning stages of writing my dissertation. I am also very much still in the postpartum phase, as I delivered my daughter less than two months before panic ensued. Needless to say, I am at a very precious stage in my personal and professional development. So I've been asking myself, what would it look like to pivot? What do I want to pivot toward?

A Pivot Toward Family

The first thing that I pivoted toward, out of necessity, was more time with my family, as a family. In the early days of the pandemic, when we were still blessed to have my husband home on paternity leave, we spent a lot of time getting to know each other as a new family of four. I learned so much about my son as a big brother. He is a natural caretaker. He immediately embraced this role and grew very protective—of me while I was pregnant and of his sister when she was born. I also learned that family is very important to him. Not only is he a caring and thoughtful person, but he is also fiercely loyal. Any activity that we did, he always asked if we were doing it as a family. When we took family walks, he always made sure to look behind him to make sure he could still see me as I struggled, still recovering from my C-section.

At times, this made me extremely uncomfortable, and I had to sit with those feelings. The concept of family can be difficult for me. I did not grow up in a two-parent household, and there were not a lot of family activities with either parent. I quickly realized that my son's interest in family came from a place of love, but also from a place of fear. Our family unit provided a place of safety for him. While the world around him turned upside down, he knew that safety was here, right in his home. I felt both proud and sad. It brings me joy that my son feels that safety and comfort, but because I didn't experience that as a child, I secretly long for that too.

So how did pivoting help me rectify those feelings? At the encouragement of my therapist, I engaged in more play. I bought the board games I'd always wanted as a child. We had movie nights with lots of snacks and comfort food. We sat in our driveway with chalk and drew silly faces. As I saw my son's face light up and heard his laugh and squeal, I realized that my inner child was being healed. The pandemic was triggering the feelings of uncertainty, chaos, and despair that I constantly felt growing up. Doing things that made my inner child smile, and parenting my children in a way that nurtures both them and myself, was helping me cope with the violence of the pandemic. As my son felt safe, I finally did too.

Planting Seeds of Care

The months continued to roll by, and it became very clear that there was no immediate end in sight to this catastrophe. My feelings of despair and anxiety intensified. The year before, when my anxiety was extremely high, I had purchased my first plant in hopes that it could lift my mood. Desperate, I decided to see if plants would again offer healing. Eventually my plant interest shifted to gardening. Maybe it was when we visited a local farm and my son pointed to a plant and asked if he could have it as "his" plant. I hadn't realized that he had been watching me take care of my plants. Little did I know, he had chosen a tomato plant. As I learned to care for the plant, my excitement grew when baby tomatoes sprouted.

Gardening has been the unexpected pivot that I needed more than anything. Before the pandemic, I had no interest in growing my own food and had only recently become interested in plants. But as I watched the economy around me collapse, I realized that it made sense to start seriously considering self-sustainability for our family. I began learning as much as possible about gardening. My husband would wake up to me nursing our daughter while watching videos about soil. I can't explain the joy that I get when I am in my garden. I have plants both in containers and a raised bed garden. My husband and I built the raised bed ourselves—a project I never would have considered before COVID. I believed the idea that I wasn't strong enough to take on building things because I'm a woman (which was internalized sexism and misogyny that I hadn't realized). But after building a raised bed—a relatively easy project—I became motivated to take on other projects I've pinned to Pinterest boards but haven't actually started. I have no idea what harvest I will have from the plants I've grown, but I'm proud of myself for trying something new that I can always improve upon.

Gardening requires lots of focus and attention. I have to slow down while I am caring for my plants and take notice of their condition and needs. It is a form of self-care. Slowing down to feel soil in my hands, or to delight in a new tomato or new flower, has made me so appreciative. It is also a reminder that new life is possible. My inner child rejoices when I see a new bloom or a new leaf unfurling. Caring for my plants forces me outside. Slowing down has me filled with gratitude—for my home, for the outdoor space that I have, and for this new green thumb that I've developed.

I will always remember how my garden began, and as it grows each year, it will be a reminder that seasons bring new possibilities and opportunities. I marvel at the beautiful colors on my plants. I am in awe of how quickly growth happens with these plants, and I feel important knowing that I played a role in their growth.

Who Am I, Outside of Academia?

One of the other major ways that I have shifted since COVID has been to really sit with my relationship to academia. I have been a student for as long as I can remember. This is mainly because I was told from an early age that I am good at school. No matter how hectic and chaotic the world was around me, I always saw education as an escape. So much so that it was not a surprise when I decided to pursue a career that would essentially keep me in academia forever. I love school, so it made sense to venture toward a career that would keep school in my life always.

But once I finally started my PhD program, I never felt the pull to solely be a professor. I've always stated that I'm open to careers outside of academia (even when that isn't what you're supposed to say). My desire to distance myself from a career particularly at an R1 university became more apparent as I progressed in my program. I felt lonely, isolated, and stressed beyond measure. When I became pregnant with my daughter, in the fourth year of my program, I experienced many challenges as I tried to establish maternity leave (which I was never able to do). COVID, however, forced many of the plans that I had suggested to become standard, such as allowing me to work from home full-time using the technology that we already had in place. Academia is imploding thanks to COVID, although many would argue that many of these challenges were only illuminated by the pandemic.

It is beyond scary for this to be happening as I prepare to enter the job market in just a few months. I am terrified at the idea that everything that I've worked so hard for could potentially be pointless. But if I'm being honest, I have begun pivoting in a way that I was not expecting. So much of academic culture requires us to be "on" all the time. We have to be productive. There are no boundaries between our work and our personal lives. COVID has forced us all to come to a screeching halt. Trying to pretend that nothing is happening and to proceed forward with our work as if everything is business as usual no longer works. So now I have to sit in a future that may not include academia, and, for the first time, that feels freeing.

My therapist is having me explore what it means to *be* instead of *do*. When I think about who I was before COVID, I would describe myself in terms of my career, my identity as a student, my role as a mother. But now that it has become apparent that this pandemic will be here for longer than we anticipated and will change the world forever, who I am has also changed so much. I no longer think of myself in relation to my labor, especially the labor tied to a university. I feel so grateful for the privilege of having the time to quarantine at home and explore these soul-searching questions.

Pivot

I have had no choice but to pivot. It is scary, it is exhilarating, it is exhausting. This pandemic has laid bare so many inequalities and has challenged life as we know it. Some days it hits me so hard I can barely breathe. But I am trying my best to embrace the pivot. I am at home for the foreseeable future, and I remind myself constantly that this also means being more in control of my schedule. No longer do I have to sit for hours in my car heading to work or taking my son to school. The pivot for me has been in reimagining what my life could look like in this season. I don't know what the future holds or how long this will last. So I am choosing to draw outside of the lines and to stand tall in all the new possibilities that come from watching a garden bloom or playing as many games of Uno as I can stand with my son. I am surrendering to a pivot that brings me closer to the person that I've always dreamed of being—just not in the middle of a pandemic.

7 • SISTA CIRCLE

COVID and Community Care as Warfare

Dominique Garrett-Scott

I WENT TO MISSISSIPPI LOOKING for something. In hindsight, I recognize that it was healing. I did not know that at the time, 'cause I was just running. I had been stuck in a one-bedroom apartment for days and days and days. And days. I was not well. The plague had wiped so many away. And the numbers kept (keep) going up. We never mourned together. A man had cracked open my chest, took all of my stuff, and walked away with my peace. My older brother was trapped in a cage hours away. My PhD program still demanded reading and writing and reviewing and researching and teaching and responding to emails and all of the graduate student things. Black people kept dying in front of me. And it all happened without my permission. They didn't care that I had nothing to give. Nobody gave me a minute to find my footing, to let me catch my breath or my balance. I needed the world to stop. But instead, every day just got worse. I was not well.

I started to hate being awake. I was tired. The kind of tired that sticks to your ribs. Tired to my marrow. But I could not sleep. Cocktails of sleeping pills and cheap wine were my means of clumsily tripping into fitful slumber. But even in sleep, there was no rest. When Black folks say, "No justice, no peace," we are really telling hard truths about ourselves. It's an act of trying to put the burden on our backs back on you. There was no peace for me. I could not find the comfort I so desperately wanted. My dreams were so vivid. Where, oh where, was the escape? Black people kept dying in front of me. I was not well.

I continued my unhealthy relationship with social media. I logged on to feel some semblance of human connection, only to be triggered by some grotesque image, video, or opinion. People debating about our access to life. Black men telling me, us, how repulsive we were to them. Videos and pictures of police with knees on necks and batons battering bodies. I would

49

close the app and remark on the violence only to open it again and crawl back into the cycle. Black people kept dying in front of me. I was not well.

So, I packed a suitcase, filled my gas tank, and hopped on I-35 North to Jackson, Mississippi. I went back to this place to fill myself up. If you had told me three years ago that I would be coming *here* looking for healing, I would have thrown a belly laugh in your face. But home is complicated that way. In 2017, I ran from Mississippi. After years of activist and organizing work, the white terrorists with their cops and their courts ran me up out of there. They chewed me up, spit me out, and never thought twice about it. A past vowed to never return. And yet, here I was, on I-35, trying to find my way back. I called my best friend, Jas, to tell her that I would be arriving around 11:00 p.m. I showed up on her doorstep limping, barely upright, with a heart so heavy. I was not well.

I needed my community. Not the family forged through birth and blood, but the one I carved out on tables of bones and spades. My sista circle. I slept on that couch and let my community nurse me back to health. Pull me back from the ledge. Lift me up from the dark place that I had waded into. I was hip-deep in something so sad that even now I still don't have a name for it. I wanted to be well.

That weekend, I rode around four deep in my little two-door car screaming Big K.R.I.T. lyrics as we darted around potholes. I lay in a hammock in a backyard surrounded by wonder women. Healers in the thick of a plague. My medicine women. Soothsaying soul savers. My God, my God. I filled my time with belly laughs and lip gloss exchanges. Freestyle circles and Styrofoam cups of Kiki (my homegirls' name for tequila). Homemade meals and long drives through back roads thick with trees. I cooked breakfast—that's how I say I love you—and swayed to Marvin Gaye. We talked about ancestors and alters and gods and revolution. We watched *Real Housewives of Atlanta* for hours and hours. They showed me how to work a professional camera. I shot my first photoshoot.

My friends saved me.

From what—I don't want to name it because I don't know what to call it. It's not that I wanted to be dead, but being alive became more tenuous than I had hoped for. I wanted to lay it in somebody else's hands and let them have it for a while. I needed help with my healing. They helped me get well.

The dangerous imbrication of constant displays of state-sanctioned antiblack violence, a global pandemic handled by a grossly negligent government, and the pervasive misogynoir in popular media sucked the light out of me. In *A Burst of Light: Essays*, Audre Lorde states, "Caring for myself is not self-indulgence. It is self-preservation, and that is an act of political warfare." But what happens when our reserves are too low to preserve ourselves? What do we do on the days when it is easier to wither away? How was I supposed to self-care my way out of that place when I could not take care of myself? The social isolation made self-preservation impossible. I had to ask for help. I had to get back to a place where I could take care of myself.

I write this piece as an ode to my sista circle. I am ever grateful for the abundance of love they pour into me. I thank them for their ever-present recognition of my humanity and the stickiness that comes with it. I appreciate their grace and gentleness as they made magic hum from the mundane. Thank you, my sisters, from the thickest parts of me.

I hope that these words also serve as a call-in to other Black women and femmes out there who need to ask for help. The Super Black Woman stereotype violently excises our humanity. This ideal Black woman who, like Atlas, can hold the weight of the world on her shoulders. She is the primary caretaker, the breadwinner, the one who can endure beating after beating and still stack her back to simply take it. She is not you. She is not who we should strive to be. You should not do this alone. We are stronger together.

Bibliography

Lorde, Audre. *A Burst of Light: Essays*. Firebrand Books, 1988.

8 · REST

Shenée L. Simon

AS I TUCK MY KIDDOS in at night, I whisper to them, "Rest well." Giving them a sense of peace, safety, and security. To allow the day to wash away. Who tucks me in and whispers to me to "rest well"? I lie awake and wonder: What is rest? Who defines rest for me?

Rest is essential for our existence. Science says we need it for optimal function of our bodies and minds, for our mere survival.
Our creator rested, to take a well-deserved break from creating or to simply breathe deeply and observe and marvel at the beauty of creation.

Rest is peace, rest is safety, rest is security. Why do we rob ourselves and others from the beauty and necessity of peace, safety, and security?

Rest is resistance to what the world demands. I recently heard an activist share—

where you give your time,
you give your energy, and
where you give your energy,
you give your LIFE!

What am I willing to give my life for?
Am I willing to not rest for the sake of death or the sake of being used and abused by spaces that don't give me life?

We must resist as feminists OUR borrowed responsibility to do all the work—
to carry the mission,
to plant the seeds,

sow the seeds,
gather the seeds, or
reap the harvest, or
maybe to till the land.

Why should we resist the act of rest? Mother Earth doesn't take it all on simultaneously; she rests, she sets life in motion; cycles, ebbs, and flows are products of her existence. She rests, she leans into the season and understands and demands the change of the season and her response to the season.

Are we listening to her?
Are we listening to ourselves?
Are we listening to the earth, our ancestors, our breathing, our heartbeat?
Do you know the rhythm of your heartbeat?
Do you know the beat of your pulse?
Do you know the vibration of your breath?
Do you know?
Do you listen?
. . . If we don't know or listen, then no one else will either.
. . .

What is rest? Who defines rest for me?

Gently whispering in your ear, "Rest well."

Land Acknowledgment

Stewarding land occupied by the Chickasaw people from 1600 to early 1800s. The 1830 Trail of Tears forced relocation of Chickasaws and other Native American tribes.

Rest in the Mississippi, May 2020

The Mississippi River has many names:
- Ojibwe: Misi-ziibi
- Dakota: Mníšošethąka
- Myaamia: Mihsi-siipiiwi
- Cheyenne: Ma'xeé'ometáá'e
- Kiowa: Xósáu
- Arapaho: Beesniicie
- Pawnee: Kickaátit

and yes I call her SHE as her waters flow through me. She is the keeper of my memories, my stories, my tears, my history, and she restores me physically and spiritually. She is the mother to me as I am to my beautiful children, who were held within my waters and flowed out of me.

She is my place of rest; she remembers the 1919 Yellow Fever that took away so many that the Memphis bluff had the lowest habitation in its his-

SheFlows: Mississippi River. *Photograph by Shenée L. Simon.*

tory. Her waters washed away the tears, fears, diseases. Each ebb and flow was filled with a memory, a story from the past, and brings the remembrance back to us again.

In 2020, almost a century later, she continues to flow, shine, and reflect the lessons of the past and creates a path to our future. She gives us a place to rest, renew, refuel, rinse, and rise again. Rise and renew stronger, higher, fresher, always holding space and our memories.

The Labyrinth, June 2020

Inanna was my "Birthing from Within" guide. Calling the name, spirit, and presence of the Mesopotamia goddess to illuminate my birthing path.

Not just any path, the labyrinth, with its intricate details, spirals entangled twists, turns, direct yet predictable and unpredictable in the same vein.

A frightful space to navigate alone or in the dark and even in the light of quarantine.

Labyrinth, Sacred Ground. *Photograph by Shenée L. Simon.*

Slowly guided into her center, yet unsure of how or if or when you will reach the center or the end. Could they be one and the same?

Will we rest? Will we pause as we enter? Will we run?

Will we rest or pause when we exit? Will we run?

It was designed and created as a place for peace, rest, reflection, or prayer, yet why does it feel so confusing and uncertain?
A path to nowhere but somewhere—how do we reconcile this?

The earth is birthing something from within, birthing life, death, healing . . . rest. Forcing us to rest, to reflect, to pray, to heal, to die
to confront confusion, uncertainty.

Yet urging us to emerge more powerful, stronger, and gain strength each time we reenter and exit.

Inanna, my birthing guide in 2010 and again in 2020. Grant us love, beauty, justice, political power, and peace, as we will NEED it as we exit the labyrinth.

PART II · ACADEMIA EXPOSED
Resistance and Inner Reinventions

2. nepantla . . . torn between ways

You can't stand living according to the old terms—
yesterday's mode of consciousness pinches like an out-
grown shoe. Craving change, you yearn to open yourself
and honor the space/time between transitions. Coyolxauhqui's light in the night ignites your longing to engage with
the world beyond the horizon you've grown accustomed to.
Fear keeps you exiled between repulsion and propulsion,
mourning the loss, obsessed with retrieving a lost homeland that may never have existed. Even as you listen to the
old consciousness's death rattle, you continue defending its
mythology of who you were and what your world looked
like. To and fro you go, and just when you're ready to move
you find yourself resisting the changes. Though your head
and heart decry the mind/body dichotomy, the conflict in
your mind makes your body a battlefield where beliefs fight
each other.

"NOW LET US SHIFT," 549

9 • MIS REFLEXIONES DURANTE LA CUARENTENA

Katie L. Acosta

I ENTERED THE ACADEMY BECAUSE I love social justice. At the time, I naively thought that becoming a sociologist would somehow facilitate my activism. I was wrong. Mary Romero traces sociology's activist roots to the earliest days of the discipline whereby those who devoted their skills to applied and activist work were pushed to the periphery—their efforts silenced and their work erased in the interest of establishing sociology as an objective social science (Romero 2020). The emphasis on objectivity and on researchers' remaining detached from the research they produce has limited sociology's potential and contributed to its being a hostile environment for scholars of color, who are repeatedly discouraged from pursuing scholar activism.

Still, for a long time, sociology was a vehicle for me to study inequalities, to practice feminist leadership, to use my very presence in the academy as a corrective for the marginalization and exclusion of *mis hermanas* in higher education. For years, I thought this was enough. But the more time I have spent in the academy, the more I've struggled with its commitment to neoliberalism. The values of a neoliberal institution have come at a cost to the values I hold most dear. Like so many other scholars of color, I have found the academy's goals in stark contradiction to mine. I have the privilege of being a tenured professor, and with that has come the opportunity to reflect: Is it worth it? The question circled my mind for months before the pandemic. As the pandemic hit, the answer became increasingly clear: No.

Joining the academy took me away from the immigrant community that has nourished my soul since childhood. I spent my childhood first in the Dominican Republic and later in New York City, entrenched in ethnic enclaves where Caribbean migrants were the majority, where everyone looked like me. No matter how far away I am geographically, this will always be my community. My work as a university professor has taken me to the southern parts of the United States, where there are few Dominicans and where the hostility toward immigrants continues to grow. It didn't hit me all at once how painful this geographic shift would be, but what was once a dull craving for connection with my *vecinos* and *tías* and *bodegueros* has become a desperate need as intense as one's need to breathe. It's a new feeling to be in a place of despair, weathering a public health crisis, uncertain about my health and that of those I love and not able to access the comfort of physically touching *mi familia*. My chosen and origin families—*mis tías, primas, amigues,* and the *doñas* who cared for everyone's children and encouraged us to go to church—are the ones I have always turned to when in crisis. This time, I found myself hundreds of miles away with no ability to safely travel. As the weeks turned into months, I longed for my *tías'* hugs, the comforting smells of *la vecina cocinando*, the sounds of telenovelas, of salsa, bachata, y merengue. I longed for the Spanish that would surround me at every turn. I longed for my community. COVID-19 has robbed me of the feeling of safety that comes with being among my people. Instead of feeling *mis tías'* embrace, I am plagued by the fear that if we risk physically coming together, we risk infection.

In the first weeks of the pandemic, my emotions were a mix of fear and anger. Anger for the precarious position the United States found itself in and for the many disadvantaged citizens who are paying the biggest price. Fear for those I love who are essential workers, incarcerated people, and the immunocompromised. I have found myself paralyzed to act on these emotions. As a feminist scholar activist, my life is fueled by the social justice work that I do. But all of my social justice efforts have been thwarted in the face of COVID-19. The community activism that had previously sustained me has been interrupted, leaving nothing but raw, placeless emotion.

I have rarely allowed myself to cry during this crisis. My pain is dwarfed in front of those I love. My family, many of whom are employed in the service industry, have risked their lives for the comfort of others. All while being humiliated by privileged citizens who are afraid to come near them for fear of contamination. If ever we have forgotten who keeps this country running, let our current situation be a reminder that the undocumented, immigrant BIPOC who care for your children, bag your groceries, and stock your shelves are the linchpin of this economy. The apathy with which these low-wage workers have been treated during this pandemic reveals the ugliest truths about the United States in late capitalism—in the interest of stabilizing our economy, our most disenfranchised residents will shoulder the largest risk.

I am painfully aware of the statistics indicating that Latinx people are infected with COVID-19 at disproportionate rates when compared to white people. I've watched young, vibrant people succumb to this merciless virus or survive it only to be later decimated by the aftereffects. A FedEx driver brought a package to the door this morning. In it was the box my mother had purchased to hold the cremated remains of my cousin, who died a few weeks prior of COVID complications. I want to feel angry for him, for his untimely death, and for the sterile way in which we have been forced to mourn him in this time of social distance. But what I feel isn't anger. It is sadness. And so, I honor the sadness. I am indebted to Audre Lorde for teaching me that self-care is an act of radical self-love and resistance. Through engaging in self-care, I say, "Fuck You!" to the oppression that aims to break me and mine. I deny it the pleasure of consuming my body. I deny it the pleasure of stealing my joy.

In spite of the many losses, for me COVID has been un arrebato—it has rocked me to my core and reminded me that even at its best, the academy will always be a liminal space for those who look like me. My belonging within it will always be tangential. The academy will always show me in big and small ways that its buildings were not made for me. That my inclusion within its walls is provisional.

Gloria Anzaldúa helped me name my experience in the academy. She helped me name my existence in nepantla. This summer, members of my university joined those of other institutions in Georgia to push back against the board of regents' guidelines that masks be recommended but not mandated on our campuses. The irony of it all is not lost on me. I work at a largely commuter university with a student population composed predominantly of people of color—African American, African immigrant, and Latinx students. These students are largely first-generation college students who live in multigenerational homes. And while many long for the opportunity to return to their campuses to reconnect with their college community, it is reckless for the board of regents to ask them to do so in an environment where masks and vaccines are both optional. For it will not be only they who absorb the risk of exposure to COVID-19, but also their familias.

Without question, students deserve the opportunity to reclaim what is left of their college careers. They need the opportunity to interact with one another and their professors in meaningful and immeasurable ways to foster their growth, not just as students but as young adults. They deserve the chance to create the lasting memories that college is supposed to offer them. But there are countless ways that administrators and the board of regents can support those efforts without contributing to exacerbating the spread of COVID-19. They have simply chosen not to do so. Still, I am grateful because the actions of administrators and the board of regents in Georgia have sent me a message loud and clear. One that I have received. No matter how much education I have, how much I have sacrificed, or how many hours of labor I have dedicated to the academy, I am disposable. And so are my students. Within a neoliberal institution, faculty, staff, and countless sanitation workers shoulder the risk of keeping the university running. We, alongside our students, will risk infection while upper administrators remain in their offices.

And so, I am clear that it's time to make important changes. No longer can I allow my commitment to feminist activism to be squeezed into the parameters of my obligations to higher education. Instead, I must make my obligations to higher education fit my larger commitment to feminist activism and social justice. It is time for me to channel my advocacy and my tenacity toward fighting inequality in my communities. For now, that means returning to my work supporting newly arrived immigrants and refugees in Atlanta. It means safeguarding this work and my other activist endeavors from the university demands that repeatedly threaten to pull me away from them.

I don't know how the story of the COVID-19 quarantine ends for me, but I am also not afraid of it. I'm facing the awfulness with respect for the deadly virus that it is but also with gratitude for the reminders it has gifted me. The intense fear and anger I feel are reminders that it is time to reprioritize my goals. Higher education has consumed me in a way that has made it easy to forget my priorities. The problems of the academy scream loudly and insistently. Those who love me do not. For too long, I have let myself tend to that which is loud, that which is in front of me, and ignored what is important: my roots, my comfort, my home.

Increasingly, the values of a neoliberal academic enterprise have been at odds with my feminist goals. Even within my discipline of sociology, clear divides have arisen among those who see their scholarship as a primary goal in and of itself and those of us who see our scholarship as a vehicle for social change. These dichotomies sadden me, and I've long resisted choosing sides, but if I must—my decision is clear. I cannot change the neoliberal values of higher education: its elitism, obsession with *U.S. News & World Report*, and constant pandering to legislatures and donors who care not about our students or their educations. But I can protect my commitment to social justice and not lose sight of the fact that justice work brought me to the academy in the first place. I can channel that passion toward holding my discipline and higher education more broadly accountable to integrating community advocacy into its mission.

My biggest hope for higher education is that it will take more seriously a feminist obligation to serve the local community. I have become increasingly disappointed in the lack of support available at the university level for community engagement. Institutions of higher learning are in a fundamentally privileged position over the communities where we reside. Yet their relationships with these communities are often limited to research participation recruitment. Colleges and universities must take more seriously a commitment to community care and do so in the interest not just of furthering a scholarly agenda but of reenvisioning knowledge production by ensuring that the community is central in this process.

I am not alone in my frustration with higher education's neoliberal values. I hear it from colleagues around the country and from students in my classrooms. If colleges and universities are to remain relevant in a post-pandemic United States, their leaders will need to think more critically about their commitment to informing policy and to building a legacy as a community partner. These efforts would require a full restructuring of university goals and outcomes. Romero offers that for sociology, an important first step is to reclaim our commitment to social justice efforts. Another is to reward knowledge production for the general public and not just our elite peers. Further, colleges and universities can make other revenue-neutral efforts in the interest of fostering more accountability with the local community. Colleges and universities can formally integrate community involvement into their expectations for promotion and tenure, and facilitate faculties' incorporating community engagement opportunities into their pedagogical goals. Higher education has become singularly focused on alternative revenue streams through increasing student enrollment, over-relying on contingent faculty, tapping into an international market, and developing more online programming. These efforts have compromised higher education's roots as institutions of knowledge production and dissemination in favor of a corporate enterprise that prioritizes revenue above all else.

Before her untimely death, Gloria Anzaldúa wrote about bridges in the academy—about feminists of color as bridges who possess the ability to unite people in programs and departments divided by our differences and siloed in our offices. Anzaldúa taught us that feminists of color are the nepantleras who can remedy the fractures that exist in higher education. The question is whether universities will grant us the space to be that bridge—to foster community collaborations, to move departments beyond our differences, and to unite us under common goals. I don't know whether colleges and universities will capitalize on this moment to nurture the feminist bridges, but I believe that if they don't, the university will undoubtedly begin to lose its relevance.

Para mis hermanas in academia, I offer the reassurance that you already possess all that you need to find your way within or outside of these walls. Anzaldúa's theory of spiritual activism offers that for each of us the tools to pursue our activist efforts lie within ourselves. Through reflexivity and growth as individuals, we become stronger, more grounded, and more driven in our efforts toward transformative change. To that end, it is important that we not allow academia to discourage us from embracing our histories. The experiences we enter the academy with are essential in nurturing our activist endeavors. Should we choose to remain in higher education, we must remain grounded in who we are, where we come from, and what we have grown through because therein lie the tools for our survival. My biggest hope for *mis hermanas* is that we all allow the COVID-19 public health crisis to be the arrebato that sets us on the path to conocimiento. In the words of Anzaldúa:

> We are ready for change.
> Let us link hands and hearts
> together find a path through the dark woods
>> step through the doorways between worlds
>> leaving huellas for others to follow,
>> build bridges, cross them with grace, and claim these puentes our
>>> "home"
>>> Si se puede, que así sea, so be it, estamos listas, vámonos.
>> Now let us shift.

Bibliography

Anzaldúa, Gloria. *Light in the Dark / Luz en lo Oscuro: Rewriting Identity, Spirituality, Reality*. Duke University Press, 2015.

Romero, Mary. "Sociology Engaged in Social Justice." *American Sociological Review* 85, no. 1 (2020): 1–30.

10 • GLOBAL GEOGRAPHIES OF COVID-19

María Luisa Amado

I PROMPT MY STUDENTS TO realize the intersections of individual and society and biography and history, which C. W. Mills (1959) envisioned as the crux of sociological thinking. I also invite them to explore the underlying connections between peoples and structures in the vastly globalized stage of local lives worldwide. Amid the COVID-19 pandemic, the broadscale proportions of the virus make more visible the links between seemingly scattered places, dispersed peoples, and overlapping voices that speak of uneven geographies of suffering and pain. Ostensibly distant snippets of reality, unfamiliar vignettes of daily life in far-off localities across the world map, become less remote, yet, in many cases, less accessible. As I prepare to teach in fall 2021, online or in-person, I draw on examples from my everyday experience as a Panamanian, an employee, an immigrant, a daughter, a woman of color, and a member of an increasingly unstable middle class.

Some time back, I received a WhatsApp call from my *ahijada*, my goddaughter, in Panama City. She spoke about the total quarantine enacted across the country to contain the pandemic. Her stories of the quotidian hustles of neighbors and kin spotlighted the fracturing of livelihoods, resources, and means of survival for working people in times of COVID. In Panama's dollarized, service-oriented economy, close to half of the workforce make their living in the informal market as self-employed peddlers, whose incomes depend on street sales and ventures along busy roads. In this sort of gig economy common in the global south, joblessness takes qualitatively larger proportions when a total curfew is in place. For street vendors in cities like Panama City, public spaces closed off to the public because of COVID are the everyday workplace, the shop floor, and a primary means of livelihood.

Out of work and sheltered in place, my goddaughter, Maura, has been schooling her five minor children at home. She described the hardships of keeping up with lessons and homework in a virtual classroom out of her underserved community. Maura lives in Gonzalillo, a semirural neighborhood in the outskirts of Panama City made up of winding, half-paved/half-dirt roads and asymmetrically spaced houses of wood or unpainted concrete. Many are expanded to include overflow rooms for redoubling families. In Maura's home, there are nearly ten residents but no computer or internet connection. Her five children, spread across the K–12 school curricula, take turns on a single cell phone to keep up with virtual classes and complete assignments during the pandemic.

After "WhatsApping" with my goddaughter, I dashed from the phone to the computer to attend a Zoom meeting with a group of college teachers, my colleagues. That day, like many other days, I was the only brown face on the grid of square boxes that divide up the screen during virtual meetings. Feeling unheard and frustrated, the faculty at the school where I teach wrestled with fears of joblessness and a discernible sense of powerlessness in the institutional microcosm of a small, liberal arts college. Camouflaged by the economic effects of the pandemic, a deficit stemming from the administration's actions threatened the college's survival. The school's board of trustees, backed by their corporate know-how, confronted the crisis by downsizing and "rightsizing" labor, student services, and academic programs. I am familiar with this neoliberal approach to financial recovery. It mirrors the structural adjustment programs imposed by international financial institutions in Latin America to contend with the countries' external debt in the early 1990s. Laying off employees and slashing social services are constant factors in the mystical formula of technocrats, be they CEOs at the World Bank or vice presidents at a four-year college.

In this context, more than ever, I kept up with articles and reports about the status of higher education. And so, I found one that highlighted the relevance of sociology in the analysis of recent changes in the administration of academic institutions. The corporatization of colleges and universities was critiqued a century ago by sociologist T. Veblen at a time remarkably similar to the times we live in today:

> Just over a century ago, the same year that the Spanish flu struck millions around the world, the American sociologist Thorstein Veblen diagnosed a malady of a different sort: the control of universities by businessmen. "Plato's classic scheme of folly," he wrote, "which would have the philosophers take over the management of affairs, has been turned on its head; the men [*sic*] of affairs have taken over the direction of the pursuit of knowledge

[. . .] It has become a truism to say the coronavirus pandemic will change everything about higher education. But few discuss who should shape this change. The faculty? The student body? The public? Or the business-executives trustees that Veblen believed were destroying the essential nature of the academe? (Romeo and Tewksbury 2020)

I shared these concerns with my father, a former economist, whose disciplinary-focused viewpoints have not always aligned with mine. I telephoned him in Panama that night, like all other nights all year long. I have lived in the United States for twenty-six years, yet I still call home at least twice a day. When my mother died six years ago, my international communications gained new connotations. I took an active role in domestic affairs from afar, especially in coordinating the shifts of two ladies who stay with and assist my now-ninety-six-year-old father. My older brother in Panama does his share, but the gender expectations that cast women into nurturing roles demand my consistent help and daily remittances of love and care.

The work of care and kinship in times of COVID-19 pose unique predicaments for immigrants whose families remain at home. Such "labor of love" requires juggling roles and enduring the anxiety and uncertainty caused by the pandemic in two concomitant yet physically distant emotional fields. The complex gender dynamics involved in situations in which women employ other women to care for their kin is further complicated when the paid caregiver is an immigrant too.

Lorena, who takes care of my father every day, came to Panama from Honduras when a steady stream of Central Americans began to emigrate both north and south of their homes. Having left her children and parents behind, the care chain that starts with her was disrupted locally and remade transnationally across a web of paid and unpaid care work. So, who is taking care of the nanny's children? This question—extensively examined in the social science literature about transnational motherhood (Hondagneu-Sotelo and Avila 1997; Parreñas 2005)—gains new resonances during the pandemic in the context of geographic distance and travel restrictions.

When borders become sealed and entry/exit gates shut down, the experience of migration resembles a suspended journey. This metaphoric limbo turns tangible for those held up at the fortified gate that divides south and north, the Mexico-US border. For asylum seekers, the pause compelled by the pandemic intersects in complex ways with the physical and status immobility imposed by equivocal restrictions and power inequalities. Barred from interaction outside detention camps, they bear a range of health risks beyond COVID-19 as they wait confined in crowded tents, a gridlock between relocation and deportation.

Complicating her disquiet, Lorena found out that her oldest daughter undertook the journey north. Their migrations in opposite directions amp up their distance in more than one way. Sheltered in place in Panama City, Lorena wonders where her daughter is. She is most likely still in transit, caught up in the obverse duality of migration and detention.

As I continue preparing to teach sociology in a yet uncertain fall semester, I take note of a few lessons to share with my incoming class. For example, in times of collective threats such as pandemics, long-ignored, endemic inequities become "social problems," more ubiquitous the more social institutions exceed their "functionality" and threaten to collapse. In a seeming paradox, this viral pandemic that has required us to maintain social distance has also prompted us to become more aware of our inter-connected life circumstances.

Bibliography

Hondagneu-Sotelo, Pierrette, and Ernestine Avila. "'I'm Here, but I'm There': The Meanings of Transnational Motherhood." *Gender and Society* 11, no. 5 (1997): 548–571.

Mills, C. Wright. *The Sociological Imagination.* Oxford University Press, 1959.

Parreñas, Rhacel. "The Gender Paradox in the Transnational Families of Filipino Migrant Women." *Asian and Pacific Migration Journal* 14, no. 3 (2005): 243–268.

Romeo, Nick, and Ian Tewksbury. "You Can't Trust the Businessmen on the Board of Trustees." *Chronicle of Higher Education,* June 30, 2020. https://www-chronicle com.ezproxy.guilford.edu/article/You-Can-t-Trust-the/249087.

11 • SEEKING REST AND RESTORATION
Toward the Eradication of Academic Capitalism
Karina Santellano

WHEN I WROTE THE FIRST draft of this essay in May 2020, I was in my home in Los Angeles, California, under a citywide curfew that began at 6:00 p.m. Black Lives Matter protests had erupted just a few miles away from my Crenshaw home, across the nation, and even around the world. This global civil unrest came after almost three months of pandemic life: a life completely turned over on its head. Like most people around the world, I had reorganized my bedroom to fit a home office. On-campus activities, professional conferences, and social events were confined to Zoom, exacerbating the loneliness that already characterizes a PhD program. In addition to this, the growing number of COVID-19 cases and deaths, specifically in Black and Latino communities, including in Crenshaw and in southeast San Diego, where my parents live, made it difficult to focus on my academic work. The murders of Black people doing everyday things like sleeping, running, and simply *existing* in society by racist police and vigilantes led to mass outrage, and rightly so. As protesters had taken over city streets, they were met with police violence in the form of tear gas, rubber bullets, forceful pushing, and police cars driving into crowds with no regard for human life.

However, despite (and because of) the chaos, pain, exhaustion, and uncertainty since March 2020—including the loss of my grandfather to COVID-19 in November 2020 and my dad's miraculous recovery from it after a six-month hospitalization in 2021—I have experienced sharp clarity about the importance of rest and restoration in my life and in academia.

As a daughter of Mexican immigrants and a first-generation college student, graduate school has been yet another complex web of trauma to navigate. To say the least, graduate school was not what I thought it would be. In college, I loved my research experience with my senior thesis and the liberation I felt setting my own agenda and managing my own time. Yet in graduate school, I learned that as soon as you enter, you jump on the hamster wheel of a particular type of productivity. "Graduate school is training for faculty life," faculty members say. Of course, this makes sense, as graduate school is a time where one gains critical skill sets important to knowledge production. However, what I witnessed is a dangerous race, one where the academic job market is valued over one's mental, physical, and spiritual health. There are accolades one must collect in the form of grants, fellowships, and journal publications. There are forms of cultural, social, and human capital that one must have to secure that highly coveted tenure-track job. Faculty call it "professionalization." *So, this is like a business?* I wondered my first year as I sat in my weekly professionalization seminar. What happened to centering the well-being of marginalized folks? What happened to caring about people? What happened to doing work that matters for social good? I spent my first years of graduate school wondering, *Is this what graduate school is?* and *Is this what academia is?*

After I completed my coursework, my qualification exams, and my dissertation prospectus, I realized how mentally, emotionally, and physically exhausted I felt from the academic and service work I was doing. Of course, much of what I was doing I felt passionate about, but I needed a respite from the hamster wheel of all sorts of labor. And somehow the universe seemed to hear my request, my need for a break of sorts, for some quiet, for some time to lay my head on my pillow, to breathe, to not rush anywhere. The closing of public life as we knew it afforded me time to reflect and rest for the first time in years.

Given the closing of public places, including gyms, at the onset of the pandemic, I finally took time to take in my neighborhood in a way I had not prior to COVID-19. I began to take purposely slow walks around my neighborhood. Other times, I went on runs to feel the fresh air on my face. These steps outside, in nature, were liberating, soothing, and healing for me. I wondered why I had not given myself this time and opportunity to love myself enough to rest. Little by little, I could feel myself coming back. By that I mean that I began to feel complete and whole again, no longer mentally and physically discombobulated, pulled this way and that by academic and service responsibilities. Although some folks in academia stress work-life balance, it is hard to achieve or even attempt to achieve such balance when the hamster wheel of productivity is too treacherous to get off. I felt grateful to have returned to myself.

After more than a year and half since the start of the pandemic, I have had the opportunity to think about the questions and feelings that I have experienced in my graduate career. And as I mentioned, I grappled with these questions as my own immediate family members were fighting COVID-19. Navigating the grief of losing my grandfather and waking up every day when my dad was on a ventilator was the hardest thing I have ever had to do in my life. Experiencing this extremely tumultuous stage of the pandemic felt like life was sending multiple signs telling me to rest, focus on my health, and embrace slowness.

I realized that what I was feeling in graduate school were the symptoms of academic capitalism or the adoption of neoliberal market logics by universities. In *The Slow Professor: Challenging the Culture of Speed in the Academy*, Maggie Berg and Barbara K. Seeber explain that this is due to the rise and intensification of the corporate university, which emphasizes increasing workloads, a sped-up pace, and marketability. In other words, the university structure has not escaped but rather played a part in reinforcing neoliberal hyper-capitalistic logics in society. As such, academic capitalism makes us think that there is not enough time to do what we need to do. This translates to overworking and obsessing over publishing and external funding validation. Academic capitalism has infiltrated why and how research is done. Instead of a grassroots approach to research inspiration (i.e., we notice something or experience something, perhaps an inequality, and want to learn more about it), research is driven by the priorities of funding and grant institutions. Students hoping to be faculty members one day must navigate these market logics, and often play into them, to hopefully reach their career goal. What is the result of academic capitalism? Berg and Seeber explain that the rat race has led to less interest in self-care and less collegiality, collaboration, and community building in our home departments.

Is it possible to eradicate academic capitalism? I wonder. Is there hope for academics and academia? To counter academic capitalism, Berg and Seeber advocate for the Slow movement and they borrow from Wendy Parkins and Geoffrey Craig to reflect on it. In their book *Slow Living*, Parkins and Craig assert that slow living "is not a counter-cultural retreat from everyday life . . . not a return to the past, the good old days . . . neither is it a form of laziness, nor a slow-motion version of life." Instead, it is "a process whereby everyday life—in all its pace and complexity, frisson and routine—is approached with care and attention . . . an attempt to live in the present in a meaningful, sustainable, thoughtful and pleasurable way."[1] The Slow movement mantra resonates with me because it is not antithetical to research, knowledge production, learning, and finding ways to share our work with broader audiences. Rather, all these academic things I have listed can be compatible with the Slow movement, if we make them so.

Reflecting on my own experiences in academia, I ask: How do we build a more humane academia for graduate students of color? How do we embrace the Slow movement, as discussed by Berg and Seeber, to do this? I know I am not alone in feeling the effects of overwork in graduate school. Therefore, to adopt the Slow movement, I believe we need some structural and cultural changes. To assist graduate students, academic institutions need to provide livable wages and comprehensive health insurance to graduate students. Why is this important? I am nearing the end of my graduate program, and I can think of so many instances where graduate student colleagues and I have had to struggle to access basic needs like food, housing, and healthcare attention (including mental health). For example, when I first arrived in Los Angeles in 2016, my school year stipend was less than $25,000. So, before accounting for taxes, I was earning about $2,000 a month. This did not stretch the entire month. I had to take on weekend babysitting jobs for white families in wealthy Santa Monica and borrow from family members to survive. Only when graduate students threatened to form a graduate union during my second year of graduate study did my university decide to increase our stipend to $30,000. While a $30,000 stipend is a bit better, Los Angeles is also one of the most expensive cities in the country, so again, monthly stipends did not go very far. Graduate students with limited safety nets across the country must take on various side jobs to continue the PhD journey. Some of us provide financially for family members. I often chat with graduate student friends about the extra jobs we have had to take on during graduate school and the insensitive suggestions that faculty members un/intentionally make, like putting expenses on a credit card and learning how to budget to make it through the summer. How can we "move the academy forward," as many academics say, without being valued enough as humans to be provided with the resources to live a healthy life? We must support the well-being of graduate students by providing fair stipends and comprehensive health insurance. As living costs increase in many cities in the country, these academic institutions need to regularly evaluate whether their stipend is set to meet those living costs.

The overwork obsession also needs to end. I think tenured and tenure-track faculty can play a big part in this cultural change within their departments and across academic disciplines. For example, academics I know rarely talk about taking days, much less weeks, off. Many academics continue to work through the summer and sometimes through the holiday season. Of course, this is not the fault of the individual. Instead, it is academic capitalism and the intense demands embedded in academia taking hold of our brains, bodies, and spirits. After deep reflection during the pandemic, I have come up with some things I plan on doing when I am a faculty member. As a faculty member, I want to be forthcoming with my time off (whether that be due to holidays or for arbitrary days and weeks that I prefer to not work). I believe this is important to do because it helps graduate students realize that they, too, can take their rightly earned and necessary days and weeks off to rest. I would also think about creating graduate-level syllabi that promote learning and health because, again, they are not mutually exclusive. When I say *syllabi that promote learning and health*, I mean doable amounts of reading (perhaps select chapters), collaborative assignments, and personal workdays to work on the class final project or optional one-on-one meetings about the class rather than in-class sessions. While it may take a few tries to figure out what may work best for teaching in this way, I am driven by the question, How can I teach the material that needs to be taught without turning students into exhausted anxious zombies? Although I cannot control other classes or other factors in students' lives, I can model centering well-being in the classes I teach.

However, these two changes I mention, and others, need to be supported by a complex structural multilevel effort of improvement. I strongly believe that I cannot simply say that faculty should resist academic capitalism without acknowledging tenure expectations or the financial divestment in higher education in this country. In other words, structural changes must accompany these directions. The tenure process needs to be drastically reimagined. With a set amount of time to prove that you are an expert in your specific field and an important member of your university community, the pressure is on. For qualitative sociologists like myself, journal articles and a published book are often necessary to achieve tenure at research-heavy institutions. Meeting these expectations is often extremely time-consuming and difficult. For example, hearing back from a journal about a submitted manuscript can take months and sometimes longer. Working on the manuscripts themselves can be challenging when one is also teaching and doing service work. As plenty of research in education shows, women of color faculty often do much of the service work on university campuses, including advising student groups, mentoring students of color, and sitting on diversity, equity, and inclusion committees. Yet service work and activist work, whether on campus or in a community outside of campus, is not valued greatly toward tenure. One way of reimagining tenure is to count service work and activist work toward tenure so that faculty can do important work that they feel compelled to do without fearing that they will lose their jobs. There are multiple ways to be a contributing member of a university community that are worthwhile for employment and promotion. In a world of destructive climate change, a multiyear pandemic, widening income and wealth inequality, and so many other dire things, why support any systems or procedures that bring stress to people? In every realm of society, we need to look for ways to improve the livelihoods of our colleagues and friends. Tenure as an academic procedure and system is too archaic, too exclusionary, and too unequal to exist in its current form.

In addition, colleges and universities as well as state and federal governments should invest in the vulnerable fleet of university teaching labor: graduate students and non-tenure-track faculty. Today, about 70 percent of college faculty are off the tenure track (Griffey 2016). Adjunct faculty receive low pay and very little to no employment benefits, and they experience challenges to forming community with students and other faculty (Douglas-Gabriel 2019). While the adjunct experiences vary across institutional type (public or private), whether there is presence and success of union efforts and other factors, the point is clear: We are not investing in higher education during a time when more and more students of color are entering college, particularly at public colleges and universities (Mitchell et al. 2019). We need to ensure that their professors are invested in—so that they can participate in—students' intellectual development. State and federal divestment of higher education has made it harder to achieve this. For example, in 2015, Congress allotted almost $600 billion toward the military in discretionary spending while allotting $70 billion toward education (National Priorities Project 2021). States, on the other hand, have historically provided more aid to higher education institutions, but investment has steadily decreased since 1990 (Pew Research Center 2019). Since then, colleges and universities have increased tuition and looked for ways to reduce spending. This has contributed to the adjunct-ification of academia. University administrators, too, should ask themselves whether their budgetary decisions prioritize the well-being of their current and future community members. The suggestions I have elaborated above are a small part of a larger dialogue that academics across disciplines should think more deeply about and make plans to act upon.

The pandemic has been a completely unexpected, challenging time for all. In my own complex pandemic stages of both peace and grief, I have found clarity on loving myself enough to rest when I need to rest and on the directions that academia should take to improve conditions for graduate students of color. We must fight back against academic capitalism through multiple combined cultural and structural changes, like doing what we can as individuals and groups as well as advocating for the reimagination of the tenure process and advocating for state, federal, and university funds to end the exploitation of vulnerable workers on college campuses. For this to occur, we will need creative, innovative risk-takers at all levels, including, but not limited to, graduate students. As I think about what should be done to eradicate academic capitalism, I also recognize the multitude of challenges that graduate students of color are navigating inside and outside the university walls. Many of us have experienced the inequalities that the pandemic and recent racial uprisings have exposed. We are simultaneously dealing with structural injustices in multiple realms all the time. As we continue to face COVID-19 and the fight for intersectional justice, we will need to center loving ourselves enough to rest. Let's care for ourselves and reimagine new futures.

Note

1. See Parkins and Craig, *Slow Living*, for more information on the original quote (2006, ix). See Berg and Seeber, *The Slow Professor*, for more reflections on the Slow movement (2016, 11).

Bibliography

Berg, Maggie, and Barbara K. Seeber. *The Slow Professor: Challenging the Culture of Speed in the Academy*. University of Toronto Press, 2016.

Douglas-Gabriel, Danielle. "'It Keeps You Nice and Disposable': The Plight of Adjunct Professors." *Washington Post*, February 15, 2019. https://www.washingtonpost.com/local/education/it-keeps-you-nice-and-disposable-the-plight-of-adjunct-professors/2019/02/14/6cd5cbe4-024d-11e9-b5df-5d3874f1ac36_story.html.

Griffey, Trevor. "Decline of Tenure for Higher Education Faculty: An Introduction." The Labor and Working-Class History Association, September 2, 2016. https://www.lawcha.org/2016/09/02/decline-tenure-higher-education-faculty-introduction/.

Mitchell, Michael, Michael Leachman, and Matt Saenz. "State Higher Education Funding Cuts Have Pushed Costs to Students, Worsened Inequality." Center on Budget and Policy Priorities, October 24, 2019. https://www.cbpp.org/research/state-budget-and-tax/state-higher-education-funding-cuts-have-pushed-costs-to-students.

National Priorities Project. "Federal Spending: Where Does the Money Go." Accessed September 23, 2021. https://www.nationalpriorities.org/budget-basics/federal-budget-101/spending/.

Parkins, Wendy, and Geoffrey Craig. *Slow Living*. Berg Publishers, 2006.

PEW Research Center. "Two Decades of Change in Federal and State Higher Education Funding." October 15, 2019. https://www.pewtrusts.org/en/research-and-analysis/issue-briefs/2019/10/two-decades-of-change-in-federal-and-state-higher-education-funding.

12 • THE PhD CANDIDATE AS AN ESSENTIAL WORKER

Negotiating Dignity and Stigma During COVID-19

Fatima Suarez

I NEVER THOUGHT I WOULD be an essential worker, but here I am, hustling with humility and dignity. Working at a grocery store is exhausting. I work about thirty hours a week, earning sixteen dollars per hour. As a doctoral candidate who is in the middle of writing her dissertation, I am accustomed to sitting down at my desk for long periods, to the point where now I have shoulder and back problems. To cope with these issues, I write in forty-five-minute increments and then I walk around and stretch for fifteen minutes. This strategy helps me work without being in too much pain. But now, working in the grocery store, after being on my feet for a six-hour shift, I relish the opportunity to sit down and not get up.

Prior to April 2020, I was living out of state on a prestigious residential, dissertation-writing fellowship; I lived there for eight months. I was beginning to write the third chapter of my dissertation when California went into lockdown. I moved back to Goleta, California, in early April because I was worried about my fiancé, who was very stressed after losing his job as a server in a restaurant. A thirty-five-year-old man, he is ineligible to receive unemployment benefits. I used to worry about him for different reasons, and now I was concerned about his mental health. He joined me in our new apartment two weeks after I arrived. Although I was still on a fellowship, I quickly realized that it would not be enough to cover our household expenses. It was also impossible for my beloved to find a job during this crisis. All his work experience was in the restaurant industry, and the restaurants that remained open were not hiring. Watching him in such despair as he struggled to find work without success broke my heart. Anticipating this financial hardship, I got a job as an essential worker in a local chain supermarket.

This is my first non-university job. When I was an undergraduate, I did not qualify for work-study, and my parents, particularly my father, actively discouraged me from working while I was enrolled. He said, "Por eso yo trabajo, para pagar tu escuela así tú te enfocas en tus estudios" ("That is why I work, to pay your tuition so that you can focus on your schoolwork"). Although my father worked in construction and my mother was a stay-at-home parent, they managed to pay for the college education of their four daughters.

My new job responsibilities as a courtesy clerk include sanitizing shopping carts, baskets, door handles, and checkout stands; cleaning bathrooms and breakrooms; managing lines at checkout, and bagging customers' groceries. These responsibilities are quite distinct from my graduate student responsibilities. During my first shift, which was on a particularly hot day, I stood outside of the supermarket, wearing a fluorescent yellow safety vest, for four hours, collecting carts after customers left them scattered across the parking lot and then sanitizing them. Previously, working as a graduate student, I would go outside as much as possible to get some sun after having sat inside at my desk, thinking and writing, for hours on end. Now, I wish to be indoors. Although I quickly learned how to keep up with the rhythm of the job, I was confronted with the dangerous realities of essential workers during a pandemic. Although essential workers were aware of the health risks at the beginning of this pandemic, we were less prepared for the social risks that followed. For instance, when I was managing the checkout lines during one of my shifts back in early June 2020, a white male customer raised his hand in a Nazi salute and shouted "Heil!" at me after I reminded him and his partner to stand in line according to the store's safety guidelines. This was not my first incident of this kind. A few weeks earlier, I was at loss for words when a white woman shouted at me, "I am an American! I have a right not to wear a face mask! You are crazy and a sheep!" when I asked her and her kids to wear face masks inside the store. During these unfortunate incidents, I felt disempowered because I could not respond for fear of losing my job. Those who know me know that *yo no me dejo* (I'm not intimidated), but during these situations, I had to let it slide. These sentiments about mandatory social distancing guidelines are not unique to Goleta. Across the country, many people openly refused to follow these guidelines, protesting states' shelter-in-place policies. We are essential workers on the front lines of multiple battles, feeling unsafe on multiple fronts.

When I am at work, my partner cooks our meals, cleans our apartment, washes and folds our laundry, and brings me lunch during my break. Meanwhile, he is internally struggling to reconcile who he is and what he is doing at this time with the dominant ideas of what a man is supposed to be. He feels guilty and ashamed that I had to find a job during a public health crisis and that he could not financially support me. He feels unworthy. Almost every evening, while we are watching television or going on a walk, he gets quiet, pensive, and he tells me, "Me siento avergonzado porque no proveo más. Tú eres la que estás proveyendo en este momento. Me siento incapaz de no poder proveer" ("I feel ashamed that I don't provide more. You are the one who is providing right now. I feel powerless for not being able to provide"). But I know that without his caring labor, I could not do what I do.

He often raises the issue of my family's perception of him and our relationship as a source of anxiety and embarrassment: "¿Qué van a decir tus padres si se enteran que me estás manteniendo?" ("What will your parents say if they find out that you are financially taking care of me?"). His concerns are not baseless since my family has yet to acknowledge our relationship. They disapprove of him: "Él no está a tú nivel" ("He is not up to your level") because he is not college-educated and therefore will not be able to be a good provider. I tell him that housework is *real* work and that there is dignity in doing it. My feminist reframing of housework, though, is not enough to assuage his concerns. He repeatedly claims, "Yo lo hago porque te amo, no porque tengo que hacerlo." ("I do [the housework] because I love you, not because I have to"). My fiancé's words echo the findings of research with Hispanic househusbands: Viewing the nontraditional division of labor as temporary, forced by economic necessity, allows unemployed men to maintain self-esteem and self-respect. Under the traditional patriarchal division of labor, there is honor in paid work, not housework, for men. *Ser un hombre honorable*—being an honorable man—is consistently reflected in the stories of the Latino immigrant and working-class men participating in my dissertation project.

On the other hand, I am hesitant to share my newfound employment with my parents, friends, and colleagues. I do not think they would understand. I fear being judged. I am worried about telling my parents because I fear they would think, *Tanto sacrificio que hemos hecho para venir a este país y trabajar duro nomás para que tú estés trabajando en una tienda ganando un diario mínimo* (We have sacrificed so much to come to this country and work hard so that you can work in a grocery store and earn a minimum wage.) I have also not shared this story with my dissertation committee for similar reasons. My mentors have invested their time and energy on me because they believe in me and my potential. They often praise me as a "star," and I have built a respectable reputation in my department among peers, professors, and staff. What would they think if they found out that their "star student" is an essential worker? *Maybe she is not committed to academia?* My parents and mentors have built me up to be this good daughter, good and serious student, and a role model for others to follow. In their eyes, Fatima can do no wrong. The pandemic has knocked down the legs that sustained this pedestal.

I decided to tell my colleagues (all professors) with whom I was in the fellowship program because I had grown very close with them over the past eight months. Their reaction made me feel very guilty. One of them asked me, "Why would you choose to expose yourself?" and "Why did you get this job when you have a fellowship?" When I heard their remarks, I wanted to say, "Well, maybe because I can count how many paychecks I have left on one hand," but I swallowed my words. These were friends who, over the course of my knowing them, had shared progressive views on social issues, but when faced with my situation, they made me feel ashamed because I was working in a job that was "beneath me" as an academic-in-training. The way they reacted to my employment made me feel like they might believe they were above minimum-wage workers in some way. I was so disappointed. When I shared this incident with my coworker, a Chicano in his seventies who had lost his job due to COVID-19, he said, "What a shame. These people think they're better than everybody just because they're smart. These are the folks who are teaching our children, and yet they think so little of us."

At that moment, I had to confront a harsh reality. Will I become an elite academic who is so far removed from the realities of working people? As a seventh-year graduate student, I am standing outside of the gates of academia. Is this what is waiting for me behind these gates? We live in a capitalist society where who you are is grounded on what you do for a living. Value is distributed based on the type of job one holds. Stigma is placed on manual labor and prestige is placed on intellectual labor. I invested so much in academia that I had internalized its elitism. What else can explain my hesitation to openly share this part of my life? But this pandemic has allowed me to see myself for who I truly am. I am a humble and honorable person. I am no stranger to hard manual labor. I was raised in a working-class home in a working-class community. One of the lessons I learned from my parents, who worked as children, is to work hard. At the age of eleven, I helped my dad unload rebar from his pickup truck. I also mowed the lawn and washed my dad's truck. Being an essential worker does not take away from who I am; on the contrary, it reveals who I am fundamentally, especially in a moment of crisis.

The pandemic has created a lot of uncertainty for me. My future plans of going on the job market, getting married, and graduating are at a standstill. The future is unclear, but I am clear about the type of academic I want to be because of the valuable lessons that I have learned from this pandemic. Despite my curriculum vitae, I am still a working-class Chicana at heart who is willing to work a stigmatized job with dignity. I want to be an academic who is not elitist and who treats everyone with respect, regardless of their job title. What I can bring to academia is humility. Whenever I stand in front of a classroom or conference room, I will remember these experiences and I will communicate these lessons, because now we know that those who were deemed "essential" during this crisis will most likely not be present in those exclusionary, elitist academic rooms.

In Retrospect: One Year After

The COVID-19 pandemic has challenged and transformed our understandings of work, raising the question of whose work is essential or nonessential for the functioning of everyday social life. The categories of "essential" and "nonessential" did not exist prior to 2020. When states began to lock down in March 2020, policymakers designated certain industries as "essential" to prevent total social collapse, including food and agriculture; healthcare; transportation; warehouse and delivery; and industrial, commercial, residential facilities and services. "Essential" signifies value. When a worker is deemed essential, it means that their labor is valuable and important. The tragedy of this new typology, though, is that the category of essential has not translated into material or status value for workers. Most essential workers are still underpaid, overworked, and lacking basic labor protections, like paid sick leave. During the pandemic, many were required to work without personal protective equipment. I started working at the grocery store shortly after the workers' union won an additional "hero pay" of four dollars per hour for each frontline worker. Workers in other food and retail sectors were also given "hero" or "appreciation" pay. "Hero" or "appreciation" pay, though, suggests that one is not already a hero and that their work is not already appreciated. This essential work is what people do every day—before, during, and after a global pandemic. So, why is the "hero pay" not the normal wage? I am concerned that we call these workers "essential" or "heroes" to discursively obscure the exacerbating inequalities caused by the pandemic, deluding ourselves into believing that appreciation can replace material compensation. The labor that was once obscured has been rendered visible by the pandemic. The structural conditions that facilitated its invisibility, however, remain the same.

On the other hand, there is an assumption that academe is its own type of essential work, which is afforded a higher level of status. Academics, specifically sociologists, are responsible for examining how social inequalities take shape, how they change over time and across historical eras, and what processes reinforce them. Moreover, sociologists hold society accountable for the social ills people experience by making them visible. Our role as sociologists, then, is to explode the category of essential, pointing out the discrepancy between identifying certain workers as "essential" and truly regarding them as such. Instead of assuming the inherent value of academe, we need to earn it by communicating why these workers are indispensable and to understand the processes that render service work as low-class work. Our essential work is to speak truth to power.

In May 2021, my partner and I got married in a private ceremony in Las Vegas, with friends and family watching via livestream. Despite all the awfulness of COVID-19, the pandemic taught us new ways of being, learning, and un-gendering. To alleviate the mental stress of not working, my husband started walking in the morning and afternoon, biking, and painting. For more than fifteen years, he has always worked two to three jobs, leaving him little time to develop hobbies that make him happy. Now, my husband understands that there is more to him than just being a hard worker. He also learned that he is more than capable of taking care of our home. During our conversations about having children, he tells me, "Yo me quedo en la casa a cuidar a los niños y tú puedes trabajar" ("I can stay home and take care of the kids and you can work"). Although the pandemic has halted gender equality at the macro level, it has also created new ways of un-gendering in our relationship.

For a long time, I, too, was always working (even on weekends), identifying solely as a graduate student, an academic-in-training. This meant that I mostly interacted with people who were also in academe. The pandemic introduced me to people who I would otherwise not have met. Working alongside people who are trying the best they can to make ends meet reminded me that it is a privilege to be in academe and to do research that I am passionate about. As academics we can dictate our work schedule, which I realize is a *huge* advantage. The insights I shared early in this essay come from the positionality of a graduate student. Graduate students are constantly striving for recognition, a sign that we belong in academia. So, we aim for the fellowship, grant, award, a publication in a top-tier journal.

We learn, though, that there is often rejection in academia. On the other hand, I received all forms of recognition during my term as a grocery store clerk, including Employee of the Month, free groceries, and excellent performance reviews. I contemplated how the minimum-wage job judges people on their performance and the academy judges people on their worth.

I no longer work at the grocery store, nor am I a graduate student. I, however, still consider these tensions, especially now, as I will begin an esteemed postdoctoral fellowship at a prestigious institution in the fall. Through this pandemic, I learned that I want an academic job on my own terms. I don't want my job to have control over my life. To do this, I do not work after 5:00 p.m. on weekdays or check my email during weekends. I read nonacademic books at bedtime. The pandemic raised a new level of consciousness for me, where I negotiate the contradictions that being an academic and essential worker raised. The pandemic forced me to inhabit those two spaces simultaneously, living in what Chela Sandoval calls a "third space." As a Chicana academic who grew up in a working-class, immigrant home, I was aware of these contradictions before, but this awareness was intensified by the pandemic. It's one thing to theorize these tensions; it is another to live them. Due to the COVID-19 pandemic, people have become aware of what is important to them. What we do from now on will be forever shaped by our experiences living through this crisis.

Note

I would like to thank Annie Hikido and Liliana V Rodriguez for helping me explain my ideas when I was suffering from writer's block.

13 • EPISODES

Letters to Myself
Kiana T. Murphy

Pause.
Rewind.
Play.
Forward.

I can't gather the pieces together. I am generally unwell. The year 2020 is a hindsight vision on fast-forward.

The words: Iran, war, coronavirus, George Floyd,[1] Oluwatoyin Salau,[2] Breonna Taylor,[3] Dominique "Rem'mie" Fells,[4] heat wave, locusts, plague, TikTok, social distance, viral, Karen, immunocompromised, statues, diversity, denounce, call out, testing, picket line, immunity, Black Lives Matter.

The images: all refracted by a screen.

The sounds: fireworks.

Pause.

I am back home and my mother is laughing. No.
I am in Philadelphia and I am laughing. No.
I am back home, my childhood bed is warm but I am cold,
and I can't figure out who these people are around me.
I was in a room before, an examination,
the people only had mouths and asked me questions
saying qualifying exam over and over and

then I am in my childhood bed
it is winter
and I can't stop thinking about the word
displacement. Dis-place-ment. Ten years, in pursuit of education,
and at this moment, my home is under siege by monstrous development,
and here I am writing papers, and I do not know where I am.

4.15.2020

Audre Lorde says you can carry light
it is okay to let it touch you shake you up
and let you see darkness for the friend it is

we are mothers of our grief holding refuse
let it touch you even if you would die
let light change you even if you
would die
let light move you even if you
die

breathe in, breathe out

4.22.2020 *Parable of the Sower* Opera Adaptation by Toshi Reagon (List of Songs, Listening for Refrains)

"What You Goin' Do?" "Take Me to the Water?"
"New World coming, everything goin' be turning over, where you
    goin' be standing when it comes?"
"If I feel all you feel, would I know you better" "You think you
    can't, but you will, you will" "Grab Pack and Run"

5.12.2020 Notes from Job Placement Meeting, or Words Remembered

post-doc / lecture / visiting professor / dossier / MLA / abstract /
pull together / teaching / sample / sample / sample / committee /
three chapters by august / materials / recommendation /meeting
/ interview / mock / comportment / complete / faculty / polished
/ submit / send everything / syllabus / job market / job market /
market / market / market / send

5.19.2020 Notes from Alternative Careers Meeting, or Words Remembered

reflect / professionalize / collaborate / results / write it down / keep track / imagine / explore / my plan / options for success / 800 paths / network / LinkedIn / Google / talk about yourself / who are you / profile / test career / experience / materials / practice / handshake / appointment / advising / click here

6.10.2020 An Email, A Response

I can't stop thinking about the email notices from universities, from companies (from all over) making major (keyword: rhetorical) shifts to align with Black Lives Matter. The empty refrains seem to be their own insidious kind of violence. While the university gets in supposed alignment, there are students (mostly underrepresented students) being shuffled quickly out of dorms due to COVID-19, some returning to unsafe homes and some to nothing at all. Minimal efforts to provide essential workers on campus, graduate students, and other personnel the financial support to sustain the effects of closure, all the while sitting on millions of dollars of endowment doused in blood.

From: The University
Subject: Restitution

The University Announces ███████████████████
████████████████████████

A Message
███
████████████████
████████████████████
████████████████████████

We████████████████████████erected █████ █
████████████████our campus████████████████
████████████both now and into the future██
████████████████████████████████
████████████████████████ to allow slavery

██████ This is undeniably ███████████████████████████
██████████████ consistent with our University's core values, ████████
███████████████████████████████████ inclusion and diversity.

███████████████████ We ████████████████████████████████
███
██
advocated for slavery████████████████████████████████████
████.

███
██
████ we are grateful for ███████████████████ the institution of
slavery██
██
██████ its trustees, including our founder ██████████████████
██
█████████████

███
███████████████ announcing████████████████████████████████████
███████████████████████████ further steps to█████████████
place████████████████ statues and██████████████████████████
████████████████████ increase██ diversity██████████████████
█████████████ our firm commitment██████████████████████████
████████

██
██
██
██
██
██
██

While ███████████████████████████ pressing███████████████████
██ forward
expeditiously █████████████████████████████████████

██

racism ███ infected ████████████████████████████

█████████████████ how we operate █████████████████. We

believe ████████████████████ in ███████████ this path.

Notes

1. And more.
2. And more.
3. And more
4. And more.

PART III · BEYOND VIRTUAL CLASSROOMS
Education Reimagined

3. the Coatlicue state . . . desconocimiento and the cost of knowing

You realize you've severed mind from body and reversed the dichotomy—in the beginning you blamed the body for betraying you, now you blame your mind. Affirming they're not separate, you begin to own the bits of yourself you've disowned, take back the projections you've cast onto others, and relinquish your victim identity. Ésta limpia unclogs your ears, enabling you to hear the rustling of los espíritus; it loosens the constriction in your throat, allowing you to talk with them. Claiming the creative powers and processes of the unconscious (Coyolxauhqui), you thank your soul for the intense emotions y los desconocimientos that wrung consciousness from you. Though you try to thank the universe for your illness, emotional trauma, and habits that interfere with living fully, you still can't accept these, may never be fully present with the pain, never fully embrace the parts of self you ousted from consciousness, may never forgive the unconscious for turning hostile. Though you know change will happen when you stop resisting the dark side of your reality, still you resist. But despite the dread and spiritual emptying, the work you do in the world is not ready to release you.

"NOW LET US SHIFT," 554

89

14 · COMPASSIONATE PEDAGOGIES IN A PANDEMIC

Reflections from Latina Scholars

Leisy J. Abrego, Andrea Gómez Cervantes, Briceida Hernandez-Toledo, Leigh-Anna Hidalgo, Lucia P. Leon, Joanna B. Perez, and Iris M. Ramirez

IN THE MIDST OF THE current global pandemic, we have read wide-ranging advice about how to maintain our professionalism in academia, how to stay productive, or, on the contrary, how to turn our backs on all expectations of productivity. With a focus only on individual strategies, none of those approaches have felt quite right for us. As community-engaged Latina scholars, we have a practice of facing adversity collectively.

Academia Before the Pandemic

Institutions of higher education function structurally and culturally to reproduce social inequalities that have been exacerbated during the pandemic. Privileges and rewards go to those who already have resources; who grew up using the terms that many of us were hearing for the first time in class; who can pay for software and laptops, parking, and nearby housing—all of which make student life more manageable. Without such resources, navigating higher education has not always been a positive or empowering experience; it can be isolating and even hostile. At different moments in our trajectories, we have been those students who not only are the first in their families to go to college, but also lack financial and cultural resources to navigate the institution. These particular moments sometimes broke our spirits and fueled our imposter syndrome.

Many of us have struggled to make sense of vague calls for "professionalism" as we navigate the many unspoken rules of academia. And before we understood that much of it is based in middle-class norms, we sometimes felt like imposters for not recognizing the acceptable codes in these spaces. Academia, like much of US society, champions individuality and meritocracy. The expectation is that we present ourselves assertively as leaders, promoting our own accomplishments and publicly claiming our expertise to gain academic fellowships and promotions. These values can feel deeply contrary to how we were raised to respect humility above all else. We stay humble by downplaying our individual merits, but we gain strength by remembering the collective efforts and sacrifices that have contributed to who we are. Our accomplishments and successes belong to our communities because it is on their shoulders that we reached these heights.

We are motivated to become scholars who transgress academic culture. While each of us has taken a different path into academia, our journeys have consistently been guided by our personal and political commitments to social movements and to our communities. As self-proclaimed nerds, we also share an affinity for learning and teaching and a keen interest in pursuing challenging questions through research. As a result, it felt natural to pursue academia as a place where we could merge our community commitments and research to engage more deeply with the issues we care about. Here, we found our calling to keep creating spaces for emerging scholars who are similarly committed to community-engaged social justice scholarship.

In our schooling experience, teaching spaces have, at times, been transformational. Professors like Grace Dávila, Julie Davis, Anita Tijerina Revilla, Seline Szkupinski Quiroga, Janna Shadduck-Hernández, and others across institutions inspired us and made us feel at home. As educators, they facilitated our intellectual growth and helped us navigate expectations. They also connected us to resources and helped us apply to scholarships, internships, conferences, and research programs. Beyond the intellectual guidance, some even aided us directly by providing books and money out of their own pockets when we couldn't afford tuition, school supplies, or other basic needs. They taught us that our families' and communities' stories are important and deserve to be told in all of their complexity. We learned that we could thrive in academia precisely by remaining connected to our communities and our values.

We survive and thrive in academia by maintaining multiple commitments. We continue to prioritize the well-being of our families and communities, both within and outside of the academy, even while we meet deadlines, prepare lectures, and serve the university. We conduct research that lays bare the structures that create and sustain inequality while also bearing witness to the creativity, pain, and resilience of multiple communities. When things align well, we are able to care for our students, our families, our communities, and ourselves. Often, though, we are hit by crises.

Academia During the Pandemic

During this global pandemic, long-standing crises in academia and the world have been exacerbated. Online teaching has shifted classroom dynamics, impacting student relationships and learning. While we may virtually connect with our students, the inability to physically build community as a class has made it difficult to interpret discussions. Also, we find ourselves figuring out how to critically conduct and sustain research remotely, how to develop relationships and networks of support that are usually accessible at conferences, and how to cultivate and benefit from emotional support electronically.

For many of us, caregiving and familial obligations are not new responsibilities. The challenge during the pandemic is that the vulnerabilities of our family members make their health more dire. Many have lost jobs or had health complications. While we share our colleagues' concerns about the state of the world, personal well-being, and academic work, we are again confronted with the underlying inequalities that are more drastic and direct during a pandemic. Moving in with parents and taking care of family members' basic needs, like medications, groceries, housing, and healthcare, are just new layers of responsibility. In addition to in-person caregiving, some of us continue to have close ties to family members in other states and countries that are ill-prepared to deal with the pandemic, resulting in added responsibilities to send money for basic needs. And during justified national protests, we are called to support the Movement for Black Lives in multiple ways.

While the pandemic has made our personal lives more visible in the context of our work lives, the impacts are uneven. Many of our colleagues either have more resources for caregiving or do not have the additional responsibilities of being caregivers. For instance, while many are struggling to stay motivated or are concerned about needing to shift their research design, some of our struggles are about juggling homeschooling, childcare, and writing, on top of organizing to get food and cash assistance to community members and frontline activists. And while some express sympathy, too often educators uphold the system and practices that overburden students with academic work.

Our Response During the Pandemic

In this new world we're confronting, we are reinforcing our commitment to transform academia. We facilitate spaces of learning that acknowledge, validate, and incorporate students' experiences and funds of knowledge. We employ a compassionate and active approach to reversing inequalities that are critical in students' ability to continue their schooling. We consider ourselves fortunate when students trust us enough to be vulnerable, when they share that they cannot afford textbooks, cannot access internet services or electronics, or are generally unable to concentrate and produce the kind of work we would typically expect. They may be dealing with the loss of loved ones, with economic challenges, or with food insecurity. As instructors, we can model compassion by adjusting assignments, experimenting with instructional materials (films, breakout rooms, lectures, group work, creative projects), minimizing exams, and providing direct aid.

As a group, we encourage building community by connecting with other scholars who share similar values and experiences. In our case, we do this by organizing virtual writing groups, sharing goals through electronic documents, exchanging book chapters and grant applications, and sharing ideas through emails, phone conversations, or virtual meetings. Our exchanges are based on equal reciprocity with the expectation that it is okay to *not* be okay right now. We heed the public health call for physical distancing, but we commit more fiercely to supporting one another in creative ways. In these virtual and telephonic spaces, we express compassion for each other by being present and flexible with expectations of ourselves and of each other. We center our humanity by checking in about life (inside and outside academia), sharing resources, and sending memes to laugh and alleviate stress.

As a new approach to collective support, during the first several weeks of stay-at-home orders under COVID-19, we wrote this piece collaboratively in a monthlong process that allowed us to be vulnerable about our particular challenges. Our conversations became generative and regenerating as we learned new details about each other's lives. Committing ourselves to weekly meetings (with the flexibility and grace to lovingly understand when someone cannot be present) fosters a sense of stability and community when we know that we will show up for each other next week and the week after that—whether or not we happen to be thriving at research, writing, and teaching. We celebrate enthusiastically when someone in our group completes their master's thesis; files their dissertation; earns a job, grant, or fellowship; or is designated chair of their department! We also support each other when our articles or grant applications get rejected, and we affirm the value of each other's work and of our presence in the institution.

Building and sustaining community has been essential to our survival in academia. Because we have done this collective care work through multiple and ongoing crises—including presidential election results, immigration policy changes, the rolling back of rights for transgender people, and police brutality against Black people—we feel well equipped to continue to cope and adapt collectively in the uncertainty. Compassionate pedagogy is our philosophy and our praxis. It is based on the understanding of cycles of oppression and resistance that shape the university and propel us to imagine new spaces. Now more than ever, it is critical that we continue molding and transforming our previous approaches, weaving in communal strategies to persevere in the years of uncertainty to come. As we face the possibility of recurring moments of quarantine and we fight nationally in support of the Movement for Black Lives, we encourage more scholars to abandon the individualistic values of academia. Let's envision a new university rooted in compassionate pedagogies and community, one that stands in honest solidarity with those fighting to end anti-Blackness and the oppression of racialized groups.

Note

An earlier version of this piece was first published on the website Latinx Talk: Research, Commentary, Creativity, on June 17, 2020. The authors retain the copyright to their work. The original text includes hyperlinks to publications that might be of interest to the reader. The original text is available at https://latinxtalk .org/2020/06/17/compassionate-pedagogies-in-a-pandemic-reflections-from -latina-scholars/.

15 • PEDAGOGIES OF A BLACK FEMINIST QUARANTINE

Rituals of Womanist Teaching in the Wake of 2020

reelaviolette botts-ward

Abundance. *Photograph by Reanna Norman. Reanna Norman is an Afro-Okinawan photographer and storyteller. This piece was originally published in blackwomxnhealing's 2019 exhibit,* This Sh*t Is for Us *(blackwomxnhealing.com/thissh-tisforus).*

This creative reflection details my process of curating a virtual learning community rooted in a radical Black feminist healing arts praxis.[1] Written in the same format as my summer 2020 course syllabus,[2] this multimedia poetic essay maps five phases of ritual undergone to birth an online site of sacred communion. In some ways, this text is designed as an instructional guide for Black feminist educators invested in reimagining virtual pedagogy. In other ways, it is a call to healing for Black women, an invitation into another way of being in this world and the next, a leaning into virtual life-making on our own terms. This is a rejection of "business as usual" Zoom culture and a reframing of the virtual classroom as a liberatory site of convening that offers new possibilities for home-based integration of text, theory, and praxis.

Black Feminist Healing Arts: Reading, Writing & Livin' a Womanist Praxis of Care

Phase One: Curating a Syllabus

Don't Touch My Crown. *Photograph by Sydney Forneret, Oakland, California, 2019. Originally published in blackwomxnhealing's 2019 exhibit* This Sh*t Is for Us *(blackwomxnhealing.com /thissh-tisforus).*

My first undergraduate course as lead instructor. I type out the name on a blank Google document, wondering how to make a world of womanist safety on-screen, how to bring care to life on Zoom, how to embody a labor of love within a virtual syllabus for a virtual class that grounds itself in the real?

I proclaim this process ritual. Write the weight of 2020 into syllabus.

Name desire for course to be oasis in the midst of the wake. Name healing as wake work,[3] as possibility in the wrath of impossibility, as what we do in the midst of perpetual dying.

Bring art into the space of the page. Place homegirls' photography of pre-quarantine slay alongside Audre Lorde, Alice Walker, Alexis Pauline Gumbs. Place neon paintings alongside nude-colored cartographies to signal complexity. The palimpsestic remnants of crisis.[4] The art of survival.

Invite students to use Black feminist scholarship as compass into self, into communion, into wholeness. Center creativity as praxis. Name song and dance and film and book as medium, as art, as text. Study each with equal rigor. Place Beyoncé's *Lemonade* in conversation with Noname's "Song 33" in conversation with Shange's *For Colored Girls*. Put "it feels right to me" in conversation with "spirituality . . . [as] the basis of art."[5] Assign self-care ritual for 40 percent of grade. Assign final project creative production of choice. Encourage every student to discover her own creative power within.

Each week is themed—soul care, communal care, ancestral care. Each week is outlined alongside an image. A link to a film. An autographed self-portrait. Each week witnesses the merging of hood and holy, sacred and unraveling. The document ends with an extended list of texts. Virtual platforms. Books. Articles. Films. Songs. Albums. To direct students to more than one hundred Black feminist creations that six weeks could not hold. Invite students to add their own sources. A collectively curated guide, for us and our homegirls to be well.

My student proclaims, "This syllabus is a work of art." She mirrors my intent. To force the page, to hold the holes of Black femme humanity. To force the screen to stretch for the capaciousness of our convening.

Phase Two: Centering Praxis

June Jordan's *Poetry for the People* as the model. Mikki Kendall's word as intent. Centering homegirls and hood girls and all the femmes at the margins of acceptable Black womanhood. "So many feminist texts . . . written about girls like me, instead of *by* girls like me."[6] So many courses taught *about* disrespectability and wayward lives,[7] but so few *embody* this mode of refusal in the process of pedagogy. So many classes hint at care yet do not inhabit a healing pedagogy within the framework of course structure.[8] How do I curate a course that centers the poetry of the people, the citation of the communal, the curation of homegirls, the care of colored girls who are still considering suicide because the rainbow is enuf?[9] How do I place Alexander's *The Black Interior* and Sharpe's *In the Wake* and Hartman's *Way-*

Queendom. *Photograph by Sydney Forneret, Oakland, California, 2019. Originally published in blackwomxnhealing's 2019 exhibit* This Sh*t Is for Us *(blackwomxnhealing .com/thissh-tisforus).*

ward Lives in conversation with wounded women who are wayward and wandering and forgotten?

I name this course a 'round-the-way Black girl methodology made real. Invite students to show up in headwrap, bonnet, house robe. Let locs be tightened and edges be greased on-screen. Allow mamas and babies to brush braids on-screen. Let students show up as their unapologetic selves on Zoom for the first time. Name that care as praxis. Center beauty supply and dollar store and laundromat as radical sites of Black femme self-making. Name Black women's survival an art form. How a mother "adorn[s] with flowers whatever shabby home [she is] forced to live in."[10] How a teacher "make[s] a path through the wake."[11] How a sister creates "livable . . . spaces and places in the midst of [the] unlivable."[12] How unhoused Black women of the #37MLK encampment offer the most rigorous ontology of intersectional world making in the face of global crisis.[13]

Invite community into classroom, for no one could teach 'round-the-way healing arts better than Black women who make life beyond the academy. My homegirl from Texas who is a self-made curator, my homegirl from the Bronx who makes films. Lean into the "productive **dissonance** that occurs as we work at the edges of disciplines, on the margins of social life . . . in the vexed spaces between academic and nonacademic communities."[14] This is Black studies. Communiversity. Community and university collide. Become one—one collective virtual Black feminist convening.

Phase Three: Cultivating Self-Sanctuary

Borderline: An Ode to Self Care. *Photograph by Jasmine Sozi, Oakland, California, 2020. Originally published in blackwomxnhealing's 2021 exhibit* #blackgirlquarantine *(blackwomxnhealing .com/blackgirlquarantine).*

I begin our journey with six steps to curating virtual sanctuary.

Step one: *Identify a safe space in your home.* A praxis of Black feminist survival. With an understanding of the limitations of home safety, and a reckoning with the spectrum of precarity Black women experience at home, I invite students into a new relationship with the domestic sphere. Though home may not always be safe, I challenge students to imagine an oasis in the midst of chaos. Like the #37MLK encampment, where Black women drape tents in interior design decor, I ask, What might it feel like to lean into a closet, a corner, a tub, a space in a room, a liminal, ephemeral escape from the chaos of the home? Like Harriet Jacobs,[15] might we find a small corner of freedom amid the claustrophobia of quarantine? I ask, "Where do you feel most safe in your home? Where do you feel most secure? Most sure? Most held, nurtured, affirmed?" I invite my students into a new place. Inside the home. Inside the self. I am in my sacred corner and I invite them to curate their own. "Thank you for inviting me to move away from this desk, where I sit on Zoom all day, and into my bed, under my blankets." A Black girl student finds that comfort is essential to the Black feminist virtual classroom.

Step two: *Identify a sacred object*. I hold Hanu, my sacred stuffed unicorn, and let students know she is my lucky charm. I speak about inner child healing, how in my process of mourning my "inner[blackgirl]child,"[16] I discovered a girl whose spirit was murdered and rebirthed in me. The unicorn became her symbol of self-recovery, a reminder of all the Black girls who have died in me, all the ones I do this work for, the ones longing for levity and transcendence. I ask students to identify their sacred object, something tangible to touch and hold, something tactile to keep one's feet on the ground, to root one's spirit in nurtured soil. An amethyst stone statue at the corner of an altar. A white waxed candle from a grandmother who practiced Santeria. An obituary. A note. Something to hold close at every convening. To remind ourselves who we are and whose we are and why we are doing this work.

Phase Four: Cultivating Communal Sanctuary

The Daughter of Mother Earth. *Photograph by Sydney Forneret, Oakland, California, 2019. Originally published in blackwomxnhealing's 2019 exhibit* This Sh*t Is for Us *(blackwomxnhealing.com /thissh-tisforus).*

Step three: *Make a community playlist*. "Who y'all like to listen to when you alone with yourself?" I ask my students to fill the chat with all their faves. Jill Scott. Erykah Badu. SOL Development. Tasha's "Lullaby" and Jamila Woods's "Holy." We spend the first ten minutes of convening listening to the tunes that bring us back to ourselves.

Step four: *Make a community care covenant.* "What do you wish to ground our space in? What will we commit to as a community of learners longing to be well?" We use the chat to ask for what we need. Care. Vulnerability. Necessary silence. Acceptance. No shame. Rejection of systems and structures that keep us from being whole. I take each request and compile a covenant of care that demands we show up differently, for ourselves and for each other.

Step five: *Repeat collective affirmations.* "What do you wish to repeat to yourself to help you be well?" We place pain and purpose in conversation as we work to name new scripts. *I am brave. I embrace the parts of myself I was taught to fear.* Use the chat to teach each other love languages we never knew we needed. *I am theory. I am knowledge. I am worthy of learning and unlearning.* I take each love-bound affirmation and compile a fragranced note of tenderness. A stringing together of words and phrases that remind us we are whole, we are hurting, we are healing. We read our collectively curated affirmation poem at the end of every class.

Phase Five: Sacred Ritual

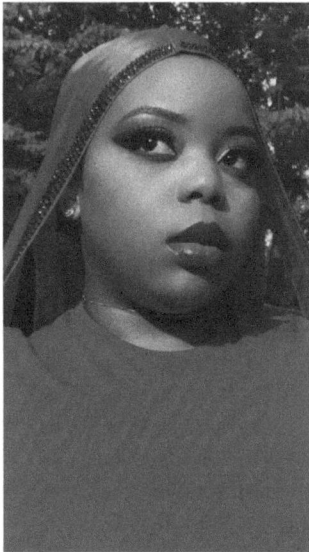

REVE(A)LED. *Photograph by Kandace Moore, West Orange, New Jersey, 2020. Originally published in blackwomxnhealing's 2021 exhibit* #blackgirlquarantine.

We begin each class with meditation. An invitation into breath. An awareness of body and all the ways it needs to move. Gratitude for flesh that is theory that makes art. Harpist from the Hood playing in the background.[17] Let harp lead us home, into the self, into the healing we have longed for.

We transition from the breath to the pen. From the harp to the hymn. Playlist of 'round the way rude girls and gin-sippin' blues girls blasts through speakers. We do not speak. Just listen. Just vibe. Just write. Ten minutes, nonstop. No picking up pen. Let hand move words cross page unfiltered. Express. Relief. Release. How heavy it is to be Black and woman and wounded; how freeing it is to let yourself name that in intimacy. No one will read your writing. It is only for you. Hold your journal close and know it is one of the truest sites of self-convening. Write about how *Hood Feminism and Home-girls* gave us permission to be ratchet and brilliant and broken at the same damn time. How Aja Monet and Sunni Patterson affirm the wildness of our womanhoods. How in our "mother's gardens, [we] find our own."[18]

Share out. Three souls to a breakout room. Five minutes each. Read or speak or be silent. Breathe or think or dream. Whatever you need to feel well. Shower yourself with words you need to hear, with words from texts that saved our lives. Use your five-minute share to locate the root of trauma, to name harm, to cry and shed and be seen, to remember the dis-membered body.[19]

Come together again. Share out. What was said in breakout groups that resonated? What would you like to affirm of a sister/comrade/friend? Snaps and claps and "sis I feel you," tears and love and virtual hugs. We are learning to hold each other. We are learning to hold ourselves.

Self-care/communal care check-in. One song long to write in the chat all the care you need in this moment. What do you need from us? What do you need from you?

Spend the rest of class flipping through slides of Black feminist artistry. Centering quoted texts. Reading art as text. Naming all the ways the words of Black feminist foremothers became the ground I stand on.

Notes

1. For additional reflections on Black feminist healing arts as a theoreti-cal framework, please visit reelaviolette botts-ward, "Black Feminist Healing Arts: A Making of Pedagogy and Praxis," *Synapsis: A Health Humanities Journal*, accessed February 14, 2025, https://medicalhealthhumanities.com/2024/08/14/blackfeministhealingarts/.

2. Please go to www.blackwomxnhealing.com/blackfeministhealingarts for the syllabus.

3. Christina Sharpe, *In the Wake: On Blackness and Being* (Duke University Press, 2016).

4. Christen Smith, *Afro-Paradise: Blackness, Violence, and Performance in Brazil* (University of Illinois Press, 2016).

5. First quote from Audre Lorde, "Eye to Eye," in *Sister Outsider: Essays and Speeches* (Crossing Press, 1984). Second quote from Alice Walker, *In Search of Our Mothers' Gardens* (Harcourt, 1983).

6. Mikki Kendall, *Hood Feminism: Notes from the Women That a Movement Forgot* (Viking, 2020), xii.

7. Saidiya Hartman, *Wayward Lives, Beautiful Experiments: Intimate Histories of Social Upheaval* (W. W. Norton and Company, 2019).

8. I acknowledge the ways in which the academy makes this an impossibility and leaves vulnerable folks who refuse to comply with institutional norms.

9. Ntozake Shange, *For Colored Girls Who Have Considered Suicide / When the Rainbow Is Enuf* (Scribner Poetry, 1975).

10. Alice Walker, *In Search of Our Mothers' Gardens* (Harcourt, 1983), 239.

11. Sharpe, *In the Wake*, 7.

12. Sharpe, *In the Wake*, 7.

13. #37MLK is a community of unhoused Black women in Oakland that provides communal care through the creative production of homemaking.

14. Brittney C. Cooper et al., *The Crunk Feminist Collection* (Feminist Press, 2017), xviii.

15. Katherine McKittrick, *Demonic Grounds: Black Women and the Cartographies of Struggle* (University of Minnesota Press, 2006).

16. reelaviolette botts-ward, *mourning my inner[blackgirl]child* (Nomadic Press, 2021).

17. Destiny Muhammed, also known as Harpist from the Hood, is a harp player who centers communal epistemologies in her sonic art practice.

18. Alice Walker, *In Search of Our Mothers' Gardens* (Harcourt, 1983), 241.

19. Jacqui M. Alexander, *Pedagogies of Crossing: Meditations on Feminism, Sexual Politics, Memory and the Sacred* (Duke University Press, 2005).

16 • IMPERFECT CRITICAL LOVE

The Shadow-Beast During Pandemic Times

Gema Cardona

THE UNCERTAINTY OF THE PANDEMIC that impacted the entire world is quite familiar to me. I have felt this uncertainty before, deep within my Brown skin. The kind of uncertainty that takes power over bodymindsoul. The kind of uncertainty where isolation turns into vicious psychic pain rather than the opportunity to listen to calming meditative tunes in your mind. It was in the summer of 2019, to be exact. I found myself alone in my home with my two-year-old son. That summer I was unemployed, left without funding from my graduate program, and without stable childcare. There is a saying I learned at a very young age: *sacar energía/esperanza de donde no existe*. It translates to "find energy/hope from where it doesn't exist." That summer my energy had been drained because the raw realities of our broken system had done their job of taking from my essence what always maintained that *dicho* true—my soul. The dicho is calling us to do the impossible; it's asking us to reach into what does not exist; it's moving us to reach into our souls *cuando todo se está derrumbando a nuestro alrededor*. In its philosophical sense, the dicho is calling for a spiritual response to healing in times of woundedness.

What guided me in responding to the pandemic differently compared to the summer of 2019 was becoming more in tune with my Shadow-Beast. The way that I arrived to what Gloria Anzaldúa calls the Shadow-Beast— or forbidden inner knowledge—was being in complete and utter "chaos" of my deepest emotions, which Audre Lorde (2007) and bell hooks (1994) refer to as the *erotic* or *eros*. Emotions are a source of knowledge. Feeling pain—in our hearts and bodies—is emotional. The emotion of pain that has been coming to the surface while in isolation during these pandemic times was not from being in physical contact with others, but rather from being in a constant state of remembrance of past painful experiences. For me, this forbidden inner knowledge meant embracing my imperfections. My imperfections reside in being a *wounded subject*. The emotional chaos while in quarantine has been a constant questioning of what belongs to me and what emotional baggage is a deep internalization of what white patriarchal society inherently believes I am. The isolation has forced me to return to old feelings and insecurities about my intersecting identities of first-generation college student, Brown *mujer*, and Brown single motherscholar.

Before we can speak of our woundedness, we must understand the origins of our pain. In the past year, I have been floating in an ocean of pain that feels like it has taken over me. Mind paused; body numb; spirit broken. I could not make sense of the pain. Making sense of this pain meant embracing my imperfections. It meant accepting I am a wounded subject. The pandemic was quick to bring me to a place of messiness with all my emotions that had been kept hidden away in my body (Cruz 2001). When someone tries to embody perfection, they are truly fearful of failure. In a white patriarchal society, being *perfect* means fitting the "norm"—that which is white, male, heterosexual, middle/upper class, and abled. The same goes for love. When we try to love perfectly or find the perfect love, we are afraid to truly love. Similarly, the consistent practice of perfection is painful because it is a denial of our true essence. We cannot deny how we have been wounded—whether it be prior to the pandemic or while navigating during pandemic times. If we could name a *blessing* during these pandemic times, it would be a reflection of how we might be consenting subjects to the practice of perfection. This blessing is essential because it unmasks our obsession as a society to love perfectly and to love that which is constructed as the perfect subject.

Perfect love does not exist; it is merely an illusion. Yet the emotional consequences it produces when we inherently believe in it as truth are real. Love is "unconstricted"; it is "rooted in a committed willingness to struggle persistently with purpose in our life and to intimately connect that purpose with what [Freire] called our 'true vocation'—to be human" (Darder 2011, 180). *Unconstricted* means that love does not have a structure or set of instructions. I have been afraid to truly love because I have been believing the lie that love will only [eventually] lead to pain. The reality is that love is the solution to healing our pain as colonized wounded subjects. Part of this healing work means loving our pain and loving our wounded selves.

Before we can use the healing powers of love, we must clarify the underlying *mentiras* of our Shadow-Beast. Anzaldúa (1999) explains that our understanding of the Beast tied to "sexual lust" is one constructed and projected onto our Beast by "heterosexual males" (42). She then says that when we come to realize this lie—that our Beast is sexual lust—we see tenderness in the Beast. This tenderness, especially when it is a "sign of vulnerability" is so "feared that it is showered on women with verbal abuse and blows" (Anzaldúa 1990, 383). This idea and realization—that to be a Brown feminist means to embrace *tenderness*—has been transformative and radical for me, while also painful to navigate in a world that circulates around racism, sexism, and other systems of violence. Seeing this tenderness in my Shadow-Beast has radically transformed how I imagine and practice love, as both a mother and an educator.

This tenderness has allowed me to vulnerably ask: How can we love when we have been oppressed, wounded, and traumatized? How can we love in a world so obsessed with irrational violence? I refuse to accept that the solution to violence is more violence. Yet I understand it is sometimes the first mechanism we use as wounded subjects of a wounded system. It is sometimes the survival mechanism we use as wounded subjects. More than wounded and broken subjects, we have become heartbroken subjects.[1] How can we love as heartbroken subjects? Especially when we have been heartbroken countless times, we have lost sense of what love feels like. Ultimately, how can we love in a wounded world during pandemic times? First, we must clarify our definition of love in relation to emotions, particularly pain and fear. This is because one of the greatest effects of coloniality is the colonial wound, which holds valuable knowledge. I find this forbidden knowledge to be tied to how we can redefine love as decolonial, which promotes healing between self and others (Ureña 2017). Part of this healing is understanding how love does not have to be perfect and unveiling the lies we have been conditioned to believe about love.

Loving imperfectly and critically means embracing ourselves as wounded subjects. The controlling image of being a *strong mujer* has produced an unrealistic ideal by which to constantly live by. The notion of *imperfect critical love* means emerging and transcending into a spiritual space of facing and dialoguing with our Shadow-Beast with the intention of understanding how healing emotional pain will produce more loving relationships. Prior to coming to imperfect critical love, I was living life and teaching simply by transmitting information without pausing to deeply reflect on how trauma and pain from navigating education as a first-generation Brown *mujer* was producing loveless interactions with others. This did not mean I did not *care*, nor that I did not take a "critical" approach to how I was teaching about race and gender, for example. Rather, it meant that I was unaware of the loss in potentially transformative professor-student interactions because I had not truly learned to love myself as a wounded subject from all the oppression that was in constant motion around me. Ironically, I was teaching and lecturing about oppression *without* inviting my oppressed body to enter the classroom. In essence, this also shut the door for my students' oppressed and fragmented bodies to enter the classroom. Imperfect critical love is, as hooks (1994) describes the erotic, "to enter the classroom 'whole' and not as 'disembodied spirit'" (193).

Imperfect Critical Love in the Private Sphere: Unveiling the Fear of Love

The first important aspect that bell hooks tells us in *All About Love: New Visions* is that "deep affection" does not properly define love; it is only one ingredient of love. True love means learning to encompass various "ingredients," as hooks (2000) says: "care, affection, recognition, respect, commitment, and trust, as well as honest and open communication" (5). Drawing from the work of both M. Scott Peck and Erich Fromm, hooks (2000) defines love as "the will to nurture our own and another's spiritual growth" and writes that when we have this understanding of love, we cannot claim we love when we practice being "hurtful and abusive" (6). What is most important in this definition is the aspect of the spiritual, which is tied to "our capacity to be more fully self-actualized and be able to engage in communion with the world around us" (hooks 2000, 13). Part of my own process of self-actualization has been the realization that men (including men of color) have been socialized to lie and I have been at the core of this dynamic. At the core of said dynamic, as womxn of color, we also begin to lie in order to please others. hooks (2000) describes the heart of justice as being able to tell the truth. Yet from an early age sexist socialization teaches us to lie as a means to avoid getting hurt or hurting others (hooks 2000). I find that this sexist socialization is also a fear of allowing love into our lives.

The reality is that not everyone consistently practices being courageous in loving and living. The reality is that there is an immense *fear* to love and be loved. This fear derives from the constant practice of perfection and lying. The practice of perfection, of impeccability even, derives from fear of making a mistake, of getting hurt, or of hurting another. To practice perfection is to lie in the process. For me, critical love is *imperfect*, and it holds the possibility for transformation and liberation. An *imperfect critical love* means unveiling the fear of love that exists within ourselves and in the world and understanding the erotic as part of our self-actualization.

Imperfect Critical Love in the Public Sphere: The Classroom as a Site of Love

In my years of teaching, I consistently have heard students express their desire to excel academically. At times, it feels like they are trying to impress me and gain my approval. As we transitioned to remote learning, I thought that, based on all the chaos in the world, including all the antiblack racism and those impacted by COVID-19, students would not be as preoccupied with grades and the stress that accompanied trying to receive approval from their professors. I found this not to be the case—there was still the overwhelming stress of trying to be the *perfect student*. Many times, this was tied to the reality that their academic standing was strongly correlated with receiving much-needed financial aid during a time of crisis. This was something that could not be dismissed, especially in a pandemic. I could not blame the students. What I could decipher was that higher education, even before the pandemic, did not embrace the kind of love that allowed students to have flaws—to be imperfect and still feel loved with all their imperfections. That meant deeply reflecting on why love was so scary. In many ways, I feared facing my own practice of perfection, as that is what I had used as a mechanism to survive my own navigation of higher education and the world as a Brown *mujer*.

Before I can provide my students with a truly humanizing education, I have to first emerge in a process of self-actualization (hooks 1994) where I define and construct my own humanity as a Brown single motherscholar. As I began to transcend from a fragmented understanding of love, I came to understand love as encompassing *courage* by actively tackling fear. This is what Antonia Darder (2011, 181) describes as a "courageous vulnerability of . . . humanity" when reminiscing about the time she witnessed Paulo Freire show deep grief over the death of his wife Elza during a professional presentation. Our emotions for what impact us as educators should be welcomed into the classroom. This promotes humanity in teaching and learning, especially in such uncertain times.

Loving and Teaching During Pandemic Times

In *Teachers as Cultural Workers: Letters to Those Who Dare Teach*, Paulo Freire's second letter, titled "Don't Let the Fear of What Is Difficult Paralyze You," deserves our ultimate attention when teaching during pandemic times. Freire (2005) makes the connection between fear and difficulty in the context of understanding a text. Understanding a text, as Freire has made clear in his other work, is parallel to understanding the world. When faced with difficulty, the *fearful subject* can either face the difficult situation or be *paralyzed* upon being faced by the difficult situation. The problem is not that fear exists or that we are fearful subjects—this is part of our humanity. The problem is when we are paralyzed by fear, we cannot overcome the difficult situation.

Embracing imperfect critical love means that we see our own humanity and that of our students when we face fear, which has been inevitable in what has been unveiled during these pandemic times. In teaching from a place of love, we should not force our students to face the difficult situation, but it should be set as an example. More than facing the difficult situation, Freire explains that we should not be ashamed if we do not fully understand what we have faced. Our *gran maestro* Freire's understanding of the fearful subject helps us to avoid paralysis, which our *gran maestra* Gloria Anzaldúa (2002) has similarly described as the Coatlicue, or third space, which is the state of being in deep despair and hopelessness. This state of being is what paralyzes us.

Fearless educators do not exist. Transformation during difficult times has meant that we face fear up front. It is part of our humanity to humbly accept that we have experienced fear to some capacity during the pandemic. Motherhood has taught me this. As a mother, I have also witnessed my son come in contact with fear through his own child imagination. I cannot tell my son—a Brown boy—to not be afraid. I would be teaching him early stages of machismo—that a man is fearless and is thus never afraid. Fearlessness is another mask of perfection. As a mother, I walk alongside my son to explore and identify what makes him afraid and find a solution that makes him feel empowered. The same goes with our students. As educators, it is our responsibility to identify fear, uncertainty, and confusion and address them in the classroom. Before we can act upon this fear in the classroom, we must consciously understand how it exists within us. This entails tapping into our spiritual activism (Anzaldúa 2002), which will be messy and imperfect. Our spirit is perfect in its own imperfection. Our spirit is peaceful, but it is also a Beast that is waiting to be unleashed. Our spirit is a balance between inner peace and inner chaos. This is love—that which is both peaceful and chaotic. This love never abandons us.

Note

1. Ríos-Rojas (2020, 162) argues that we must experience heartbreak in order to "*feel* an otherwise" and become conscious of grand narratives that reproduce oppression in order to move toward greater justice. Given this, there is a necessity for breakage.

Bibliography

Aigner-Varoz, Erika. "Metaphors of a Mestiza Consciousness: Anzaldúa's Border-lands/La Frontera." *Melus* 25, no. 2 (2000): 47–62.

Ahmed, Sara. *The Cultural Politics of Emotion.* 2nd ed. Edinburgh University Press, 2014.

Anzaldúa, Gloria. *Borderlands/La Frontera: The New Mestiza.* 4th ed. Aunt Lute Books, 2012.

Anzaldúa, Gloria. "La conciencia de la mestiza: Towards a New Consciousness." In *Making Face, Making Soul / Haciendo Caras: Creative and Critical Perspectives by Feminists of Color*, edited by Gloria Anzaldúa, 377–389. Aunt Lute Books, 1990.

Anzaldúa, Gloria. "Now let us shift . . . the path of conocimiento . . . inner works, public acts." In *This Bridge We Call Home: Radical Visions for Transformation*, edited by Gloria Anzaldúa and AnaLouise Keating, 540–578. Taylor & Francis Group, 2002.

Darder, Antonia. "Chapter 9: Teaching as an Act of Love: Reflections on Paulo Freire and His Contributions to Our Lives and Our Work." *Counterpoints* 418 (2011): 179–194.

Freire, Paulo. *Teachers as Cultural Workers: Letters to Those Who Dare to Teach.* Expanded ed. Westview Press, 2005.

hooks, bell. *All About Love: New Visions.* William Morrow, 2000.

hooks, bell. *Teaching to Transgress: Education as the Practice of Freedom.* Routledge, 1994.

Lorde, Audre. *Sister Outsider: Essays and Speeches.* Crossing Press, 2007.

Ríos-Rojas, Anne (Anna). "'Pedagogies of the Broken-Hearted': Notes on a Pedagogy of Breakage, Women of Color Feminist Decolonial Movidas, and Armed Love in the Classroom/Academy." *Frontiers: A Journal of Women Studies* 41, no. 1 (2020): 161–178.

Sandoval, Chela. *Methodology of the Oppressed.* University of Minnesota Press, 2000.

Ureña, Carolyn. "Loving from Below: Of (De)colonial Love and Other Demons." *Hypatia* 32, no. 1 (2017): 86–102.

17 • FEMINIST THEORY, DISABILITY JUSTICE, AND THE COVID CLASSROOM

Michelle Velasquez-Potts

Spring 2020

Over the years I've thought a lot about how punitive the classroom is, how between the classroom and the teacher exists a dialectic relationship informed by discipline, punishment, ableism, and policing. I want to reflect on how COVID-19 has reinforced what many of us already knew about how intrinsic ableism and punishment are to higher education and how both only further the logics of the prison industrial complex (PIC) inside the classroom. In doing so, I hope to push myself in continuing to imagine transformative approaches to education in light of COVID-19 that are grounded in relationality, care, and my own femme embodiment.

On the role of the PIC in higher education, scholar activist Margeaux Feldman writes, "The PIC can be seen quite clearly through the university's investment in ableist policies and practices, which shape the classroom as a space hostile to disabilities and chronic illness."[1] Such ableist policies take the form of bureaucratic protocol that requires documentation in order to qualify for accommodations, refusal to accept late work, pressure to drop the grade of work submitted after the due date, rigid policies around absences and tardiness, and an overreliance on campus police in the event of a mental health crisis.[2] My own pedagogy has historically been shaped by ableist policies such as these, presented to me as a graduate student instructor as the only effective way to "run a classroom." I have spent this past year reflecting on the normalization of punishment in higher education and trying my best to unlearn those ways by interrogating the content and structure of my syllabi, addressing access needs within the physical and virtual space of the classroom, and interacting with my students in ways that are trauma informed and relational.

As a result, being in the classroom the semester that COVID-19 hit felt life-affirming and generative. I had multiple conversations with students about their individual access needs, chronic illnesses, mental health challenges, and disabilities. These conversations felt vulnerable while still cognizant of boundaries. As such, this meant checking in with students about what their needs were even if they hadn't gotten accommodations yet, whether they knew what resources were available, how they felt about those resources, how they envisioned doing the work and showing up, and in what ways they could show up. Together, we negotiated due dates, attendance, and varying needs around how to approach course material that was not only theoretically dense but also thematically heavy due to the course's emphasis on the intersections between gender/race/sex and violence. This isn't to say it was a perfect semester and that every single student had all of their needs and desires met, nor that they even liked me as an instructor, but I can say that the relationship I cultivated with my students was predicated upon communication, relationality, and an awareness that we are all embodied subjects whose needs have historically not been met by the institution of schooling.

Once classes went online in March, my only priority was to make sure my students felt as safe as possible, given the precarity and uncertainty that came with an unprecedented pandemic. Mutual aid and disability justice have much to teach us about what it means to rely upon radical collectivity to have our needs met when it comes to food, housing, and emotional and physical caretaking—all the things that make us interdependent beings constituted by one another. My students were understandably stressed, anxious, and scared for the remainder of the semester. Many of them were coping with sick or dying relatives, some needing to get jobs quickly, as their parents had lost theirs, and some managing their own chronic illnesses and disabilities. I thought a lot about what it means to be there for them during this time even as I couldn't do much for them, or myself, given the circumstances. Yet despite the difficulty of this time, for me, refusing the university's investment in the overproduction of material labor meant nurturing what Morgan Bimm and Margeaux Feldman call a "femme pedagogy," or recognizing "teaching as care work" and taking seriously our shared vulnerabilities inside and outside the classroom.[3]

The university itself as a neoliberal institution makes it nearly impossible to really be there for one another; its entire structure is predicated on individualism and an ethos that encourages and rewards doing too much to the point of illness and severe psychic unrest. The work never ends, especially for BIPOC folks struggling to get by from within. I subscribe to this, too, as a woman of color who is contingent faculty. I write this in the midst of too many deadlines, nights of insomnia, and a general sense that I'm very close to a breakdown. Often it's much easier to take care of our students than ourselves. And caretaking itself is a gendered category that often falls entirely on the shoulders of women and femmes. COVID in many ways has crystallized what many of us have known for some time—that feminized labor already manages and maintains life itself during the most quotidian of times, and even more so during a pandemic. Caretaking, for me, both in and outside of the classroom is a central part of who I am, but it's also undeniable that the demand and overreliance on the labor of women of color is killing us, and Black women in particular. Feminized and racialized labor is also a concern for feminist pedagogy and disability justice. As we imagine the university post-COVID, I hope we continue to evolve the conversations that women of color feminists have long been leading regarding these concerns.

Here, *femme* is a useful heuristic, as many writers and activists, such as Mia Mingus and Leah Lakshmi Piepzna-Samarasinha, conceptualize femme as practice rooted in lived experience used in the service of collective liberation. A femme practice of care understands care as continuous, not temporary. But in a culture that is so terrified of and cruel toward sickness and difference, care is usually understood as a means to an end, which is to say, health or wellness; otherwise the sick person becomes a burden, disposable. Indeed, practices of care historically are feminized, and I think that's why in some ways care is resisted by so many, but it's here I think that femme survival and care practices offer us so much.

Viewed through this lens, what disability justice—in addition to coming from a long line of sick women—has taught me is that although it's normalized to think about pain, illness, and bodily and cognitive differences as pathological and in need of cure, these differences are part of what makes being and caring for others all the more beautiful. The problem is our culture's deep-seated ableism, which keeps us from cultivating the skills to actually care for one another and, more, to want to care for one another. In the wake of COVID, I see how many for the first time are considering how we might better be in relation with one another, that our bodies are precarious, and that this is only a problem because structural reasons make it so that livability isn't guaranteed for all people. This, to me, is deeply imbricated in the logics of the PIC, its logics so insidious that many educators feel inconvenienced by accessibility in the classroom and truly believe that the only way to address mental health differences and trauma is by calling campus police.

With COVID-19 and global uprisings for Black liberation, I'm committing myself to reflecting and thinking more deeply about what my responsibility as a feminist educator and abolitionist looks like in the classroom, where any disability politics must also be one rooted in Black liberation. Most of my teaching is about gendered, racial, and sexual violence, enacted both by the state and interpersonally within our various communities, and so I must continuously reflect on what it means to teach about violence without reproducing that violence, about bringing care and a transformative justice approach to my pedagogy. With renewed calls to defund the police on university campuses, and conversations and resources around mutual aid, I want only to continue nurturing my femme pedagogy—its softness and vulnerability—in service of a feminist abolitionist classroom and world.[4]

In Retrospect

I wrote the above paragraphs at the end of spring 2020, after spending the final six weeks of the semester on Zoom. I wrote it because I wanted to reflect on what my students taught me throughout the semester about flexibility, communication, listening, and compassion. Before COVID-19, I tried my best to interrogate the content and structure of my syllabi, accessibility within the space of the classroom, and ways of interacting with my students that are trauma informed and relational. As such, COVID only solidified the importance of a feminist pedagogy that prioritizes ongoing conversations with students about their individual access needs, chronic illnesses, disabilities, and university accommodations. This is to say, teaching at the onslaught of the pandemic taught me a lot about disability justice in the classroom. When it became clear we would still be online the following year, I felt much more prepared and thoughtful about how to structure the syllabus. I found that practices such as establishing group agreements, using collaborative note-taking, and allowing for Zoom cameras to be off were only some of the ways to resist ableism on an institutional and personal level. I also felt even more committed to integrating disability studies texts into my feminist theory syllabus as a way to continue thinking with my students about how any feminist praxis, in and out of the classroom, must be one that is informed by anti-racism and disability justice.

And so, my spring 2021 Feminist Theory syllabus spoke to our very immediate moment in the midst of the pandemic and how it related to reproductive justice, disability, transformative justice, and abolition. Each week on Zoom, someone would volunteer to take discussion notes, a practice that facilitates accessibility while also creating an archive of what resonated for us collectively from lecture and discussion. The notes we took, I think, speak to what ended up being a semester-long preoccupation with what texts and ideas do and how to engage with feminist theory in political and ethical ways—ways that facilitate being in better relation with ourselves and others, and the ecologies that surround us. The course's guiding questions included, *What is a feminist and queer response to violence and harm, and how can we address this question drawing from the lessons of feminist antiviolence movements and disability justice and abolitionist teachings?*

Central concerns for the course were also relationality, interdependency, and care—how to enact all three toward abolitionist and crip futures. Considering this was an undergraduate course, my students were surprisingly interested and attuned to the fact that there were specific questions the syllabus was seeking to answer and a larger set of political and ethical preoccupations animating each week's readings. We also had several guest speakers join us who were longtime community activists and international scholars, and all expanded our perceptions about what it means to enact a feminist politic informed by lived experience while also remaining deeply invested in the work of theory. Indeed, our guests all demonstrated a commitment to what Cherríe Moraga and Gloria Anzaldúa call "a theory in the flesh." There was an openness to building connections from inside and outside of the classroom.

I wouldn't have been able to do this without my students sharing their own embodied experiences while reading and thinking with the texts. We engaged in many discussions about what theory is and what it does. What does it mean to read and write and engage in knowledge production collectively? Thinking with my students about the different forms and uses of theory within a feminist and queer context helped to demystify what we've come to understand as "high theory" in the humanities, and, as such, we approached our weekly texts through the framework of creativity and expansiveness. Our forms of writing and expression would sometimes feel more technical and other times more self-evident. I stressed that the point isn't to like every single text on the syllabus but instead to get a sense of what's useful to each of them on an individual and collective level, what's interesting and engaging. When is it worth wading through the density of a text, and when do you leave it behind? And in the context of a global health pandemic, can theory mobilize us to form care networks or facilitate ways of understanding our present moment in new and perhaps even comforting ways?

Reconsidering Theory in a Pandemic

As such, reflecting on the trajectory of my spring Feminist Theory class in the midst of so much precarity, uncertainty, and grief has made me think about the multitudes of feminist theories that exist and what it would mean to consider theory itself as a form of care. My Feminist Theory syllabus started with two foundational texts in the field of women's and gender studies. Hortense Spiller's "Mama's Baby Papa's Maybe" and the *Combahee River Collective Statement*, respectively, asked us to consider who gets to be the subject in US nationalist history and who has been made into its object. Spiller's text left a deep impression, it seemed. In part I think this is due to its difficulty, at the level of its theoretical form but also the complicated emotions it invokes. It's a text that demonstrates the power of theory and the centrality of Black feminist thought to a variety of fields, but in particular women's and gender studies. To theorize one's relationship to gender, sexuality, and history, all in the language of one's choosing, became a sort of guide for how we might understand the transformative power of theory and self-determination. We concluded the semester with the intellectual/creative/political work of adrienne maree brown's *Emergent Strategy* and Alexis Pauline Gumbs's *Undrowned*, which offered us new ways to engage with not only one another but also the world around us by way of land, water, and animal/ecological life.

The discussions we had about these texts solidified for me that relationality is a pressing concern for feminist theory. Also, it became apparent throughout the semester that relationality is at the crux of why so many students decide to major in women's and gender studies. For their final discussion post, I asked that my students posit their own questions or concerns about feminist theory, or to reflect on their own experience engaging with theory. Had their thinking around what constitutes theory changed at all? Or what possibilities did they see in using theory toward feminist politics, if any? Often, theory is dismissed as something abstract and immaterial. And of course it sometimes is, which is why I prefer the plural "theories," because there are so many kinds, all of which do different things. But I also invited them to think through what theory *does do* or what possibilities it holds to enact change in the world and within themselves.

What's possible when you sit with a text and let it become something other than what you thought, when you let the misrecognition of the text lead you somewhere else? I think we can hold questions of accessibility and utility while also being open to the performativity of the text, which is to say, being open to what the text does or could do. There's a privilege in playing with language one day a week and seeing what you come up with. Of course, not every week is interesting, and sometimes it's zoning out and annoyance with what feels like an over-performativity of linguistic jargon. However, we hold out for the weeks in between, when something, anything happens. Theory is hard, but it's also playful, important, absurd, and infinitely creative. It gives language to a set of problems and feelings that in the context of the feminist and queer classroom have been with us for some time. Ultimately, cultivating a feminist classroom during a pandemic was also a reminder that theory is deeply collaborative, a way to practice care for the self and for one another.

Notes

1. Margeaux Feldman (@softcore_trauma), "Policing Ability and Mental Health: The Prison Industrial Complex in Higher Education," Instagram, July 11, 2020, https://www.instagram.com/p/CCghwukg7tz/. It is also available on Facebook at https://www.facebook.com/photo/?fbid=155130302773553&set=pcb .155130619440188.
2. These examples are adapted from Feldman, "Policing Ability and Mental Health."
3. See Morgan Bimm and Margeaux Feldman, "Towards a Femme Pedagogy, or Making Space for Trauma in the Classroom," MAI, January 27, 2020, https:// maifeminism.com/towards-a-femme-pedagogy-or-making-space-for-trauma-in -the-classroom/.
4. For more on abolitionist efforts to defund the police, see Mariame Kaba, "Yes, We Mean Literally Abolish the Police," *New York Times*, June 12, 2020, https://www.nytimes.com/2020/06/12/opinion/sunday/floyd-abolish-defund -police.html. For more on disability justice and interdependency, see Mia Mingus, "Access Intimacy, Interdependence and Disability Justice," *Leaving Evidence* (blog), April 12, 2017, https://leavingevidence.wordpress.com/2017/04/12/access -intimacy-interdependence-and-disability-justice/.

PART IV • IMMIGRANT HEARTS

"Stay Home" . . . but Where Is Home?

4. the call . . . el compromiso . . . the crossing and conversion

Knowing that something in you, or of you, must die before something else can be born, you throw your old self into the ritual pyre, a passage by fire. In relinquishing your old self, you realize that some aspects of who you are—identities people have imposed on you as a woman of color and that you have internalized—are also made up. Identity becomes a cage you reinforce and double-lock yourself into. The life you thought inevitable, unalterable, and fixed in some foundational reality is smoke, a mental construction, fabrication. So, you reason, if it's all made up, you can compose it anew and differently.

"NOW LET US SHIFT," 558

18 • ON BECOMING MY OWN REFUGE

A Palestinian in the US-Mexico Borderlands During Pandemic Times

Maissa Khatib

IN JUNE 2020, I RECEIVED a call for papers on personal experiences and perspectives during the pandemic period. When I read the call, I instantly felt anxious and uncomfortable, as the listed questions to consider for the writing were uncommon. The questions ranged from a very personal experience of social distancing due to the COVID-19 pandemic to an objective perspective on required feminist intervention during these dizzying times. All my academic life, I have been trained to avoid the "I," the self, in order to generate "quality" work. It is not easy to open up and disclose my personal feelings and experiences in my writings. I felt a resurgence of self-doubt. This time my self-doubt focused on two things: my relationship with the English language—more specifically, writing in English—and the fact that I needed to include self-reflection about the pandemic. But after talking with my friend, a feminist scholar, I felt encouraged to document my struggle as the first step to tackle my self-doubt, so I decided to embark on this writing journey.

It is very challenging to let my struggling, hidden identity be in the open. I am a Palestinian refugee who was born in the early 1970s; I was raised in Lebanon. My mother is Lebanese, and my father is a Palestinian refugee who was forced to leave his country with many other Palestinians in 1948 after the Israeli occupation of the land and the declaration of the State of Israel. He was eight years old when he sought refuge in Lebanon. Being a Palestinian refugee in Lebanon was not the only challenging force; being a woman also took its own toll on me. *Al nisa'*—the women—were targeted during the Lebanese civil war and numerous Israeli invasions of Lebanon; we, women, were always at high risk to be raped and killed. I was *al akhar*—the "other"—who was unaccepted and systemically forced to leave. I struggled to lead a life where I was not accepted and needed to remain hidden.

Migration became my only hope to have a chance for a better life. Fate chose the United States to be my destination. In 1995, I moved from Lebanon to El Paso, Texas, as a wife at age twenty-two. While I was establishing my life in a new place and trying to adapt to all the changes, raising my two children and working on my education, my three-year-old daughter was diagnosed with brain cancer. So, I had to relocate to Houston, where my daughter received her treatment. My first encounter with the lack of accurate information and prejudice against Arabs and Muslims was there in the hospital. Some physicians and nurses provided instructions based on subjective, generalized, and distorted information about my race and ethnicity. After a year, we returned to El Paso to resume a "normal life." Things got harder after September 11, 2001; stigma and prejudice haunted the lives of everyone in my immediate and extended family. Living in the United States had for many years reinforced the walls I built to hide my identity, numb my pains, and remain silent.

COVID-19 has imposed on us a remote/virtual lifestyle. It is new and a bit difficult to adjust to, but this has urged me to revisit and examine my life journey and to explore new things, such as enjoying different genres of books that I have not read before, gardening, and journaling.

Some time ago I read *Siddhartha: An Indian Tale*, by Hermann Hesse. I enjoyed learning about Siddhartha's spiritual search and fulfillment, emphasizing self-assertive individuality. I have followed in Siddhartha's steps: I fast, wait, and think. I added another step, too: journaling. Through journaling I am connecting with my inner self, which I had ignored for so long and which had become a stranger. I am finally becoming my own refuge.

Today, as a Palestinian American woman, an academic, and a feminist, I am finally able to recognize that El Paso has made me feel welcomed and valued, just by looking back at my life journey here and how I prevailed, despite the many painful racial and sexist experiences and personal challenges, due to the support I received from various people in El Paso. I am now able to confidently say that in El Paso I do belong and that to some extent this is home (*watan*), a word that did not exist in my daily vocabulary. As Darwish (2003) poignantly states, "I am from here, I am from there, yet am neither here nor there. . . . I have learned and dismantled all the words in order to draw from them a single word: *Home*" (Darwish 2003, 4 and 7).

Sometimes I still question my relationship with this city, and sometimes

I find myself in an in-between space. The name of this city literally means "the pass"—the best mirror reflecting my life journey. The pass has been a source of mobility, change, and hope for me. Even though El Paso after all these years has become the place of the familiar, where it is comfortable and safe, I still sometimes feel the urge to return, but I'm not sure where to? Lebanon has never granted me the sense of homeland, and Palestine has been an imagined homeland that was drawn through my father's story-telling about his childhood. What I am sure of is my mutability, how easily I change (and I am changed) from one thing to another, how unstable my spaces and places are—and all because of the missing foundation of my existence, the lost ground of my origin. I can also say that as I continuously cross visible and invisible borders, my thinking process undergoes a dislocation and relocation and shifting of mental, social, and physical boundaries, where I realize I am a refugee but I am also a witness. I am alone, but I feel the strength of all the women in the world.

My most recurring questions these days are: How has this pandemic affected me personally, and what have I been doing that I can claim as meaningful and satisfying for me as a Palestinian American feminist living on the US-Mexico border? How are Arab Americans and Muslim Americans dealing with these pandemic-imposed changes? What is the impact of COVID-19 on women, and what can feminists and women's rights activists do to sustain the attained gains and keep going onward? What has been done to address health disparities and injustices? What do we need to do to recover and be better prepared for crisis in the future?

Over the span of a quarter century in El Paso, here I am today, a Palestinian American immigrant woman. I am also the mother of the three-year-old girl who was diagnosed with cancer and who recently died at age twenty-four, now trying to reshape her parenting in a way that maintains her connection with her son, a recent college graduate, and shield him from grieving. I am an academic whose current job situation confirms the absence of support for female junior faculty and the fact that the evaluation tools in place only acknowledge one's publishing record. I am an academic who cherishes aspects of her career and invests in areas that do not count much in being considered for a promotion. Through my job, I have been trying as a feminist educator to create the conditions for students to be aware of critical local, national, and international issues, to feel empowered and be active citizens. I create innovative pathways for students to critically examine various structures of "isms" and realize the interconnectedness and interdependence of our lives across borders. Students in my courses expand their learning beyond the classroom and textbooks, participating in projects and activities where they engage with local and global communities. Court observations on domestic violence cases, volunteering at the Center Against Sexual and Family Violence in El Paso, and service-learning at centers for women who have experienced domestic violence in Morocco and Jordan are part of my women's and gender studies courses.

I have to admit that I do still have heavy moments, feeling anxious and overwhelmed and pessimistic about all the developments of this pandemic and the concurrence of the justice movements Black Lives Matter and Me Too. These movements have brought to the forefront two deeply rooted American epidemics: racism and sexism. I am concerned that in this chaotic period, which started with a failure to contain the pandemic and continues with uncertainty around the ability of the three available vaccines to fight the current variants of the virus, the presence of too many conflicting factions, and the rise of hatred and violence, women will lose ground in our long journey of fighting for freedom and gender equality.

Today, Arab Americans, Middle Eastern Americans, and Muslim Americans are still invisible populations. There are no accurate statistics about the number of Arabs and other Middle Easterners. There is still no clear racial and ethnic identifier for us. In the case of the census or any demographic survey, the only options I can choose for my race are "White," "Not Hispanic," or "Other." Arab Americans are a historically understudied minority group in the United States, and their health needs and risks have been poorly documented. During this pandemic, the only news coverage of the Arab and Muslim population in El Paso that was posted on the *El Paso Times* website was an article from *USA Today* about how Muslims in the United States are observing Ramadan, a fasting month, during the COVID-19 pandemic. While there is no paucity of stigmatizing representation and unfavorable visibility of Arab Americans in the mainstream media, there is not much documentation about the varied roles we play and contributions we make, or information about our health and well-being. In schools and textbooks, terrorism is erroneously discussed as an exclusively "Islamic problem," completely ignoring the prevalence of domestic terrorism in the United States. What do we know about Arab American and Muslim American healthcare providers, patients, and caregivers during this pandemic? Things have not changed, and we are still in need of inclusive initiatives that give space at the table to the silenced and the forgotten. The emergence of the COVID-19 pandemic and public health crisis have exposed this reality of underrepresentation and misrepresentation of minority groups, widening health disparities where they have become more visible and undeniable.

As the COVID-19 pandemic deepens, economic and social stress coupled with restricted movement, social isolation measures, and gender-based violence are increasing exponentially. Many women were forced to "lock down" at home with the men who abuse them at the same time that services to support survivors were disrupted or made inaccessible. Gender inequality is still heavily affecting women in the private and public spheres. There are various areas where gender inequality is intensely impacting women's lives. First, the burden of the gender pay gap and unpaid work still has not been recognized, reduced, and redistributed. Second, compounded economic impacts are felt especially by women and girls, who are generally earning less, saving less, and holding insecure jobs or living close to poverty. In addition, there is a global expectation that a woman should spend hours every day cooking, cleaning, and caregiving to keep her family going, but generate no income. The unequal distribution of unpaid work disempowers individual women. Third, intersectional invisibility (Purdie-Vaughns and Eibach 2008) is another impediment that has been impacting the lives of women of color. The daily life of these women is shaped by the intersection of racism and sexism. Their unique and complex stories of injustice and inequality are not recognized.

Gender inequality has excluded women from decision-making positions and acknowledgment of contributions throughout history. For instance, women have not been considered or integrated into the design of the curriculum of many programs, services, and supplies. Most medical schools' curricula are based on 150-pound white males. During this pandemic, we have also witnessed how women are excluded even when it comes to medical supplies. For instance, healthcare providers need personal protective equipment (PPE) that fits in order to protect them from exposure to infectious diseases. The PPE that is delivered to hospitals and clinics is often designed for men, even though 80 percent of health workers in the US are women, according to the US Bureau of Labor Statistics (2018). Also, currently, most heads of states are men, and women still hold fewer than 20 percent of key leadership roles worldwide (Bureau of Labor Statistics 2018), even though during this pandemic we have all witnessed how nations led by women, such as New Zealand, Germany, and Taiwan, have better contained the virus.

Here we are still battling long-standing and deeply rooted injustices, have experienced lack of leadership with the Trump administration, and have never had a female president, all of which has urged me to think of feminist interventions that we critically need now. We cannot ignore that women's history is full of trailblazers in the fight for equality in the United

States. But where are we now? What is the situation of women in this country today? Why are women still facing discrimination and experiencing high rates of various types of violence and abuse? I believe that the most important question is what feminists need to do now, when the system and its institutions fail to protect women from discrimination, harassment, violence, and gender inequality. We all know that gender inequality lies at the center of all forms of gender-based violence. Feminists need to take important steps to be able to face new challenges as the COVID-19 pandemic has erupted and exposed deeply rooted structures of discrimination and racism.

This is a call for action that requires essential changes and a unified agenda. First, we need a feminist task force that consists of two teams. One team will focus on scholarship and research that leads to policy change, while the other team will be on the ground working closely with women through free programs and interventions for empowerment and development. Mainstream feminists need to critically reexamine their strategies and implement needed changes to effectively address women's challenges today. Second, we need to question our modes of knowledge production and expand beyond the gendered epistemology (Rahman 2018) to be able to acknowledge the plurality, diversity, and intersectionality of various factors affecting women's lives, such as race, ethnicity, class, age, sexual orientation, disability, and physical appearance, among others. As feminists in the past challenged the notion of "sameness and sisterhood" and how it controlled and dictated the production of knowledge and silenced nonwhite women, mainstream feminist scholars today need to challenge their built-in privilege of being academics, scholars at risk of exploiting communities and engaging in extractive research. We must acknowledge Patricia Hill Collins's concept of how women belong to two social worlds: the dominant group of women (academics) and the oppressed group of women.

More feminist scholars need to climb over the walls of academia and reach the general public. Our work should consider the general public's capabilities of access and understanding. We also need more feminists to shift gears and move beyond academic and conventional work. We have to work on two major goals. First, scholarship should be action-based, that is, targeting policy change and bringing awareness and providing empowerment through designing and delivering innovative community engagement projects. Second, we need more feminists in the field listening to other women, using these firsthand encounters and the voices of oppressed women as the impetus for policy change, ensuring women's protection, access, and equality in all sectors of society. More feminists are needed on the ground walking next to other women, strengthening sisterhood, overcoming differences to empower selfhood in the face of male-dominated power and control structures and combating outdated social and cultural attitudes about women and men.

COVID-19 is not only a challenge for global health systems but also a test of our human spirit, an opportunity to remake our world. Recovery must lead to a more equal world that is more resilient to future crises. Feminists need to use this pandemic as a catalyst to eradicate gender inequality. We, all feminists, need to focus on how to empower women and girls to speak out and have agency in the face of sexism, racism, classism, and violence and participate equally with men in decision-making at all levels. We need to build each other up! This is my focus now in all this chaos. I hope it will be yours too.

Bibliography

Bureau of Labor Statistics. "Labor Force Statistics from the Current Population Survey: 2018." https://www.bls.gov/cps/tables.htm.

Darwish, Mahmoud. *Unfortunately, It Was Paradise: Selected Poems*. Edited by Sinan Antoon and Amira El-Zein. Translated by Munir Akash and Carolyn Forché. University of California Press, 2003.

Hesse, Hermann. *Siddhartha: An Indian Tale*. Penguin Classics, 2002.

Purdie-Vaughns, Valerie, and Richard P. Eibach. "Intersectional Invisibility: The Distinctive Advantages and Disadvantages of Multiple Subordinate-Group Identities." *Sex Roles* 59 (2008): 377–391. https://doi.org/10.1007/s11199–008 –9424–4.

Rahman, Fatima. "The Merits and Limits of a Gendered Epistemology: Muslim Women and the Politics of Knowledge Production." *Journal of International Women's Studies* 19, no. 1 (2018): 20–33. https://vc.bridgew.edu/jiws/vol19 /iss1/3/.

19 • FROM TOKYO SUBWAY TO BERLIN U-BAHN

A Radical Rethinking from Intersectional Womanness to Interconnected Humanness

Jingqiu Ren

HAVE YOU BEEN TO TOKYO and used its labyrinthine subway system? The two operators, Tokyo Metro and Toei Subway, together run 13 lines with more than 280 stations, covering the entire city and connecting various local, express, and bullet train lines.[1] Having been there many times, I still get anxious every time I transfer between lines. There are different fare gates going in and out of platforms; long and winding walkways up and down the stairs leading to giant intersections, where directional signs can point in eight divergent ways; and separate platforms to access different trains going the same directions. It is an amazing feat that over 10 million people use it daily without getting utterly lost in the maze,[2] like I constantly fear that I may do every time I visit. The complexity reflects the distinct business interests of various transportation entities. To clearly differentiate financial interests but still deliver a connected and functional system, redundancy, complexity, and bureaucracy are unavoidable. It takes an enormous amount of planning, engineering, administration, coordination, and execution to keep such a behemoth system running smoothly every single day. I have marveled at its accomplishment but at the same time wondered about the cost-benefit outcome of its complexity. Financial gains may be ascertained from each operating company's balance sheets. However, what about the hidden costs of time people lose while walking for kilometers through many transit gates just to catch the next segment of the line? What about the environmental impact of powering the air-conditioning and illuminating the extra underground network due to its complicated interchange patterns? What about the potential danger of congregating and dispersing a massive number of people through the interchanges as they navigate through the Byzantine system in times of an infectious disease epidemic, like the COVID-19 pandemic we are facing right now?

What the Tokyo subway system made me ponder, even before the pandemic arrived, however, is how much my life as a woman actually resembles such a complicated system of parallel and diverging lines running in different directions with undecipherable calculations of tangible and hidden costs and benefits. It is 2019 and I can see, for instance, distinct tracks with their own stations along the lines I run on as a graduate student, a professional, a daughter, a wife, and a mother of two preteen boys. They require daily activities that occur in either the same or different times and spaces. I check my watch, fill in my planner, follow the reminders on my phone, and try to run multiple apps in my brain to compile and process information in order to formulate appropriate responses. The society we live in has made it so that the destinations of being a good student, professional, daughter, wife, and mother are somehow controlled by different entities with diverging and often competing interests. But there is no "superwoman." We can't run full speed in our professional or academic life while attending to everyone else's needs in the family without missing a beat. We can only turn off the camera and mute ourselves on Zoom when we need to cook dinner for the family, supervise children's homework, and check the pharmacy app to see the status of parents' prescriptions, all at the same time.

We hurry between the lines of our parallel lives, rushing through those monstrous interchanges where the signs point in eight different directions, glancing at our watches, checking the schedules of the next train, and calculating how we may hop on and off different platforms to make it to the end of the day. We pride ourselves in being able to multitask and keep up with the enormous burden of running such a system smoothly. And like the Tokyo subway system, we hardly stop to think about the hidden costs of its complexity. How does one calculate the net profit when you missed your child's first step but aced your conference presentation? What if the prestigious academic position you worked so hard for all these years finally extends an offer to you but requires your husband to quit his promising job to relocate with you? What cost is there to a society if half of its members need to trade off gains on one role with losses on another, when the society needs to accumulate all positive gains on all of her roles in order to achieve maximum welfare for the society as a whole?

Such was my intersectional life as a woman before the pandemic arrived.

COVID-19 brought a fresh understanding of my intersectional identity to a whole new level.

My daily life as a woman didn't drop its demands when the coronavirus brought the world to a halt in early 2020. Classes and work have moved online. Then there is the concern of bringing back the virus to my elderly parents and immunocompromised family members when going out to get necessities. I contemplated wearing a face mask from the very beginning. But I often had to carefully appraise my surroundings before deciding on masking. My fears were not unfounded. My own sociological research analyzed numerous face-mask-related anti-Asian discriminatory incidents reported in the Stop AAPI Hate incident database between late March and mid-April 2020.[3] I have come to realize that as an Asian, as an immigrant, and as a woman, I am far more vulnerable in this pandemic. The largest categories of anti-Asian incidents I analyzed consisted of marking mask-wearing Asians as the source of the disease and asserting their foreignness or inherent socio-racial inferiority.[4] These discriminatory incidents took the forms of both verbal and physical assaults. Asians were called names. They were accused of having brought the disease here and were told to go back to where they came from. Paradoxically, some were also attacked for not wearing masks in the early days, when mask-wearing was sparse among the general public, because a "diseased" racial identity was imposed on the victim.

As a recent immigrant, it jolted me from vaguely basking under the halo of "model minority" right back to the terror of being despised as the "yellow peril." The significant increase of Asian immigration started in the late 1960s, at which time the concept of "model minority" began circulating in the contemporary social consciousness. As a latecomer immigrant, I was shocked to rediscover the social power of the majority to set the identity and narrative for us as racialized "others." The capriciousness of such power can raise Asian Americans to be the "model minority" when it served the purpose to accentuate the undesirability of *other* "others," namely Black Americans. The renewed racialization as the "yellow peril," though, throws us back to the nineteenth-century San Francisco slums. I hear loud and clear the words uttered in the California State Senate report of 1878 on Chinese immigration: "Impregnable to all the influences of our Anglo-Saxon life, they remain the same stolid Asiatics that have floated on the rivers and slaved in the fields of China for thirty centuries of time."[5] As minorities we fail to remember that whether we are regarded as "honorary whites" or "imposter whites" entirely depends on which framing better serves the political, economic, or cultural benefit of those with social power at any given period of history. COVID-19 made it clear how our identity as Asians and as immigrants is socially ephemeral, "shape-shifting to respond to the nation's most pressing questions."[6] My research on face-mask-related discriminatory incidents reported in the Stop AAPI Hate database reveals that the majority of the victims of pandemic-related racism incidents are Asian women attacked by white men (see notes 3 and 4). Although it is not surprising that systematic sexism perpetually denigrates women in all aspects of social life, the physical and emotional menace of such incidents increasing due to the pandemic becomes pervasive enough that I find myself becoming extra vigilant in public, so as to not provoke any potential attacks.

The complexity and stress of navigating life as a woman and as an Asian immigrant during the COVID-19 pandemic made me wonder why we should continue as usual the life arrangements we have long taken for granted, when the life around us is being upended by the most unexpected events. It leads me to this—the Berlin U-bahn. Berlin's subway system is so impressive because it is exceedingly simple. Subway entrances are located in predictable locations; there are no long and labyrinthine underground walkways and no complicated platforms. You set out for where you want to go, buy a ticket, hop on, and get there. It is the polar opposite of the Tokyo subway. Its simplicity and effectiveness resulted in a sudden epiphany of how we should really be living our lives: not running mad on separated tracks with different identities as women, professionals, students, wives, daughters, parents, immigrants, and minorities, but moving forward with unity of the plural roles of our humanness, with purpose, bereft of distractions, and driven by our inner motivations to fulfill our dreams. The Berlin U-bahn runs on an infrastructure designed with such clarity, ease, and repose in mind. To refocus our lives from competing roles to interconnected humanness, we need to rethink the invisible costs of current social arrangements that fragment the identities of women, increase their physical burden, and elevate emotional distress. Maybe by redesigning to create less complicated interchanges, easier transfers between stations, and simpler schedules for connecting lines, we will gradually move away from needlessly complicating our lives toward fulfillment of a simpler purpose of what's really important in life. After all, if the pandemic necessitates an overhaul of the entire world, couldn't it also become a catalyst for change of women's lives everywhere for the better?

Notes

1. See www.gotokyo.org for a map of the Tokyo subway system.

2. Average daily usage includes 7.6 million passengers per day for Tokyo Metro and 2.82 million per day for the Toei lines. Data provided by www.gotokyo.org.

3. The face-mask-discrimination incidents analyzed are from the Stop AAPI Hate database (March 19 to April 15, 2020). The Stop AAPI Hate website (https://stopaapihate.org) was launched as a site for voluntary reporting by people with firsthand experience of or people who witnessed anti-Asian and anti–Pacific Islander discrimination in the United States. I thank Chinese for Affirmative Action, the Asian Pacific Policy and Planning Council, and San Francisco State University's Department of Asian American Studies for launching the center and providing me access to their database.

4. Detailed analysis of these mask-related anti-Asian incidents is conducted by Ren and Feagin. See Jingqiu Ren and Joe Feagin, "Face Mask Symbolism in Anti-Asian Hate Crimes," *Ethnic and Racial Studies 44, no. 5 (2020): 746–758*, https://doi .org/10.1080/01419870.2020.1826553.

5. California State Senate Special Committee on Chinese Immigration, *Chinese Immigration: Its Social, Moral, and Political Effect* (F. P. Thompson, 1878), https:// archive.org/details/chineseimmigrati00cali_1/.

6. Ellen D. Wu, *The Color of Success: Asian Americans and the Origins of the Model Minority* (Princeton University Press, 2014).

20 • GATHERING OURSELVES IN THE COVID ERA

Revisiting Fear and Attachment Toward a Horizon of Spiritual Activism

Ana López Hurtado

Life is uncertain,
as causes and conditions for death are innumerable.
If you do not attain the confident state of fearlessness in
this very life.
Then, what is the use of being alive?

WAKING UP FROM THE DEEP SLUMBER OF
IGNORANCE, BUDDHIST TEACHING

IT IS THE END OF August 2021. The Texas heat rises to 36°C, approximately 96.8°F, as I feel sweat accumulate under my N-95 face mask. Seventeen months ago, COVID-19 first arrived in Austin. The Texas government has banned vaccine and mask mandates, leading to a health crisis with hundreds of deaths that speak of dilemmas about biopower and the cultural lack of collective consciousness that is so persistent, collectively yet selectively, throughout the United States. I have already gotten used to being stuck at the place I now call home.

The pandemic has been a site of self-transformation. I revisit my past self and encounter a vulnerable being, a human full of fear, pain, and questions about how to deal with oneself and a collapsing environment. I gather my past self and feel my old suffering. I relive my exhaustion and see myself in my old apartment, looking through the window. Among the few stable things around me, there was a dynamic, unstoppable one: the highway. I became obsessed with watching the freeway because its perpetual motion remained intact during my self-isolation. There were fewer cars after

COVID-19 hit Austin, but the movement never really ceased. I stared at the highway and thought of Slavoj Žižek. Žižek claimed that the pandemic would give capitalism "a Kill Bill–esque blow," meaning our current economic system would face its collapse. I laughed with anguish as I watched sixteen police cars mingle with the traffic, accelerating among Amazon trucks to stop Black Lives Matter public demonstrations developing in the city center. I remember feeling bad for not attending the protest, but I was so afraid of the virus and terrified of getting deported. *¿Cómo habitar(me)*, how to inhabit (myself), in the midst of this pandemic and come to terms with my lack of movement? What did stillness mean and how did fear look back then? This text is an intimate view of my experience during COVID-19. It seeks to explore the forms of fear, attachment, and transformation that flourished within, in my personal and collective experiences through pandemic times.

While COVID-19 opened a path for self-recognition and healing in the context of isolation, the pandemic also exacerbated the structural inequalities that divide humanity along the axes of race, class, gender, sexuality, and ability. It reinforced the oppressive dynamics that fix people into categories anchored to capitalism, colonialism, and patriarchy. While the most privileged people were able to safely lock down, essential workers of color were forced to get exposed to the virus because they depended on their jobs to survive. State laws and the precarious health system in this country exposed people with vulnerable health to pernicious risks. Today, as the pandemic advances, the conservative policies of the Texas government keep risking vulnerable populations by prioritizing individual liberties over collective care. This landscape of catastrophe calls for feminist interventions: communal networks built on deep inner and individual spiritual work. If we want to break through oppressive categorical fixations, we must first deeply understand our situated experience and how it is interconnected with that of others.

Today I think of ways to effectively translate my embodied worldliness and fear into words of a foreign language that will always shape an incomplete notion of myself. *Narrarme en inglés es narrarme a medias*—narrating myself in English means an incomplete narrative. I position myself in this challenging exercise of cultural, spiritual, and linguistic translation: *Aquí es desde donde escribo, mi cuerpo en casa*—this is where I write, my body at home. My place of enunciation is the privilege of confinement: I write at home because the US academy guarantees my economic stability. Although I am an alien to the state, my fellowship keeps me safe while I write from a body that questions its gender and materiality. I am not an undocumented person, I do not live in a crowded space, and my labor is not "essential." My Colombian blanca-mestiza self writes among the turbulence of social chaos and isolation embedded in many forms of transformation through facing fear. Facing dread led me to begin recognizing the attachments I made during the pandemic and further reflect on what a feminist self and collective care look like, drawing a horizon of liberation rooted in radical transformation and inner healing.

Fear

Fear began with the obsessive-compulsive disinfection of hands, clothes, groceries. The toilet paper hoarding, the alcohol shortage. It spread across empty streets as the pandemic became visible through face masks, bodies drawn apart, broadcasts of people singing on balconies, images of intubated humans in full-capacity hospitals, and silence. The perpetual silence outside filled only with the background white noise of a never-stopping highway. Just silence.

When the pandemic started, I did not know I would ever get to name fear. I felt it streaming down my forehead like sweat or going up my spine when the sound of coughing reached my ears in a socially distanced line outside the grocery store. The threat of infection and death; the uncertainty of how, when, or if I would hug my loved ones again; the guilt of contagion for not being careful enough. One of my biggest fears was getting the virus and giving it to "A," an immunocompromised person who was part of my social pod and whom I grew to love. She became the center of my self-care since her health was directly linked to mine. I cannot tell when my fear of contagion, of hurting her, became an attachment to our relationship. It was the profound spiritual connection we built between walls, in our own stillness. The way we curled up against each other as the world collapsed and left us suspended in an intimacy she decided not to name as she left without saying goodbye. Her final silence was devastating to me.

Silence would be filled with terror when inner and outer landscapes collided: The pandemic forced us inward and into our own intimate stillness. While outside, only the sound of highways echoed through lonely boulevards; inside, each person struggled with an excess of unnamed and untamed feelings that emerged with the lockdown. Fear was constantly changing. One day it felt like dry hands avoiding contact with random surfaces, and the next it looked like me staring at myself from the other side of the mirror. Sometimes fear sounded like the absence of A's voice or embrace, but it always had to do with the difficulty of dealing with one's body, one's being in solitude. The highway: white noise that blurred how the world collapsed. My chest: a black hole that swallowed the light of day while hours passed, keeping death untouched as days in isolation repeated themselves one after another. I close my eyes and I see myself there, fragmented, deciphering the transactions of being and craving embrace as dread swallowed me whole. I was truly afraid of myself. Terrified of loneliness.

Attachment

Attachment is a coping mechanism. It appears as a response to trauma or feelings of incompleteness, and it reacts to emotional cravings. According to Buddhist philosophy, it is also one of the main causes of suffering, as it nurtures the illusion of self and other as separate. It solidifies the ego. I want, I need, I am. The pandemic has taught me to identify and observe my attachments. I am slowly learning the traps of the self and how it is an obstacle to recognizing that we are one with the universe. First, it was gender. Then, it was religious practice. Last, it was loved ones. I got attached to the things I thought saved me from myself, but as I keep tracing my own footsteps, I learn more about my fear of loneliness. All these attachments and perhaps the ones I haven't recognized respond to how terrified I was of allowing myself to be still without doing anything. Stillness meant getting in contact with pain.

I summoned stillness and looked at my reflection: What does it mean to be a woman? This binary coding has traversed my body since I opened my eyes for the first time and wailed while a nun pierced my ears—It's a *she*! *She* has a vulva, this little *girl*; pierce her ears. I turn to an unthinkable anatomy of bodies undefined, bodies narrated without an obsession with genitalia. What a utopia. I do not know what "being a woman" means anymore. My body aches from the imposition of gender, the roles of womanhood. Rita M. Gross, feminist Buddhist teacher, argues that attachment to the prison of gender roles is an obstacle for achieving enlightenment. It is an iteration of the self. I let go of womanhood as a fixed concept and touch the borders of queerness. Being queer: a river of possibilities. But how to dwell in concepts that have been thought of in latitudes so far beyond mine? Can I name myself using this language that does not belong to me? Can English ever become my home? Before I could tell, I was flirting with queerness in a way I knew could mean new forms of attachment. *I am non-binary. I am non-binary. I am. I. I. I* observe the self and let myself float through queerness—the *cuirness* of the Spanish-speaking world—like a feather detached from the bird's body. Every day I choose not to limit myself to gender. I choose to exist in whichever meaning being queer—the stigmatized Latin American *cuir*—takes by the hour.[1]

I am much more than this physical body. Yet I speak my tongue, my sex remembers, and my skin still echoes centuries of violence and genocide. I am much more than this physical body, but I also was once a little girl. The rootless girl. The Catholic white-mestiza full of guilt and fear of not being girly enough, speaking loudly, disappointing *Dios Padre todo poderoso, creador del cielo y de la tierra* (God, our Father almighty, creator of heaven and earth). I am an expansive being, but this body that aches has also benefited from whiteness. I have struggled to acknowledge my whiteness without falling into a Catholic rhetoric of guilt. *Mea culpa mea culpa mea máxima culpa*. Guilt can also be a manifestation of attachment. It does not heal; it does not allow us to be accountable, to repair ancestral damage. Guilt does not bring relief in any form; it centers the self and feeds the ego. I think of positionality statements. There must be something else, because just pointing at our whiteness is not actually touching at the interconnection of sentient beings and how we reproduce oppression, how we make others suffer, and how we suffer. I sit with my whiteness. It tells me there is something I must learn from this embodiment, so I embrace my human complexity in stillness and try to cultivate awareness of how I interact with others. Maybe self-awareness through compassion will allow me to hold myself accountable in ways that actively listen to other people's needs and act accordingly. Maybe reparation needs active listening as an act of conscious presence with one another. I do not know what makes up my mestizaje, but I see and feel my whiteness as a life lesson that urges the self to listen through the whole body and decentralize itself.

Pandemic self-transformation involved identity agitations. And as I dealt with gender and race as intertwined with my Catholic upbringing, questions on spirituality kept rising through the black hole my chest was those days. Something within me has always resisted *la misericordia de Cristo, el perdón de los pecados, la resurrección de la carne y la vida eterna por los siglos de los siglos. Amén* (Christ's mercy, the forgiveness of sins, the resurrection of the body, and the life everlasting. Amen). God never spoke in a language familiar to me, or perhaps I always struggled to grasp it. But you can grow spiritual roots elsewhere. You can be your own refuge while the world regurgitates the harshness of its crisis. The first stage of the pandemic brought Buddhism to my life. It felt like a new language that touched me deeply as it swapped guilt narratives with compassion and gently taught me that the nature of our reality is impermanence and suffering.

I unfolded myself and tried to observe the enormous web of existence, the threads that unite humanity beyond the abyssal lines imposed by the capital-patriarchal-colonial junction of power. Buddhism has allowed me to understand myself in connection to others more clearly. I took advantage of the moment and observed old systemic symptoms that encounter the virus and exacerbate misery. In such a landscape of excessive pain and death, in times when profit-hungry states exercise necropolitics, it was the first time I allowed myself to stand back, embrace my own suffering, and be in the moment. Life needs space to develop, to settle down. It was too soon to theorize about what was going on; one must first embody it.

I moved out of the apartment. My new home stands five blocks away from a Buddhist temple. I started frequenting the temple, met the resident lama, and began a learning journey that transformed how I understood reality. In the Nyingma tradition, which is the school I took refuge in, you must go through preliminary practices to cleanse your karma before you receive deeper teachings on the nature of reality and emptiness. They are called Ngöndro practices and involve daily prayers and meditation; the epigraph of this chapter is included in my daily prayers. I got into the practice, prayed, and meditated every morning with my new spiritual guide. But there came a point when I became dependent on the practice to be stable. I was missing a fundamental core of Buddhist teachings: effortless being.

By then, I recall, the Texas government had already opened the state. Some people were living their daily lives as usual, going out on dates, drinking beer and dancing. But my fear of contracting the virus and infecting A kept me at home with very limited contact with the outside world. My social life was reduced to five people: Lama Pasang, A, my partner, my roommate, and their partner. We all agreed on being cautious to protect A, but my well-being depended on their companionship as my life came down to being with them. Eventually, our collective care pod dissolved, and I realized I was unconsciously expecting them to consistently hold me. I turned myself to spirituality and used it to avoid my fear of loneliness. I took refuge in the three jewels of Buddhism, but I also let my sanity depend on the militaristic imposition I created around practice: I forced myself to wake up early to pray, although sometimes my body asked me for a deeper rest. I got angry when I was not able to fulfill my daily practice, and I became obsessed with not disappointing my teacher. Buddhist practice came to release me of pain and fear by teaching me to cultivate inhabiting the present moment effortlessly, but as I became attached to a fixed idea I had of its benefits, I started suffering when things did not go as I intended them to. The days I could not practice were painful and felt endless. I was forced to be with myself and realized spiritual work needs us to befriend our shadow, to accept messiness into our lives. Attachment to practice condensed the fear of instability. Fear of instability spoke to the difficulty of facing the parts of me I wanted to ignore: my wounds. Instead of using meditation to explore my cracks and heal them through surrendering, I tried to avoid them by attaching myself to the idea of becoming enlightened.

Today I look back and feel like embracing my past self, telling them to be patient. I have come to slowly face fear and allow it to sit with me in the darkness of those nights when I randomly wake up around 3:00 a.m. I am starting to understand there is no such thing as being lonely. Maybe that is why saying goodbye to loved ones has become easier with time. Maybe that is what the pandemic taught me: Solitude does not really exist if you remember you are connected to absolutely everything and everyone around you. I gather my past and future and relax in what I can barely grasp as it changes: the present moment.

Feminist Interventions: Spiritual Activism and the Collective Sense of Spirituality

Spiritual awakening involves acknowledging the need for self-healing. However, contemplating interconnectedness helps us understand that our own liberation is linked to that of others. This is the basis of the Mahayana Buddhist path: The purpose of becoming enlightened is to help other sentient beings to achieve liberation as well. In this sense, spiritual awakening has a collective character. For Chicana feminist Gloria Anzaldúa, a fundamental part of collective healing is conocimiento, an act of knowing that exceeds rational thought and returns to the body and the ancestral wisdom we hold within us. She described conocimiento as linked to a reptilian third eye that could simultaneously look within and without ourselves. Conocimiento is the capacity of generating a dialogue between our inner well of sacred knowledge and the outer social context that surrounds us. This bodily form of knowing requires us to recognize how we are part of the interconnected net of existence and suffering. Anzaldúa also thought of her writing as healing, as a tool that mobilized her inner reflections from her deepest self to the outer world. Writing, for Anzaldúa, was a vehicle to spiritual activism: bringing the intimate lessons we learn individually to the collective and creating spaces for active listening. Spiritual activism is feminist praxis.

As pandemic times change and we slowly get to meet others again, I am dealing with new forms of fear. My ways of interacting socially have changed, and I am struggling to keep up the small talk. My social network was drastically reduced to people who have left or are leaving soon, which feeds my fear of solitude. I follow Anzaldúa's reflections on writing and make a poem out of myself. Poetry has become a way of connecting with conocimiento, touching fear, and recognizing attachment. This combination of writing and allowance helps me coexist with dread and pain without overidentifying with my feelings, which opens space for sharing my writing with the people around me. Maybe speech and holding conversations has become tougher, but poetry is, perhaps, a feminist intervention into our hurt environment. I am slowly building strength within me to let go of fear and connect with new people.

As I revisit my personal experience in COVID times and what I have learned from fear, attachment, and the self, I ask myself: What does spiritual activism look like? Spiritual activism is a feminist intervention: Sharing our inner journeys in whichever form we can weaves threads of collective connection through empathy and compassion. We see ourselves in others when we actively listen with our whole bodies and know everyone deals with fear and attachment. Hence, spiritual activism as feminist praxis allows for finding common ground that reveals the complexity of human experience. The spiritual path is an ongoing process. It has an individual character, but it cannot be fulfilled in isolation. Spiritual activism draws a horizon for collective healing. I gather myself in the Texas heat. I know I have changed in the year that has passed. I am less afraid. I also know I am slowly getting ready to reconnect with others and give shape and meaning to the collective forms of liberation through poetry and active listening. It is already happening.

Note

1. "La variación *cuir*, es la derivación fonética/españolizada/desviada/impropia que busca afirmarse y relocalizarse, por medio de la reapropiación del estigma de hablar con *acento* que pesa sobre las hablas castellanas y las coloca en una posición subalterna/defectuosa frente a la pronunciación *correcta* (con acento anglófono), del término *queer*. (. . .) *Cuir* registra la inflexión geopolítica hacia el sur y desde las periferias en contrapunto a la epistemología colonial y a la historiografía anglo-americana" (Valencia 2014, 68). (The *cuir* variation is the Spanish phonetic/deviated/improper derivation that seeks to assert and relocate itself through the reappropriation of the stigma of speaking with an *accent* that weighs on Castilian modes of speech and places them in a subordinate/defective position in relation to a *correct* pronunciation [with an Anglophone accent] of the term *queer*. [. . .] *Cuir* records the geopolitical inflection toward the South and from the peripheries

in counterpoint to colonial epistemology and Anglo-American historiography.)
Translation is mine.

Bibliography

Anzaldúa, Gloria E. *Light in the Dark / Luz en lo Oscuro: Rewriting Identity, Spiritu-
ality, Reality*. Edited by AnaLouise Keating. Duke University Press, 2015.
Chödrön, Pema. *Becoming Bodhisattvas: A Guidebook for Compassionate Action*.
Shambhala Publications, 2018.
Gross, Rita M. *Buddhism Beyond Gender: Liberation from Attachment to Identity*.
Shambhala Publications, 2018.
Mbembe, Achille. *Necropolitics*. Duke University Press, 2019.
Valencia Triana, Sayak. "Teoría transfeminista para el análisis de la violencia
machista y la reconstrucción no-violenta del tejido social en el México contem-
poráneo" [Transfeminist Theory for the Analysis of Sexist Violence and the
Nonviolent Reconstruction of the Social Fabric in Contemporary Mexico].
Universitas Humanística 78 (2014). doi:10.11144/Javeriana.UH78.ttpa.

21 • BETWEEN EPICENTERS

Mapping Anger in the Waves of a Pandemic

Paola Cossermelli Messina

The truth is, there is no better place to live than in the shadow of a beautiful, furious mountain.

CARMEN MARIA MACHADO, *IN THE DREAM HOUSE*

IN THE AFTERMATH OF A winding and multi-themed argument, my partner questions "the use of anger." We are in her room—a damp, cement-floored basement in a communal Brooklyn home, where we live with five housemates and our Bangalore-born street dog, ATM. My perplexed reaction to her question is interrupted by the synchronous vibrations of our phones and the alert message that follows: "Citywide curfew in effect for NYC: 11 p.m. on 6/1 to 5 a.m. on 6/2. Essential workers exempted." Like a cork forced into a bottleneck. A bitter liquid froths beneath it, a wave that ebbs and flows. Sometimes the liquid bubbles up just high enough to lick the stopper. Does the cork dissolve?

"Anger is useful," she says, "when there is injustice."

But aren't the boundaries of injustice porous? Like the waves of a pandemic, injustice rises and falls. Like a pandemic, it continues even when we're assured, "It's endemic now. Take off your masks. Fill your lungs with the breaths of those around you once again"; "Racism? Slavery is over. We have a diversity, equity, and inclusion representative"; "The past is in the past. Sit at a Thanksgiving meal and be grateful for everything under the sun now," except the land on which you feast, which was and continues to be full of Indigenous life and potential.

Injustice, coronavirus, and anger exist in similar ways. If they (and their variants) aren't named and examined, they will surge under capitalism, spread unabashed, and take certain lives, the more-than-human—Black, Indigenous, trans, immunocompromised—first and foremost.

In her keynote address at the National Women's Studies Association Conference in 1981, titled "The Uses of Anger: Women Responding to Racism," Audre Lorde describes a visceral imbibement of anger: "I have suckled the wolf's lip of anger and I have used it for illumination, laughter, protection, fire in places where there was no light, no food, no sisters, no quarter" (1987, 6). Anger is internalized and Lorde's primary response to racism. Its uses are all around her; it is food, shelter, the body's joyous sounding. It is also markedly different from the anger that Lorde describes as "dripping down over this globe like a diseased liquid" (1987, 6). This form of anger—a bitter substance born in the pit of one's stomach—eventually oozes out as ink on official documents that oppress and displace, or leaks as thick black oil out of the bellies of oil platforms into clear ocean waters.

As the pandemic raged through New York City in March 2020 and the first year of my PhD program in ethnomusicology continued in a new form, I wondered if some of this "diseased liquid" resided in me. Zoom arranged classmates and teachers like chocolates of assorted shades and fillings in a neat gift box. I struggled to connect with them and with what I read and wrote in a doctoral program that would extend for the next five years of my life. While my partner rallied fellow medical students to help families connect with their sick relatives and assist health workers, I wondered why my work mattered in a different way than I had in the past. It made me angry to feel that it didn't, and I was ashamed to express that. Music certainly matters and was especially important during the pandemic, though most musicians were struggling to make ends meet and forced to reimagine live performances. But my ethnography on the jukebox of Brooklyn's queer/lesbian bar Ginger's felt inescapably nostalgic, like writing an anticipated eulogy for a community.

Days before the lockdown was announced, I was getting my hair cut by a longtime, beloved Ginger's patron who also held the keys to the pool table. A few days before, we'd driven around Brooklyn to get to some of her errands. Our growing friendship dissolved as the pandemic kicked in, partly because I felt that the only tool at my disposal was my writing, and that was far from enough. This letting go was fueled not by anger as sustenance, but anger as divisiveness, driving me away from actively challenging questions around the significance of my work during the pandemic and, ultimately, letting a friendship dissolve.

This feeling was compounded by the prospect of not being able to see my family in Brazil for an unknown period of time. How could it be that after years of constantly being pushed out of this country, I was suddenly forced to stay? An O-1 visa expires every three months due to a reciprocity clause in the agreement between the US and Brazil. If I returned to São Paulo, I would be at the mercy of the US embassy's reopening and its ability to issue visas. "But you're married to a US citizen, so aren't you a US citizen too?" I feel a surge of irritation at what little understanding acquaintances and friends have of the complex bureaucratic web one must disentangle and the chunk of a lifetime that is spent navigating national boundaries. This is not the highest price paid by unwanted immigrants to this country; the opportunity to navigate national boundaries has been a privilege for me.

As a queer feminist scholar and immigrant to the United States, my body and its ambiguity is no stranger to disorientations—in the untraceable foreignness of my voice (both here and there), the hybridity of my body's femme/masc readings, and the shifting perceptions and privilege of my skin, I find myself "at an oblique angle to what coheres" (Ahmed 2006, 567). Anger can spark from one's incoherent positionality in a generative way. I see now that I could have metabolized my frustration and doubts in such a way that brought me closer to my friend and thesis project. Or, as Lorde puts it, to use anger and its fieriness as a source of light, rather than a burning agent.

When a bitter substance like anger is not given a chance to transform in such a way, it can be weaponized. White supremacists grip steering wheels with rage and take aim at crowds of protesters across the United States. Brazilian president Jair Bolsonaro—a deadly prophet, a *messias*, as his middle name declares him to be—greets his followers without a mask because, he says, "We will all die one day." Cocked guns live in his pupils as he dishes out insults at a cabinet meeting a few months before Brazil becomes the world leader in COVID-19 cases and deaths. Then, the virus finally takes hold of him too.

Yet I am not angry at the virus, which multiplied, transformed, and traveled boundlessly on its way to my body. Was it angry? The virus journeyed into me, surfacing from the cellular level as a low-grade fever that lasted one day, some fatigue, and a bout of desensitization to smell and taste. I was quarantined along with my partner for about ten days, while our housemates prepared our meals and maintained their distance. Anger rose once again, as quarantining meant being on the sidelines of mutual aid efforts for a month. Yet the virus wasn't fueled by anger. It acknowledged our willingness to cede our sociality and did not spread to others inside the house.

In the semidarkness and sticky air of the basement where my partner and I argued, anger seemed like an obstacle to consensus. But to relegate anger to moments of injustice, as my partner suggested, is not possible or helpful. Injustice isn't presented neatly and neither is anger, but its messiness is its versatility. As a bitter liquid should, it eats at the cork that attempts to stifle it.

I don't remember what my partner and I were arguing about the day New York City's curfew was announced in March 2020, but two years later on a Chilean tour boat, our anger coalesced. A glacier's translucent limbs were scattered, floating around Santa Ines Island in Tierra del Fuego, across the clear waters and light-green lands of the Kawésqar people. Vivaldi's *Four Seasons* played from the boat's speakers as we floated before the massive wall of moving ice. The concerto echoed across the water and the sudden cracking sound that resounded from the wall of ice, followed by the crashing of a chunk of glacier into water, did not disturb those enjoying whiskeys served over glacial ice.

Anger can go unnoticed, until anger is an ocean rising.

Bibliography

Ahmed, Sara. "Orientations: Toward a Queer Phenomenology," *GLQ: A Journal of Lesbian and Gay Studies* 12, no. 4 (2006): 543–574.

Lorde, Audre. "The Uses of Anger: Women Responding to Racism." *Women and Language* 11, no. 1 (1987): 4.

22 • PANDEMIC DIARIES
Immigrant Perspectives
Jyoti Puri

Personals

It's early March 2020, COVID-19 infections are just beginning to surge in the US, and tests are not easy to come by. My partner has been exposed, and soon he has symptoms and needs to see a doctor. The hospital I call early one morning puts me through to the Massachusetts Department of Public Health. But the epidemiologist cannot provide medical health, so we head to the emergency services.

The staff have their masks on, as do we. They wipe down the area with a sanitizer after checking in my partner, and they are efficient, even brusque. I tell the nurse as she is taking him away through the double doors that he needs to be tested for COVID-19, given his exposure and symptoms, but she is noncommittal.

I am alone in the waiting area, away from the reception desk. I cannot quite focus on the muted TV or something that I am trying to read. The same nurse comes back later for no apparent reason and reprimands me for lowering my mask even though there isn't another person in sight. Would that she express a similar level of concern for her patient. They don't test him for COVID-19 until he insists. They are not interested in testing me. They send us home with no specific instructions. They are keen to get us out of there.

I have been in touch with my cousin's spouse, who is a nurse, about his fever. Initially it seemed best not to alarm the family, but I need their support. I call the doctor's office, and they suggest that we return to the emergency services that, once again, are eager to be rid of us. My cousin's wife tells us how to manage the fever. A friend suggests an oximeter.

I check in with others in my Brown immigrant network, and childhood friends, two of whom are doctors, tell me how to manage the recovery and avoid a relapse. No one from the doctor's office follows up. A local public health official emails my partner, emphasizing the need for us to remain in quarantine. I don't know whether I have mild symptoms as well. I can't quite tell for sure. It feels like we've been abandoned by the healthcare system.

As the pandemic took root in the US in early March 2020, so did the fear, but this was not an equal-opportunity bug. It posed a particular risk for people on the front lines of healthcare, especially without adequate protections, people who were deemed essential workers and unable to quarantine. It posed a particular risk for Native communities, triggering a massive outbreak in early April and spikes in deaths in the Navajo Nation, which the governor of New Mexico sealed off by invoking the Riot Control Act. But draconian measures are poor remedies for a crisis caused by conditions such as impoverishment, inadequate healthcare over the life course, work that doesn't allow people to quarantine, shortage of running water, and poor housing quality.

Despite the steady drumbeat that higher rates of COVID-19 infections and higher mortality rates among people of color are due to underlying health conditions, these are symptoms rather than causes of the problems. Racial disparities overshadow the data on the virus's impact throughout the US, independent of geography and age differences. African American and Latinx people have been three times more likely to become infected and nearly twice as likely to die compared to their white counterparts due to frontline jobs, reliance on public transportation, and living in cramped apartments.[1] But the story does not stop there, for Black and Brown people are also overrepresented in the carceral system, which accounted for as much as 20 percent of all positive cases of COVID-19 in Ohio by the third week of April.

Asians have not been at as high risk as Black and Latinx communities, but we are more vulnerable than white people. My partner and I are privileged to have access to health insurance, and we live in an area with no shortage of well-equipped hospitals. But this experience laid bare how the failures of national leadership in a context already riven by systemic institutional fault lines can reverberate at the granular level and especially for people of color. The hospital that we went to had a protocol in place, but by itself that was not enough. The lack of a nationally coordinated response surfaced the gaps between various parts of the healthcare system—between local, state, and national public health agencies and the needs of people requiring assistance, between the information that circulates and what people in distress need to know. Each of us, case by case, is left to fill in the blanks, to advocate for our dear ones and ourselves. If we are lucky, we have health insurance and access to an informal network of family and friends that sees us through the crisis.

Projects

I try to resume work on my project on death and migration. Work is both a refuge from the emotional stresses of the previous few weeks but also disturbing as the reports of suffering and death in the US but also Italy and Spain fill the news feeds. Migrants are particularly vulnerable in detention centers in the US and in the hastily imposed lockdown in India.

I am distressed, feeling that I need to be able to hold it all. At the very least, I feel the need to witness as much as I can from my quarantine. The accounts and images of loved ones passing away alone in hospitals; the healthcare workers who are sacrificed by the callous ineptitude of the state, hospitals, and nursing home authorities; the incarcerated people who are pressed into service to inhume bodies on Hart Island; the hastily arranged funerals; and the online memorials are painful.

Research is at a standstill, suspended by the institutional review board to comply with the state of emergency declared in Massachusetts. I wonder how migrant communities are managing: How are the temporary closure of mosques and temples affecting them, especially through Ramadan? How are the local Imams responding? Are they performing prayers at more funeral services than usual?

Premature death, the seclusion of people succumbing to the virus, and the constraints on funerals and mourning rituals are among the reasons that this pandemic has been hard to bear for so many people. But this has always been the story of migrant death! The conventional narrative is that people are supposed to die at the end of a long and well-lived life in a place that they consider home and among people who care about them. But all too frequently, migrants lose their lives prematurely in the very process of transit over land and sea, in detention centers, and at other carceral sites. The pandemic has sharply reversed the circuits of migration, and most receiving countries have closed their borders—for example, Malaysia has endangered hundreds of Rohingya refugees by refusing to let their boats dock, and the US has exposed untold numbers of asylum seekers to COVID-19 infection through forced deportations.

Being away from loved ones who are dying, unable to return in time or return at all to say goodbye or attend funerals, is not an uncommon condition among migrants. We live in dread of the phone call with news that a loved one is dying or has already passed away. The news seems to come when you are least expecting it. Phone and video calls, photos, and memories fill the voids left by death and distance, and now the pandemic has made this migrant condition more commonplace for nonmigrants. The immigrant paradigm has become universalized.

At the same time, funeralizing in these times has exacerbated the challenges for marginalized communities. An emergency bill in Britain initially proposed cremating all bodies that had tested positive for COVID-19, including Muslims and Jewish people, despite the religious and cultural injunctions against burning. In Sri Lanka the state-imposed cremation of two virus-infected Muslims was anguishing for the minoritized community. The injunctions to cremate are part of the effort to stall the contagion, to destroy the virus as well as the body. But when the body is the path to afterlife in Abrahamic religious traditions like Islam, then cremation is abhorrent. And for Muslims, who are troublingly associated with contamination in contexts such as the US and India—accused of corrupting dominant Christian or Hindu ways of life, polluting land and water through burial practices that require no embalming or coffins, infiltrating civic life with religious fundamentalism—it is not only deathways but the very existence of the communities that are rendered precarious. As the pandemic took hold in India, the backlash against Muslim communities as the vectors of infection and contamination was swift and harsh.

Politicals

Mid-April: I am in a colloquium related to my research project, and one of the interlocutors asks if I see death as transgressive. Not really, I say, but my response is fumbled. Another interlocutor responds by taking a stronger stance—that in the US death is a social taboo and therefore transgressive. I think it's more complicated than that, but I am not able to articulate a well-considered response at the time.

On May 6, a friend posts a petition seeking to build public pressure to ensure justice in the killing of Ahmaud Arbery, which happened on February 23, 2020. Around the same time, news about Breonna Taylor's murder also starts to circulate on social media and enters the national limelight. Within a couple of weeks, it is reported that George Floyd's life had been callously, almost casually taken from him by the police. I cannot bring myself to watch the videos capturing Ahmaud Arbery's and George Floyd's last minutes, but their sacrifices also demand that we don't turn away from them.

Police violence against Black people in the US has a long and dark history that has intensified since 2016. The mainstreaming of white nationalism—as power and supremacy—has occurred through defending and promoting state-sanctioned violence on Black communities, the crackdown on Native American–led activism, Islamophobic policies, and unrelenting anti-immigration rhetoric and practices. White nationalism has served as a vector for unleashing internal war. If the Bush years were defined by external warfare and imperial expansion, then what has been said and done since January 2017 is an internal assault. In this assault, Black and Brown people are being sacrificed through willful neglect, actively supporting police violence, enacting necropolitical national policies that will ensure their untimely deaths, and biopolitical acts of omission that refuse the national leadership needed to contain this historic pandemic.

The long arc of settler colonialism and slavery, as well as its afterlife, are constant reminders that for some communities, death is not a social taboo but a state of being, leading poet Claudia Rankine to call Black life an endless state of mourning. Neither is death taboo nor transgressive for the growing numbers of Muslim migrants who have settled in the US and Canada and seek to be funeralized per Islamic guidelines. Muslim communities have sought access to Islamic burial grounds but have met with fierce local opposition from residents, and also sometimes from state officials, in dozens of cases across North America. They've had to inform and educate through media sources, to correct harmful prejudices against Muslims, and to repeatedly turn to the courts to establish Islamic cemeteries. Death, then, is a matter of ensuring dignity and asserting the right to belong to this land and its soil. It has been front and center for marginalized communities, while mainstream white constituencies have been able to privatize death. Notwithstanding the recent opioid crisis, death is not a leveler, and endemic death, death rites, and mourning are social and political matters.

Provisionals

Paying tribute to the lives stolen by police and state-sanctioned violence, the Movement for Black Lives, founded in 2014 with a group of more than 150 organizations, has released a summary for a legislative bill, the BREATHE Act. Aimed at securing justice for Black communities in the US, the bill's summary proposes transformations sweeping from divesting federal resources in carceral institutions; to demilitarizing and changing policing, prosecution, sentencing, and jailing procedures; to making direct investments in community safety. It calls for establishing educational, environmental, health and family, food, economic, and housing programs to promote justice, as well as paving the way for greater self-determination within Black communities.

Important about this proposal is its vision for institutional and structural transformation, aimed at supporting life and stalling death. It upends many of the foundational structures that are maintained in the name of securitization, while seeking to breathe new life into Black communities. Such a vision promises not only to transform Black lives, but also to bring a sea change for all of us who stand to gain from the diminishment of the carceral state and especially its impact on migrants and refugees. Its emphasis on life-affirming forms of healthcare, food, water, education, environmental conditions, jobs, and greater community self-determination echoes many of the needs of Native American communities that begin with reparations for past and ongoing harms, social recognition, access to land and water rights, education, health, cultural revival, and more.

Such restitutions will pave the way for erasing political borders, lines of control set up in the name of nation building, national sovereignty, and national security but that have actually worked to create and sustain inequalities around the world. They are the sources of international disparities—which produce states of continual wars in some areas, ensure that people in some parts of the world can thrive only if others don't, and actively exploit the lives and labor of some people in sending as well as in receiving countries. If the pandemic is reinforcing one takeaway over and over again, it is that our lives "here" and "there" are inseparable. The uprising for racial justice that has swept through the US and echoed in so many places around the world is a manifestation of the belief that harm to some is harm to all. The conviction that the lives of people anywhere are not secure until the lives of people everywhere are secure must be the foundation for reimagining and reorganizing our world.

Note

1. Richard A. Oppel Jr. et al., "The Fullest Look Yet at the Racial Inequity of Coronavirus," *New York Times*, July 5, 2020, https://www.nytimes.com/interactive/2020/07/05/us/coronavirus-latinos-african-americans-cdc-data.html.

23 • ON BEHALF OF MY SISTERS

Exposing the Invisibility of Latina Immigrants During the COVID-19 Crisis

Anahí Viladrich

THIS ESSAY REPRESENTS AN INWARD turn in my attempt to honor the contradictory feelings I experienced at the onset of the COVID-19 crisis, a time during which we all had to adapt to and create a "new normal," one that is still in the making. Since March 2020, we have been bombarded with COVID-19 news and, at some point or another during this (not-yet-over) pandemic, many of us have been dogged by persistent mood swings, yo-yo-ing between hyper-attention to the latest scientific findings and discouragement about the seemingly ineffective treatments. From the moment the pandemic first disrupted our everyday lives, many of us were forced to adapt to what has ultimately become a striking symptom of human disregard for our planet and nature. In my case, this meant devising new daily routines during an initial self-imposed quarantine, learning to navigate the technological challenges of online teaching and virtual committee meetings, and—last but not least—getting involved with up-to-date forms of academic activism and social advocacy.

Truth be told, and *con el corazón* (with heart), for the past two years, I have been experiencing an emotional roller coaster of my own. Confusion, anger, disbelief, denial, rage, self-pity, and fear of the unknown are just some of the emotions that I have been dealing with during this COVID-19 era. While at first I was paralyzed by these emotions, they have lately driven me to take action by writing, denouncing racial injustices in the Spanish-language media, demonstrating against police brutality, and joining my Latina sisters and Latino brothers in the good fight. Yes, I am grateful for having a job and being able to put food on the table while so many are unemployed, but, at the same time, I am part of a community with deep roots in different Spanish-speaking countries, and we have suffered more than anyone during these challenging times. Meanwhile, social inequalities have returned with a vengeance in the form of a structural racism that impinges on the health and survival of our African American and Latina sisters and Latino brothers (Viladrich 2020).

My past writings gave me the chance to contribute to the "politics of emotion" as I engaged with Gloria Anzaldúa's legacy through personal accounts of my own struggles as a Latina immigrant in the United States (Viladrich 2011). As an intersectional feminist, I have always seen myself—in my multiple struggles against patriarchal structures—vis-à-vis other minority women and men. I have also become quite aware that my own privilege, rooted in the acquisition of cultural and educational capital, has bestowed me with key epistemological tools that served me well in voicing both the macro and micro injustices perpetrated against ethnic minorities on a daily basis. I write this essay as a public scholar, as a Latina advocate, and as someone who is honored to speak on behalf of some of my Latina sisters who do not have the opportunity or the means to put their experiences into writing.

Why My Sisters' Stories Matter

I would like to briefly introduce you to María, a Latina immigrant originally from Colombia who, like me, came to the United States in the late 1990s hoping to make a difference in her (and her family's) life. Our similarities end there, however. I migrated to the United States as a graduate student in the mid-1990s with a student visa and the support of generous fellowships. Although my initial migratory path was anything but easy, I was slowly able to forge enough human and cultural capital to complete two master's programs and a PhD, and eventually become a full professor at the City University of New York.

María also was able to turn many of her dreams into a reality. Over the years, she saved enough money to bring two of her siblings to New York City and raised two loving daughters, mostly as a single mother. Nonetheless, she could not escape the pervasive systemic conditions created by her undocumented legal status. For more than twenty-five years, María has been working in the informal economy alternately as a babysitter, a home health aide, or an off-the-books seamstress. Her latest job as a house cleaner found her in the midst of a pandemic that made her more invisible than ever. Unlike those working in supermarkets, pharmacies, and businesses such as hardware or grocery stores, María's job did not fit within the rubric of "essential worker."

Consequently, women like María were among the first to lose their jobs when the virus struck the United States in mid-March 2020. She was not able to receive any of the unemployment or cash benefits approved by Congress and signed into law by then-president Trump. Technically, some of her friends were eligible for financial aid on behalf of their children, but they decided not to apply, concerned that it could jeopardize their ability to legalize their status in the future. Long before COVID-19 pummeled NYC, women like María were already on the fringes, barely surviving. They earned their money one day at a time, with no sick leave or medical insurance. And despite the fact that they paid taxes, they did not receive social and health benefits from their employers. To make matters worse, Latinas and Latinos in NYC presented some of the highest infection and death rates from COVID-19 and were also the most impacted by job losses and income reduction (Viladrich 2020).

During the first few weeks after the pandemic struck, María faced a dilemma. Either she could look for work and run the risk of getting infected or stay home and lose the ability to pay her bills and put food on the table. Because they were at home 24-7 during the lockdown, many of her former clients no longer needed help. They began doing their own cleaning and taking care of their own children. Furthermore, fear of contagion caused domestic workers to be seen as "potential vectors" of the virus, particularly given the fact that they depend on public transportation to get to work and typically visit several homes per week. To make matters worse, many upper- and middle-class families left the city in a modern version of the "white flight" that occurred when the white middle-class population discovered suburbia in the 1950s. Meanwhile, members of Latina/o/x communities and African Americans were forced to stay in an urban core that seemed to be taking a turn for the worse.

I initially found myself confused about how to assist María and her friends, so I decided to join them in researching alternative ways to find jobs. Along with some of my colleagues, I connected María with worker-run cleaning collectives that offered financial assistance, protective gear, and, most important, employment. We collaborated with fundraising initiatives to get supplies (i.e., disinfectants and masks) and helped raise funds through GoFundMe. We also signed petitions for extending financial and legal support to domestic workers, including the Domestic Workers Bill of Rights Act and the Heroes Act, both of which are still being debated in

Congress as of this writing. I doubt that any of the actions and campaigns I have engaged with will turn out to be a long-term solution for María, nor will it calm my sometimes-guilty conscience for not doing enough on her behalf. Still, my work has helped me channel my frustration and anxiety into proactive coping mechanisms, toward galvanizing new forms of academic collaboration with community groups that include Latinas from all walks of life.

Building Community During Difficult Times

The COVID-19 pandemic is a painful reminder that, as scholars, we do not erase our complex identities as minority members, immigrants, queer folks, transgender people, working-class individuals, and people with disabilities. My privileged academic status does not wipe away the fact that I am also a member of an ethnic minority. In fact, my status in the scholarly world makes me part of the 2 percent of Latina faculty members and less than 1 percent of the full-time faculty labor force in the United States (Torres 2020). More than ever, I am committed to supporting communities of color that not only have been impacted by the COVID-19 pandemic the most but also continue to endure social and racial exclusion along with dire socioeconomic conditions.

Anzaldúa (1993) taught us how to traverse labile boundaries. Her conceptualization of nepantla perfectly encapsulates the sense of in-between-ness that I have felt since COVID-19 ambushed us back in March 2020. For the past two years, I have been able to navigate my different identities while learning from the incredible strength, adaptability, and survival skills of María and her Latina comrades. Their fiery determination to make things work for themselves and their families is deeply ingrained in their cultural and spiritual resilience—nurtured by an extraordinary sense of self-worth continuously reinforced by a large network of family, neighbors, and fellow citizens. María and her friends have shared invaluable lessons with me on how to build strength in seemingly unbearable circumstances and, in the midst of this pandemic, have welcomed me as their ally under their collective umbrella.

The educational and social distance that separates me from the majority of my immigrant *hermanas* does not preclude me from feeling their pain or trying to do something about it. They are my friends, my sisters, and my alter egos. Just before the pandemic, we would get together at community events, birthdays, and festivals celebrating our countries of origin, events that offered us an opportunity to honor our pan-ethnic Latina/o/x communities in the diaspora. We would sing songs, eat, share stories about our children, and everything in between that allowed us to re-create virtual versions of our respective homelands. Yesterday and today, what brings us together is an ever-present awareness of our foreignness and our shared ethnic traits, a common language and cultural *habitus* (Bourdieu 1984) ingrained in our beloved music, dancing, and food.

Anzaldúa exhorted us to write with poignancy, honesty, love, and compassion for others and ourselves. Writing is indeed a form of harnessing the power of our inner truth, a way of mobilizing our collective desires while devising alternative tools for resisting racial and economic oppression. María taught me an invaluable lesson imprinted in her courage to simultaneously be bold and vulnerable, fierce and insecure, strong and weak. In the end, working with these women has become a proactive way for me to overcome my initial emotional numbness and social isolation in a time of (seemingly endless) physical distancing.

As an ally to María and others fighting against economic and social inequality, I have been able to develop coping skills, which will hopefully serve me well once this crisis is finally over. If we truly want to decolonize our writing, we must start by acknowledging who we are and are not, and what we stand for. I stand for women like María, many of whom do not speak English and cannot reap the benefit of staying at home or earning an income sitting in front of a computer. Sharing these women's stories and advocating for their rights has become my own decolonizing effort toward supporting my Latina sisters, who, today more than ever, have the right to be heard.

Bibliography

Anzaldúa, Gloria E. "Chicana Artists: Exploring Nepantla, el lugar de la frontera." *NACLA Report on the Americas* 27, no. 1 (1993): 37–45.

Bourdieu, Pierre. *Distinction: A Social Critique of the Judgment of Taste*. Harvard University Press, 1984.

Krogstad, Jens Manuel, Ana Gonzalez-Barrera, and Luis Noe-Bustamante. "US Latinos Among Hardest Hit by Pay Cuts, Job Losses Due to Coronavirus." Pew Research Center, April 3, 2020. https://www.pewresearch.org/short-reads /2020/04/03/u-s-latinos-among-hardest-hit-by-pay-cuts-job-losses-due-to -coronavirus/.

Torres, Lourdes. "Inclusion 101: The Whiteness of Higher Education." *The Hill*, February 2, 2020. https://thehill.com/opinion/education/482355-inclusion -101-the-whiteness-of-higher-education/.

Viladrich, Anahí. "COVID-19 Amplified: Deconstructing Immigrants' Vulnerability During Pandemic Times." Roosevelt House Public Policy Institute, July

16, 2020. https://www.roosevelthouse.hunter.cuny.edu/?forum-post=covid-19
-amplified-deconstructing-immigrants-vulnerability-pandemic-times.

Viladrich, Anahí. "Deconstructing the Immigrant Self: The Day I Discovered
I Am a Latina." In *Bridging: How Gloria Evangelina Anzaldúa's Life and Work
Transformed Our Own*, edited by A. L. Keating and G. González-López. University of Texas Press, 2011.

24 • WORLD MAKING IN TIMES OF REVOLTS AND DISEASE
An Observation in Four Parts
Sara Rezvi

Part 1: On belonging in the interstices of nowhere

In my homeland that is
Neither home
Nor land
I am attempting to find my way
In the in-between
Of nothing and everything

Like the coating of an envelope
Before you press and seal with a kiss
There is space for both

Part 2: A poem for every dying woman holding it together by a half-severed thread

I have words but I don't know where to put them

I have silence but don't know how to stay still

I have rage but only these smoky ruins remain

Shall I wrap them softly?
Swaddled in burnt ember?

Somewhere in the crawl space of my heart
I keep these words
I keep them quiet, I keep them safe

I fear their lighting
—a burnt match
A pathway winking into existence
To a smoldering anger undying, to worlds that I would end
with just one glance

Eternal, unvanquished, immortal

They say to women, find your voice

They say to women, find your dignity

They do not warn you
no they do not warn you

What happens when you do—

the only infinity that exists is this rage

I can no longer remember the name of the dish my mother used to prepare

—the sucking up of juices of boiled bones

What else can you call
the dripping of
savory blood
down your chin
Except a kind of feral hope?

Part 3: A poem for every healing woman stitching herself back together with a bow and arrow

After the 107th time I tried to die
a friend asked me if I felt
—like I was the same person
Trapped in this reanimated skin

The fusing together of so much put-together glass
A stitching together with bow and arrow
With fiber threaded
—pulled in and out
Until it resembles an almost-woman again

I had to pause and think for a moment
The longing to die replaced with a will to live

In these 35 years I have circled this sun
Orbited this moon
Rotated dizzy counterclockwise on this hemisphere

Fallen in love
With a man with too-long hair and blue mischief
Who whispers his love daily softly
As he strums an out-of-tune guitar

And even though this love is beautiful
It was not enough

It could not replace the deep well of self-love
I have misplaced
Somewhere in these deep crevices
Safely hidden is a place I am beginning to return

I have always been my waiting first lover
The arms reaching out
The lips pulled back
—in a crooked, anxious smile
The smell of lavender follows
As we hold each other
For the first time

though I've never known you
Salaam and welcome—
My, how much I've missed you.

Part 4: On that particular *New York Times* headline

Day 78 of shelter-in-place
We who are hurting
And are so small
Curved and hunched
In protection
100,000 and more—your breath catches
A sharp intake as the weight of
These numbers settle into your spine

10 × 10 × 10 × 10 × 10
The scale of it all ~

Let it be known that in the time
of this disease
of this revolt

The first inclination of so many
Was not the firehose
Or the ax
Nor the bullet and the too-short temper

It was instead to offer
Our own unique abundance to each other

To reach for soil
To sow a garden full of seed

It was in the smallest of things
We found our own holiness

The way the sky darkens before night
A scent of a flower
The careless winged cacophony in the trees
In this we find our humility
In this perhaps
we find our grace

Note

Some sections of this text were previously published by *South Side Weekly*, a community-based newspaper in Chicago. The author has the rights to the text presented here.

PART V · MOTHERHOOD IS RADICAL LOVE

On Being a Mother During COVID-19

5. putting Coyolxauhqui together . . . new personal and collective "stories"

Coyolxauhqui personifies the wish to repair and heal, as well as rewrite the stories of loss and recovery, exile and homecoming, disinheritance and recuperation, stories that lead out of passivity and into agency, out of devalued into valued lives. Coyolxauhqui represents the search for new metaphors to tell you what you need to know, how to connect and use the information gained, and, with intelligence, imagination, and grace, solve your problems and create intercultural communities.

"NOW LET US SHIFT," 563

25 • REFLECTIONS OF AN AFRO-LATINA MOTHERING THROUGH CRISIS

Michaela A. Machicote

I THOUGHT THIS WOULD BE a cathartic exercise, writing something that had nothing to do with my life as an academic. Little did I know that this would be an experience that left me vulnerable and exposed. It has been cathartic in the sense that it has allowed me to be honest with myself, to face that which I had pushed down for so long now. This global pandemic has left me with ample time to ruminate on what it means to be a Black mother, and what that mothering looks like during times of crisis. I think to myself, *When are Black mothers not mothering in crisis?* One of the hardest things I've had to accept is learning to live with uncertainty and neither deny nor hide behind it—to turn away from any need to justify the future, to live in what has not yet been.

Dealing with the COVID-19 epidemic has meant extra anxiety on top of the everyday Afro-Puerto-Rican-single-mother-in-graduate-school anxiety. It seems like every day my university or department drafts memos on how we are living through "exceptional" times marked by "unprecedented" precarity. I delete these. I delete them because they do not reflect the fact that for myself and others like me, every day is and has been precarious. As a Black Latina mother to a Black-Brown son, every day is marked by uncertainty as I live paycheck to paycheck trying to make ends meet. When your finances are stretched so thin that every purchase in excess of a bill leaves you racked with guilt, what is stability? Is stability working long hours that interfere with your being available to your child, while also dealing with the stress and inconsistencies of co-parenting across state lines? Surely it can't be navigating the endless Zoom meetings that leave you so fatigued and irritable that all you have left is the space to cry in the shower at the end of the day, questioning why you decided academia should be your career path? You know the answer to that rhetorical question because as a Black Latina raised in poverty, you wanted (and were raised) to believe that education was the safest and surest way out. You were taught to break generational "curses." But what if the stress of academia kills you first?

I find that baring your soul gets easier once you begin to understand that you are not the only one feeling this way (and forgive yourself for all the guilt you feel). Maybe that is a small, comforting fact. Or maybe, COVID compounded by state-sponsored genocide both exhausts you *and* keeps you up at night.

Because maybe, you, too, are stroking the curls on a baby boy—or it could be a baby girl, for that matter. My son. The same son that amid keeping him safe from the pathogens ravaging Black and Brown communities, I have to also keep safe from the genocidal agents of the state. Maybe you, like I am, are imagining the heart-wrenching video of a small Black boy being gunned down while holding a toy gun, as you watch your own son play "captain of the high seas" with the water pistol given to him by the entertainers dressed like pirates. You realize Tamir Rice was only two years older than your son is now. The world isn't much better for little Black girls, who are imagined to be five years older than they really are, angry, rebellious, sassy, and hypersexualized. Then you feel the guilt again for having taken the first vacation you could afford to take, and actually had time to take, in four years because we are in the midst of a global pandemic. But it was my birthday and I needed something to break me out of the dismal monotony of the depression I can feel trying to creep in. The mask covering my face isn't what makes it hard for me to breathe.

Maybe your son, too, is still learning about race, and why it is that little McKenzie-Apple won't play with him on the playground, and why she won't let Hunter or Kyle play with him either. Maybe, as a Black mother to a Black-Brown child, you, too, feel a hitch in your chest when your son wants to play loudly in public like most kids his age do, because you know he will not be afforded the same childhood innocence as the other kids his age who are not Black. You know you will have to remind him, again, why he cannot express joy as loud as he wants—because perhaps the best-case scenario is that another parent will shoot you unapproving looks, and the worst-case scenario is that some unapproving parent will say something to you that upsets you or your child, or the police will arrive to actually shoot you.

I wonder to myself, *Am I more afraid when he is with me or his father? Is he safer with his Black mother, who has had to learn to navigate state violence from the time she was in elementary school, but also who is still a target of the rampant anti-Blackness fueling this country, or with his Brown father, who is Mexican and surveilled in other, equally troubling ways?* I am always afraid when he is out of sight. How does his father help him to navigate the anti-Blackness of the world? Despite our conversations on what it means to raise a Black-Brown child when you are not a Black person, I am still afraid. Anti-Mexican sentiments mean my son is doubly marked. I have to trust that his father will keep him safe.

While teaching my son how to navigate the world as a Black-Brown boy, how to try his best to stay safe, I wonder, too, *What hope can I offer him of the future?* Hope is not a plan. Stealing moments of joy with him seems so much more urgent than ever before. Tomorrow is never promised, but these days it feels as if danger lurks in every shadow. The more I stay inside, the easier it becomes to see how very real my fears are that every time we step outside could be my last. One fateful interaction with a white person, or non-Black person, could change my life forever. Even the simple act of putting on my athletic clothes and going for an early morning jog has become daunting. I force myself to confront these fears because I know that I am no safer inside than I am outside (rest in peace, Breonna Taylor). Cold sweats, quickened heartbeats, and paranoia feel debilitating. I no longer sleep through the night. I feel hypervigilant. Every sound in my apartment forces me awake.

While attending Black Feminist Kitchen's "Black Feminist Summer School" workshop themed #WakeandWayward2020 after Christina Sharpe's *The Wake: On Blackness and Being* and Saidiya Hartman's *Wayward Lives*, I wrote a poem that begins with a line from Gwendolyn Brooks's poem "Paul Robeson."[1] This simple exercise allowed me to express my fears and anxieties in ways that writing this article could not, and in ways that painting could not quite capture:

> Cutting across the hot grit of the day
> Texas summers unforgiving
> Like living with uncertainty
> Hot like pavement
> Beneath bodies of Black womxn[2]
> Slammed, pinned to asphalt
> By pigs
> Unrelenting like southern heats
> So often are
> And have been
> For the last 400 years or so
> When Black bodies turned to Brown bodies

In fields
Then again to Black
On highways.
The hot grit of the day,
Periodically laced with
The loud cries of cicadas
Outside my window
Reminding me that
Fearing the outside world
Does me no good.
Bullets don't knock—
They shatter walls,
Rip through dreams.
Cutting across
The hot grit of the day,
Breaking the promise
Of a peaceful night,
Turing bedtime stories
Into elegies—
Red stains pooling
Where dreams should be.
I hold my son tighter,
As though my arms could shield him
From the world's sharp teeth.
As though love alone
could stop bullets mid-flight.
Instead, I turn to
Childhood memories:
Water hoses, broken fire hydrants
Decorated with wooden planks
Forming temporary rainbows
Cutting across the hot grit of the day.

Pushing through my fears has been one of the most challenging things I've had to do. I am one of the lucky ones; I can work from home because of the nature of academia and because I am still a student. I am able to be at home with my son instead of working in a cubicle or call center, like women I know. But I still have to leave my home to perform basic daily tasks like grocery shopping, buying household essentials, going to the post office, etc. I have to battle both the claustrophobia and agoraphobia I feel trying to build in my mind. I begin to think of my son. I wonder what hope looks like for my little one. How can I turn hope into action? I have turned our time into an intense teaching moment. Everything serves as a lesson. We have watched Black documentaries together. We have had, and continue to have, talks about what it means to be Black in an antiblack world. His understanding grows along with his vocabulary. I have been teaching him why it is important that he learn Black feminist values. I surround him (virtually) with Black feminist family and friends. I am raising a Black-Brown boy to be a Black-Brown man that values life, values womxn,[2] and protects Black womxn. I am doing my best to mother radically, making space for error because I know that I will not always get it right, and reminding myself to be gentle when I make mistakes. I insist on loving and trying my best to live, not just survive, through this pandemic, and for now, that has to be enough.

Notes

1. Gwendolyn Brooks, "Paul Robeson," Academy of American Poets, https://poets.org/poem/paul-robeson.

2. This alternative spelling of *women* refers to Black cis and trans women, femmes, and nonbinary people erased by normative womanhood.

26 • PANDEMIC BORDERLANDS

Between *la Academia* and *la Familia*
Liliana V Rodriguez

"¡MAMÁ!" SHE SCREAMS AT THE top of her lungs.

It was six in the morning, and I was more determined than ever—driven by my guilty conscience—to work on my research. My tenure clock had begun ticking a semester before, when I began my new job as assistant professor at a research university in Texas in fall 2019, and I needed to get things done. I took a sip of my freshly brewed medium roast coffee.

"¡Mamá!" she screams again.

It had been a week since both my and my oldest daughter's spring breaks were extended. With a seven-year-old and a one-year-old at home, it was clear from the beginning that I would not be able to get much of my own academic work done. My husband, on the other hand, who works for a book publisher, had been working from home for almost a year, so not much changed for him after the quarantine, except that now he had help with the kids—me.

"¡Mamá!" she screams louder.

I looked at my cup, a sixteen-ounce round, white cup, bigger than the regular standard coffee cup. It had been gifted to me when I graduated with my PhD a year before. The gold letters across it read "Congrats Grad." I could not help but smile as I recalled my graduation and the words I shared with the audience as the student commencement speaker. I hold that moment close to my heart, for as the daughter of Mexican immigrants, I embraced the opportunity to publicly thank them for all of their sacrifices.

A mis padres, mis guerreros, estoy aquí gracias a sus esfuerzos, sacrificios y constante amor. Ustedes me enseñaron lo que es tener educación, respeto, y ganas. Los he visto trabajar de sol a sol y con sus lindas manos para que nosotros pudiéramos llegar lejos. Mamy, Papy, este logro es de ustedes, lo tienen bien merecido. Los amo.

(To my parents, my warriors, I am here thanks to your efforts, sacrifices, and constant love. You showed me what it means to have education, respect, and desire. I have seen you work from sunrise to sunset with your beautiful hands so that we could be successful. Mommy, Daddy, this achievement is yours. You have earned it. I love you.)

"¡Mamá!" I hear myself yell out to my mother at the age of ten, as I frantically tried to find her within the cornfields of Michigan. Trying to make ends meet, we migrated *pal Norte* the summer of 1990. I did not want to stay with the community babysitter, so I begged my parents to let me go with them to work. *I, too, can remove the tassel from the eight-foot-tall cornstalks*, I thought. The following day, I woke up early, about four in the morning, and dressed myself similar to how I had seen my parents and older siblings dress—jeans, a long-sleeve flannel shirt over a worn-out T-shirt, a hat and a bandana for protection from the burning sun. Since my parents did not speak English, I took it upon myself to ask the white labor contractor at the cornfields to allow me to work alongside my family. He agreed without hesitation and told me I could begin on the spot. Although I was supposed to work, my parents never let me do any of the labor required. Instead, they each took half of my workload, on top of theirs, and told me to just roam through the fields. I did that from sunrise to sunset and would often get lost in the corn maze, so I would cry out to my mother to find my way back to her.

"¡Mamá!" My daughter's scream brings me back to the present. My work will have to wait—again.

Since news of the COVID-19 global health crisis spread all over the United States, my life had changed. In only a week, I became proficient in teaching online courses to university students who themselves were navigating unfamiliar territory, became a first-grade teacher to an inquisitive seven-year-old, and took on the role of a daycare instructor to an energetic one-year-old, to name a few of my newfound roles in life. My research? What research? Even though my CV looked as if I had acquired new accomplishments, I felt like anything but successful.

The more I tried, the more I lost control of whatever little balance I felt I once had in my life. I was not able to devote myself to my research, my work. Yet I was not able to give myself unconditionally to my family, my parenting, my home. I felt stuck. Stuck between my desire to succeed professionally and do what was expected of me—teach, write, publish—and my yearning to just let go and hug my family a little tighter. If there was ever a time to find balance between my personal and my professional lives, it was then. As a feminist and woman of color, separating the public and private spheres has always been a difficult task to accomplish. The global COVID-19 crisis overly complicates this situation.

"Mommy!" I hear her calling me.

This time it is my oldest child. "You are confusing me on my knowledge of adverbs!" she suddenly yells, bursting into tears. I just stand there looking over her shoulder, thinking to myself that not even my hard-earned PhD prepared me to be a first-grade teacher. A total failure.

"¡Mamá!" my baby screams from her crib.

Before being in quarantine, my husband took care of the baby while I was at work and had her nap routine down to a science. But since then, my presence at home has disrupted her schedule. She no longer wants to nap; she does not want to eat while sitting in her high chair; she throws tantrums every time we eat; she only wants me to hold her, to carry her, to feed her, to rock her to sleep. Not only am I a total mess, but I am making a total mess of her.

"¡Mamá!" She extends her arms so I can pick her up.

I take her in my arms, and together we go over to my computer to check my emails. Students are asking about grades. I need to grade. But I also need to revise that paper I have been trying to get to. She is in my arms and my back hurts. My husband offers to take her and she bursts out crying. As they walk away, I expect the cries to fade away; instead they get louder and louder. Do I grade, work on my paper that is so close to being published, or get her? My heart aches, and all I want to do is hold her. But my guilt of not performing, producing, and publishing stops me. Even though I am aware that the pandemic and the lockdowns have weighed more heavily on women academics, resulting in the decline of their research while journal submissions from men have increased during this time (Fazackerley 2020), I cannot help but feel incompetent. Feminist scholars have written about gender inequality in work extensively, but the pandemic is widening this gap (Fazackerley 2020). My feminist consciousness about these matters does not assuage my feelings of guilt, incompetence, and failure to be a motherscholar.

"¡Mamá! I hear her loud screams. They are so loud I cannot think straight. I cannot work. I cannot write. I cannot do this. My heart beats faster and faster. I feel a throbbing headache coming as I am sure my blood pressure is elevated. Since all of this started, I have gone to the doctor on three different occasions because of high blood pressure. I was prescribed medication to help control it. However, the doctor keeps telling me that I need to find alternative ways to control my stress. I need to just stop. Breathe. But instead, I cry.

"Mom! Mommy! Mom!" I hear my daughter calling me. "I'm bored. When will you be done?" Done? I have not even started. I need to compose myself. I do so just in time before she walks into my office and says, "I am hungry."

I inhale. I exhale.

I have been in this place before. A space of ambiguity. A space where I struggle to belong, to be me, to exist. It is the borderlands. The borderlands that I am so familiar with as a Mexican American born and raised in South Texas—*la herida abierta* (Anzaldúa 1987, 25). Yet it feels like a distant experience. There is so much happening in the world and others who have it so much worse. Why am I struggling to find balance, feel accomplished, be at ease with myself? The pandemic exacerbated inequalities and shed light on the flaws and fallacies of our nation, our government, and our world. It shook the very ground on which we stand and with that brought upon us clouds of doubts, fears, and uncertainties.

Amid my anxieties, I know there is a way out. There exists a force that binds the spirits of those whose pain leaves them looking for individual solutions to combat structural forces. Anzaldúa (1987, 110) calls it magic: "Here we are weaponless with open arms, with only our magic. Let's try it our way, the mestiza way, the Chicana way, the woman way." And then the unexpected happens.

"Mommy!" she says. "You make it look so easy. How do you do it?" she asks me as I am washing the dishes.

I do not quite understand what she means. I ask her.

"You are a professor, you teach your students, you are trying to publish, you have two daughters, one who always wants to be in your arms and the other who always wants your attention, you cook, clean, play with us, read to us, watch TV with us, spend time with Daddy, are constantly checking up on Grandma and Grandpa, and then with all of this going on—" she stops to catch her breath.

I look at her in disbelief as she continues to list things. I see her lips moving but I cannot hear her anymore. I am lost in my own thoughts. I see chaos all around me. Once the pandemic hit, everything seemed to fall into pieces, and since then I have constantly struggled to put the pieces back.

But in that moment, I suddenly feel different. I feel the blood of *mujeres fuertes* running through my veins. Those "nepantleras, boundary-crossers, thresholders who initiate others in rites of passage, activistas who, from a listening, receptive, spiritual stance, rise to their own visions and shift into acting them out, haciendo mundo nuevo" (Anzaldúa 2015, 571). At that moment, I think of all the strong women in my life who against all odds have been and continue to be forced to find creative and innovative ways to get things done, to keep pushing forward and lead the way because our pain is stronger than our fears. I see my mother as a child in her hometown in the municipality of Rayón in the state of San Luis Potosí, Mexico, having to abandon her studies at the young age of ten because her mother could no longer afford to send her to school. She was then expected to stay home, do chores, and babysit when she was just a baby herself. My *abuela* became a widow at the age of twenty-five and had six children to raise. To this day, I cannot even begin to fathom how she managed, but she did. I am no stranger to that which propels us forward as we fight for dignity, happiness, and survival. I have lived it, I have breathed it, and I have seen it via the strength and grace of all those mujeres fuertes who I admire and look up to because they make things happen. But I failed to recognize it. At her young age, my daughter sees the power and knowledge that exists within me, within us. Anzaldúa calls this our conocimiento, that which prompts us to "take a deep breath, shift your attention away from what's causing pain and fear, and call upon a power deeper and freer than that of your ego, such as la naguala and los espíritus, for guidance" (2015, 570). I breathe in and breathe out as I call upon my ancestors to let their wisdom lead me.

The pandemic changed our lives drastically and produced unimaginable fears in all of us. When all of this started, I became overprotective of my family, followed quarantine measures to the dot, and constantly read up on ways to avoid falling victim to this dreadful plague. My spirituality was tested and confirmed. I felt the need to protect my family by any means necessary and teach my girls how to stay safe. In actuality, without even knowing it, it has been them teaching me all along about resilience, survival, and coping as they navigate this crisis with the eagerness and joyfulness that only a child possesses. At their young age, they are already fierce mujeres. I can now see that our blood connects us all together across time, space, and generations. The pandemic is shaping not only our knowledge but also our relationships with those in the past, present, and future.

Ambivalence produces an oppressive anxiety. It magnifies our weaknesses. But it also allows for transformation. The borderlands are about struggle, challenges, and discomfort, and that is exactly what is happening now. But the borderlands are also about resilience, courage, and strength. Anzaldúa reminds me of this:

> She can be jarred out of ambivalence by an intense, and often painful, emotional event which inverts or resolves the ambivalence. I'm not sure exactly how. The work takes place underground—subconsciously. It is work that soul performs. That focal point or fulcrum, that juncture where the mestiza stands, is where phenomena tend to collide. It is where the possibility of uniting all that is separate occurs. This assembly is not one where severed or separated pieces merely come together. Nor is it a balancing of opposing powers. In attempting to work out a synthesis, the self has added a third element which is greater than the sum of its severed parts. That third element is a new consciousness—a mestiza consciousness—and though it is a source of intense pain, its energy comes from continual creative motion that keeps breaking down the unitary aspect of each new paradigm. (1987, 101–102)

The global pandemic created a sense of displacement that pushed us beyond our limits. These are difficult times. We are constantly in a state of limbo. We have been challenged to tackle unforeseen circumstances that highlight our vulnerabilities. I have been in this space before. I am the descendent of an oppressed people whose skin, language, and bodies are deemed inferior, yet they collide into a third element that gives us faith. The mestiza in me reveals herself and gives me strength to accept my vulnerabilities, accept my challenges, and embrace the unknown.

"¡Mamá!" she screams at the top of her lungs.

I got you, *mija*. I got this.

Bibliography

Anzaldúa, Gloria. *Borderlands/La Frontera: The New Mestiza*. Aunt Lute Books, 1987.

Anzaldúa, Gloria. "Now let us shift . . . the path of conocimiento . . . inner works, public acts." In *Light in the Dark /Luz en lo Oscuro: Rewriting Identity, Spirituality, Reality*, edited by AnaLouise Keating. Duke University Press, 2015.

Fazackerley, Anna. "Women's Research Plummets During Lockdown—but Articles from Men Increase." *Guardian*, May 12, 2020. https://www.theguardian.com/education/2020/may/12/womens-research-plummets-during-lockdown-but-articles-from-men-increase?CMP=share_btn_link.

27 • REMOTE REFLECTIONS

The Pandemic and Its Impact on Mothers in Academia

Mercedes Valadez

AS I WRITE THIS ESSAY in fall 2020, I can still recall the last day I stepped into a classroom to teach: March 12, 2020. It seems like such a distant memory now. After teaching that morning, I read an email from administration that, effective immediately, all in-person classes would be suspended and the remainder of the semester would resume online due to the COVID-19 pandemic. Faculty scrambled to redesign courses within a matter of days, addressed student concerns and questions, and adapted our personal lives to new workplace demands. I remember thinking, *How am I going to get through a lecture with a screaming one-year-old in the background?*

I did my best to make the online transition as seamless as possible for students. At the same time, I was dealing with the uncertainty of a global pandemic, including unforeseen new challenges. Slowly, the minimal social support network I had built up through local Mommy and Me classes ended. My support network at work through weekly Latina faculty lunches also came to a halt. My husband's employment became uncertain. At one point he was informed that he might be transferred to a site eight hours away from our residence. It was already challenging enough managing our toddler on my own four days a week, with his fifteen-hour workdays. Amid the chaos, I tried to stay present for my daughter, but it was tough. On his days off, my husband would take her out on short stroller rides so that I could record lectures. It felt like there was never enough time in the day to meet all the competing needs and demands from home and work.

In the early days of the pandemic, I thought it would be easy to create a division between home and work, but it became close to impossible. Social isolation intensified feelings of being lonely and overwhelmed. I knew that I wasn't the only one facing a new set of workplace hardships while navigating motherhood during a global pandemic. Having lost all social support networks, I sought ways to connect with others going through similar experiences.

I started reading research on the impact of the pandemic on mothers in academia and felt a strong connection. I saw my own hardships mirrored in their experiences. A colleague from the Latina faculty lunches and I began connecting over the ways that academia was failing to support motherscholars, particularly women of color. We are already underrepresented and face a host of barriers on our path toward tenure and promotion. We decided to embark on our own research to examine the experiences of tenure-line motherscholars in the California State University system. During my review of the literature, I found that most articles ended with suggestions of ways that institutions and departments could support motherscholars. In my own experience, I had yet to see my campus acknowledge and/or provide resources aimed at assisting parents and caregivers. Besides working on this new research project, I channeled my frustration into activism.

Currently, I serve as member of the executive board in the California Faculty Association (CFA) for the California State University, Sacramento, campus. During the fall 2020 semester, I reached out to the CFA chapter president and offered to create a survey to better understand the impact of the pandemic on faculty. We planned to use the survey responses to advocate for faculty needs and concerns during the next meeting with campus administrators. The survey was completed toward the end of fall 2020. The report I wrote, based on the survey results, was used by our campus CFA president to outline faculty concerns about the ongoing pandemic and make recommendations to improve department, college, and university responses. The hardships I read about in the open-ended questions motivated me to do more to advocate for faculty, particularly those most impacted by the pandemic—parents and caregivers.

Prior to becoming a mother, I was ignorant of most of the obstacles and challenges that mothers in academia encounter. From microaggressions to direct hostility, academe is not built to be mother friendly. As a woman of color and the first tenure-line Latina in my department, I was fully aware of the exclusionary practices embedded in academia. My field (criminal justice) is white- and male-dominated. Gender and racial/ethnic biases in the criminal justice system commonly extend to the workplace. While some departments strive to be family-friendly and inclusive, enacting programs or policies aimed at supporting faculty to strike a balance between work and family, others shy away from or reject those policies altogether.

I was able to find a community of support within my Latina faculty lunch group. We are a group of Latina tenure-line faculty from across various disciplines on our campus. Before the pandemic, we regularly met to discuss *la familia* (family) and *consejos* (advice) and to brainstorm collaborative research projects. While most of the women in my Latina faculty support system are long past parenting in the infant or toddler stages, I was able to connect with one colleague in particular. Our children were born two weeks apart. We bonded over denial of our basic needs in our respective departments and across campus. She was forced to pump in what equated to a small storage room. I was forced to obtain a medical note to be able to call into a faculty meeting. That medical note gave me the opportunity to nurse my daughter at home rather than run between my office or the lactation room to the faculty meeting. These ordeals pushed me to advocate for change.

During fall 2020, I advocated for affordable on-campus daycare options for faculty, paid time off, lactation stations, changing tables across campus buildings, and other needs long before the pandemic. Two colleagues and myself met with our campus administrators to highlight some concerns that respondents had noted in the survey, including lack of paid time off, parking for new and expectant mothers, basic sanitary needs like creating lactation stations separate from women's restrooms, and other issues. We repeatedly heard "no" and "we can't," but it didn't dissuade us from continuing to advocate on behalf of parents and caregivers. Progress on our agenda slowed because of the pandemic. Additionally, the colleague leading this task on our campus and I were primarily working alone, with minimal support. We took on this task amid the backdrop of managing the pressures and demands of the tenure process and parenting infants. We needed more support.

During the early months of the pandemic, I learned that our campus was not the only one pushing the administration to recognize the perils that faculty, particularly motherscholars, were experiencing during the pandemic. A group of women scholars across CSU collaborated to form a CSU-wide Parents/Caregivers Coalition. Together, we created a mission statement, met to discuss ways to support one another, and strategized to propose policies and programs to support parents and caregivers. Coalition members from a couple of campuses began organizing a proposal for the administration with a list of ways that they could support parent/caregiver faculty and other Unit 3 employees. We celebrated the news when we learned that one campus was successful in moving their proposal forward and garnered support from their campus administrators. This led to a domino effect of support for other campus-specific proposals.

I worked alongside other colleagues on my campus to craft our own proposal. We met with campus administrators and emphasized our concerns, particularly those surrounding the gendered impact of the pandemic on faculty. In the end, parts of our proposal were supported. However, when the campus announcement went out about the new ways that our campus planned to support faculty, there was no mention of the role that the group of faculty who advocated for changes and support played in crafting the proposal and advocating for the newly adopted changes. One of the most significant victories adopted from our proposal was three units of release time for tenure-line faculty to focus on research. Prior to the announcement, we were informed that they could not provide a particular group, in this case parents and caregivers, with resources and support while excluding others. We have colleagues who are thriving professionally because of the pandemic (e.g., producing scholarship, submitting multiple manuscripts, and traveling). Meanwhile, there are days when some of us feel like we are in survival mode. Some days it is hard to get a minute to write an email when you have someone tugging at you saying, "Mami, Mami, por favor" ("Mommy, Mommy, please"). The campus administration failed to recognize those most impacted by the work-life balance disruption of the pandemic. Those of us who had worked on the proposal and met with campus leadership felt like we won and lost at the same time. There was already a well-established motherhood penalty in academia before the pandemic. Now, we are forced to navigate academia amid additional disparities.

The pandemic served to amplify gender-based differences associated with childcare. Traditionally, women are expected to be primary caretakers regardless of work outside the home. However, the pandemic created even more of a shift in caretaking responsibilities. With daycare and school closures, many parents were left scrambling to adjust to their new routines and schedules. Others were forced to navigate pregnancy and motherhood without social support.

We all yearn for a sense of normalcy and want to return to the way life was before the pandemic. Both students and faculty feel Zoom fatigue and burnout after over a year of minimal human contact. However, in the rush to return to the way life was pre-pandemic, one important area of concern should not be forgotten. That is, we must continue to address the challenges and barriers that mothers in academia experienced prior to the pandemic as well as the gendered impact of the pandemic on motherscholars.

My teaching, research, and service to the community have drastically changed because of the pandemic. While it has been restrictive in some respects, it has also created new opportunities and allowed me to be more creative in my approach to research and service. My commitment to addressing the lack of family-friendly polices across CSU seeps into my institutional community work as well as my research.

Moving forward into the fall 2021 semester seems daunting but familiar. Beyond the stressors associated with living through an ongoing pandemic, I continue to adapt to seek a work-life balance. I am still processing how I will care for my now-two-year-old on my own over the next five months while my husband works out of the country.

Part of the motherhood penalty in academia is that we are expected to work like we do not have children. I actively reject this expectation. Too often we lose women of color in the pipeline between graduate school and tenure-line positions and along the tenure process. Representation matters. While my campus highlights its diverse student body, the same cannot be said about diversity across tenure-line faculty. As a first-generation college graduate from a working-class immigrant family and the first Latina tenure-line faculty member in my department, I actively work to dismantle the narrative that someone like me does not belong in academia.

I enjoy teaching online and have years of experience doing so. I feel confident in my ability to provide students with the same level of rigor and dedication in an online setting. However, the external pressures associated with research and service can feel overwhelming at times. During difficult times it is critical to remember that even as junior faculty we are allowed to say "No," "Thank you for thinking of me, but I am not available," and the like. It is okay not to be available at all hours of the day and night for meetings. Like others who have felt marginalized in academia (whether by race/ethnicity, gender/sex, motherhood, etc.), I have found ways to connect with others in similar circumstances. Within academia, I look to the Latina faculty in my professional and personal realms for guidance and support. Outside of academia, I belong to a few mothers' groups that help me take a much-needed break from academia. But, like most mothers, I need to remember that my identity isn't rooted in my profession or motherhood.

Adjusting my professional and parenting expectations has been key to helping me feel a better sense of self. Over the past two years, I have had to periodically reevaluate my priorities and boundaries. I remind myself of the mantra to put on my oxygen mask first. In doing so, I end my day with a ritual that allows me time to reflect and regroup. I also remind myself that life is about adapting to different stages, personally and professionally. It won't always feel this chaotic and busy. Before I know it, my daughter won't be a toddler anymore, and she will be more independent. For now, I will keep enjoying our daily morning walks and finding joy in the small things, like counting *árboles* (trees) with my daughter on our walks—*uno, dos, tres* . . .

28 • MyMother.doc

Rachel Yim

I

Thirty-one months ago, I split in two. No one tells you that you can be divided so easily, that you can exist in one body and also another that seems to still be able to speak and feel and make decisions on its own. Even you can't begin to see that you've been pulled apart into two until your second self is fully operating and functioning, years later, in a life that isn't its own. When I couldn't hold two people up any longer, it started to seep out of every part of me.

As dealing with anything you've been burdened with in your twenties goes, the desire to believe your own lie and to be seen overtakes you and can seem to be resolved only by pouring your love tragically, if not disingenuously, onto another temporary person. So when he told me at the end of April that he was finally leaving and wanted me out of the apartment when he returned, I realized he had called my bluff. It was only then, tearfully curled up on a couch that wasn't mine, that I realized I had spent the last year living in an apartment that anyone could immediately see never held a trace of me aside from the stacks of books claiming their tiny territory on the windowsill. To leave during a global pandemic and stay-at-home orders, I had to find the next logical place to drive, putting myself back even further to a place I had avoided.

Understanding this virus and our collective social responsibility toward its spread and one another has oscillated around the term *stay at home*. But the question of what it means to stay at home for those whose definition of home and family isn't clear cut is something I was immediately confronted with. I had tried to build a home in the apartment I had just left with a partner who wasn't there. As a result of the fear and self-doubt that sprung from this, I believed that everything about me was available to be changed and made more accommodating, even when that thought began to touch the fringes of my innermost truths and self-love. This question of doubt in relation to what it means to be a multiracial woman of color felt twice as heavy. What the outer world, including the partners in my most intimate relationships, expected from me seemed to be docility, subservience, and agreeability. In the moments when my rage and assertion of who I was and the love I needed could no longer be contained, desperately trying to fight for the first self, they seemed to run counter to what was expected of me. I couldn't help but feel like fighting for myself was turned around and weaponized against me, becoming the defining feature that was exaggerated because it wasn't expected from the body that I inhabit. At best, my partners responded to this with blame and abandonment; at worst, they responded with physical violence.

If I could believe that I should be shamed into changing myself by being called a woman who is "crazy," "damaged," or "burdened," it's easy to see how I also came to believe in the lie that my second self actually did love another. I was going through the motions of what a loving relationship is, expressing love and the hope of forever to someone even though I knew that as hard as I tried, the words would never align with my first self, who was astray.

II

The first time I read bell hooks's *All About Love*, and in the many times I've revisited the text in moments when I desperately needed direction, one passage in particular has resonated with me. The author writes:

> For most folks it is just too threatening to embrace a definition
> of love that would no longer enable us to see love as present in
> our families. Too many of us need to cling to a notion of love that
> either makes abuse acceptable or at least makes it seem that what-
> ever happened was not that bad. (6)

These words ran through my head as I drove on the evergreen-lined highway up to my childhood home in the suburbs. I knew love was nonexistent in this last relationship. I could tell from the confrontations I had with my second self in the moments that there was a disconnect between my verbal affirmations and my intentions. I knew that I was following the formula of love outlined by hooks, drawing abusive relationships into my life, in order to still feel connected to my mom. If I could accept these relationships for the crumbs that were being given, accept the blame for all wrongdoing, and make myself out to be the problem, then my inner shame could still exist and allow me to feel connected to my mother.

III

One night when I was seven years old, I woke up in the middle of the night unable to sleep, so I walked toward the glowing light of the computer down the hall and clicked on the first document I saw on the screen, titled "MyMother.doc."

I spent an hour reading and trying to process the story my grandmother, my *halmoni*, had told my mother on her deathbed three years before. She was born in a Japanese-occupied Korea in 1938. The realities of Japanese imperialism, which transitioned into the United States' occupation of the Korean peninsula over the course of her early life, defined her story and the traumas that would settle and take residence in our family. My mother noted in her recounting of my halmoni's life that she would use only the third person when describing what had happened to her. The distance created by narrating another self when looking back at her life was a tool she used to provide safety in recounting her experiences, such as her father's death from starvation, the arranged marriage and physical abuse she fought by running away in the middle of the night, her search for employment outside of prostitution in postwar Korea, and her fleeing from different jobs and towns because of the repeated sexual violence she experienced. Time alone wouldn't provide safety from the trauma she experienced in her life; a second self developed to shield the parts of her that she could hold on to for herself.

IV

When I finally told my mom that I had come across the story of my halmoni as a child, I asked her in frustration how it was possible for her to never talk about it, to never sit with what this meant for our family and how it structured the lives of the women in our family for so long. The inter-generational issues and silences of not only my grandmother's life but the racism, neglect, and institutional violence faced by my mother and her siblings when they came to America were always diminished. My mother was emotionally unavailable throughout my childhood; she was aloof, checked out, and often cruel. I was angry at her for not being more vocal about injustice and not being able to give me the love I needed, but most of all I was angry that American racism and imperialism had robbed all of us of something that it felt impossible to live without.

My mother looked at me and my pain, seeing the confusion I had been holding on to since I was seven years old. She told me that she wasn't checked out at all but that if she sat with everything that had happened to my halmoni, to her, to the way I was raised, the pain would take over her whole body and she would completely evaporate in her grief. I realized then that I was the one who hadn't been listening.

V

When I arrived at my parents' house outside of Seattle, I immediately felt like I couldn't stay at home. The weight of this feeling filled me with the familiar sensation of rage, but somewhere in that feeling, I realized that there was almost nothing to the tears and anger. It was something that was propelling me forward because as long as I still had the fight in me, as long as I still had the power to feel or do something, it meant that being united as a whole self again was possible.

I realized then that my second self, which had split from the trauma of my childhood and series of destructive relationships, didn't exist just to destroy me and create a perpetual misidentification with a life that I didn't want. It existed for the same purpose that my mother separated from her pain, the same reason my halmoni talked about herself in the third person. My self-awareness of its existence allowed me to keep a part of me safe, to know that when the second self could no longer function, who I was at my core would still be there, preserved.

Stepping into my parents' house and becoming a part of their social-distancing unit, I was immediately confronted with my two selves. The question of what it means to stay at home in a time of global crisis required me to come to terms with how home is itself structured through intergenerational, racial, and gendered trauma. The work of questioning who we hold on to, and how those attachments are structured through the social and political, is an act of love that is in turn a form of resistance. bell hooks defines love as

> the site of radical care. When we see love as the will to nurture one's own or another's spiritual growth, revealed through acts of care, respect, knowing, and assuming responsibility, the foundation of all love in our life is the same. There is no special love exclu-

sively reserved for romantic partners. Genuine love is the foundation of our engagement with ourselves, with family, with friends,
with partners, with everyone we choose to love. (136)

This act of radical care that sees love as the foundation of our engagement with ourselves, our communities, our most intimate relationships,
and what happens in our world can be thought about in relation to what
it means to stay at home and sit intentionally with the people around us.
Most importantly, in times like these, thinking about the self in terms of
its relationship to the intersecting identities that have shaped how one's
definition of home has been affected in every sense is radical work.

Unfortunately, this mediation doesn't end with me resolving all of the
divides that stand between me, my mother, my second self, and her second
self, confidently assuring me of the love that I will accept going forward.
Shortly after our argument I left to quarantine at my aunt's house, who
carved out a piece of her home to share with me as I came to terms with
how to reunite with the part of me that has been hidden for thirty-one
months. However, the time has allowed me to realize that the shame cultivated in me from a young age defined the trauma of our family more than
it defined me. I held on to these core beliefs about myself because the part
of me that wanted to be loved as a child thought that maybe if I played into
this role for my mother, I could hold things together for our family and she
wouldn't have to sit with the trauma of being an immigrant in America.

"Staying home" and the care that bell hooks outlines has forced me to
think not only about the conditions of home, but also about the bonds I
seek with other communities of women of color to build a shared space for
us all. Women of color feminism is the courageous act of working through
the past, situating and understanding it within its material contexts, while
still radically fashioning out forms of community and new definitions of
family and home. It has allowed me to see the crumbling of romantic relationships not simply as failures attributed to something wrong within me
but as the opportunity to break apart from conditions that separated me
from myself.

Bibliography

hooks, bell. *All About Love: New Visions*. William Morrow, 2000.

29 · GROUNDED WITH *MI AMA* AND OTHER VERSES

Jessica L. Sánchez Flores

IT WAS THE SMELL OF wet dirt after the rain that I craved the most. As a kid, I enjoyed eating dirt. I felt comfort when I would lick my muddy fingers after playing in the puddles during the rainy season. The tickly feeling of the rocky texture melting into my mouth made me want more and more.

> I still crave that smell
> That taste
> It reminds me of home.
> Being with *mi ama*, my sisters
> How do I continue to nurture those bonds?
> When I am not there?
> Is there a manual on how to do it?
> learn, unlearn
> Repeat.

"Sometimes bad things have to happen for good things to come out of it," I remember my grandma telling me once. *Mi ama*, now that she lost her two cleaning jobs due to the global pandemic, has been able to grow some vegetables in the backyard of her home in Santa Ana. Sometimes she sends me photos of her *tomates* and chiles. She also decided to welcome two chickens that her neighbor, a woman from the mountains of Guerrero, Mexico, gave her. I hear they like to share each other's dishes when they cook. When I FaceTime with *mi ama*, she loves showing me how the chickens roam around and sunbathe in the dirt. She feeds them the kitchen compost. Apparently, each chicken has a personality and that's why she named them the way she did. No chicken questions her migratory status.

Si viene la policía,
then we have to tell the truth.
We cannot get rid of the chickens.
We have to eat.
Fear. Is a reminder of belonging.
sin papeles.

I am miles away from her.

Pushing forward. Following a dream that I often question. I had a nightmare last night. I dreamed of my mom at a detention place. I was in line trying to cross to the other side. I asked about her. The officers said things were difficult. I fear that I will not see her again. I fear her return to a town she might no longer call home.

Always in movement,
not by choice but forced.
Displaced,
in the chaos of deciphering COVID-19
but grounded with *mi ama.*

La cosecha de cuarentena / Quarantine's Harvest. *Photograph by Elisa Flores Hernández, 2020.*

How to Make Your *Huertita en Otras Tierras*

You need the good kind of dirt. The one you get from the cow and sheep stable.
Now, my parents mix it with their compost hole in the backyard.
To plant they would have used the seeds saved from their last harvest.
But now they buy them at the closest Home Depot or Lowe's.
Sometimes they don't sell the seeds my parents need.
So, they decided to ask *mi abuelita* to bring some.
She brought *pápalo*, chiles, and calabaza seeds.
Now, those seeds are saved and used each year.

To water the plants, they had an elegant irrigation system from the community well.
Now, water from the house hose suffices.
In the summers they recycle the water from the kitchen use
So the water bill won't be too high.

La huertita aislada / Isolated Vegetable Garden. *Photograph by Jessica L. Sánchez Flores, 2020.*

To harvest they would have shared with relatives
and close neighbors and sold the rest.
Now, they still share with family and neighbors.
But what is left of the *cosecha* is stored in ziplock bags.

They take a bag out of the freezer to cook until the cycle is repeated.
They are tasty. They smell earthy.
These colorful *tomates* and chiles can be used in any dish
In a soup, with chicken, in a spicy sauce
They will sooth any hungry soul.

The same one that yearns to come back home
at a time when no human should leave their COVID-19 solitary
confinement.[1]

Night's Fire

She is not alone. I am not alone. We are not alone.

It was another kind of dream. My sisters, *mi ama*, *mi abuelita*, and *mi tía* were all harvesting chiles, talking in my grandma's kitchen in Cocula, Guerrero. We were joyful. *La cosecha* brought us together. Despite the fact that I am in Tejas, *mi ama* in California, *mi abuelita* in Guerrero. We were together.

Last night my room was on fire. That night I stayed up working late. It was a candle. An unexpected accident. A difficult year. I begin to think it was a careless act on my part. That week things were shaken in the house. Someone around us had tested positive for the virus. All I remember is gasping for air at 3:00 a.m. with a huge fire in the corner of my room. I got up and ran to the kitchen for water. The only thing that was on my mind was putting out the fire. I was scared. The water pitcher was not enough. The filter fell into the fire and melted. As I was rushing back for more water, some words whispered in the back of my head: "To turn off a fire you must use a blanket." Trying to stay focused, I grabbed the first thing I saw, a sweater, and I started to hit the flames. It might have been seconds or minutes, but I felt like they were never going out. Slowly they died out. By the time the firefighters came, the fire was out. They asked how I had put the fire out. The answer was simple: My relatives were with me the night of the fire.

We are not alone.
She is not alone.
I am not alone.

Awakening

You think of me as a pest.
Did I make you sicker with my presence,
Or with a virus that I was not aware I had?
How can we all understand what living in a pandemic means?
How can we all empathize when our upbringing is different?
Worriedness. A deep feeling of
Not knowing if I will see my parents again.
Who is to blame?
Who is to blame when one of the parents is undocumented, with health
problems, and the other is an essential worker at a grocery store?

Who is the victim?
Are we not all victims? someone said.
Yet you act as if you are the only victim here.

Lagrimitas del árbol / Tree Tears. *Photograph by Jessica L. Sánchez Flores, 2021.*

Should I apologize for the unexpected?
For what everyone fears

Getting Sick

my damp face reveals my disbelief
when I cannot afford a charge for reparations.
The dryness of my mouth stops me from yelling
desperation falls into thick tears
When the lungs are weak
the soul and spirit are crushed

your entitled attitude I cannot forget
taught me a lesson
so please, I plead you
do not press on a fresh wound
as it needs time to heal

the truth is
I am also entitled to grief
to be at peace.
Silence is not a given where I come from
But we come a long way
And for that we, too, deserve
like the tree's unapologetic tears.

Watering Down the Guilt

Guilt is what am pushed to feel. "Get over the guilt," I hear. All I feel is a big lump of emotions crawling to the center of my stomach. I should not feel guilty for getting sick, yet your attitude makes me doubt and wonder. I know I did everything not to. For some reason I enter the dark room again. The same one I entered as a ten-year-old when I was molested. It happened in a country everyone promised was the land of dreams. Not my dream. I am spiraling in the deepest of my thoughts. And in such anguish, I go down, reaching further each day, wondering then how *mi ama, mi abuelita, mi tía, mi bisabuela* might have felt.

Why does that keep happening to us? Is it because we were taught to stay quiet, to endure, to take all the hits? Yet, is there a reason why we shouldn't question?

I make myself stop by switching off the hot water in the shower, leaving the cold to hit my naked body during a quarantine shower. Let my head cool down for a minute. Let my body feel the shock of cold water to wake me from reviving traumas I thought I had overcome. I cannot accept the blame of getting sick, of being assaulted, of simply being me. Responsibility for whom or what, when things are out of my reach?

You can speculate.
You can demand.
You can talk.
You can apologize.

My intention.
My reality.
My truth.
me and the women who have come before me.

Notes

This piece was written between June 2020 and February 2021.

1. The title of this poem was inspired by the poem "How to Make Good Baked Salmon from the River" by Nora Dauenhauer. See Caskey Russell, "Tools of Self Definition: Nora Marks Dauenhauer's 'How to Make Good Baked Salmon,'" *Studies in American Indian Literatures* 16, no. 3 (2004): 29–46, https://dx.doi.org/10.1353/ail.2004.0036.

PART VI • THE WISDOM OF OUR WOUNDS
Inner Transformation Through Community

6. the blow-up . . . a clash of realities

In gatherings where people feel powerless la nepantlera offers rituals to say good-bye to old ways of relating; prayers to thank life for making us face loss, anger, guilt, fear, and separation; rezos to acknowledge our individual wounds; and commitments to not give up on others just because they hurt us. In gatherings where we've forgotten that the aim of conflict is peace, la nepantlera proposes spiritual techniques (mindfulness, openness, receptivity) along with activist tactics. Where before we saw only separateness, differences, and polarities, our connectionist sense of spirit recognizes nurturance and reciprocity and encourages alliances among groups working to transform communities. In gatherings where we feel our dreams have been sucked out of us, la nepantlera leads us in celebrating la comunidad soñada, reminding us that spirit connects the irreconcilable warring parts para que todo el mundo se haga un país, so that the whole world may become un pueblo.

"NOW LET US SHIFT," 568

30 • REIMAGINING THERAPY IN PANDEMIC TIMES
Collective Healings, Inescapable Enmeshments
Alicia Chatterjee

> Éste arrebato, the earthquake, jerks you from the familiar
> and safe terrain and catapults you into nepantla, the second
> stage. In this liminal, transitional space, suspended between
> shifts, you're two people, split before and after. Nepantla,
> where the outer boundaries of the mind's inner life meet
> the outer world of reality, is a zone of possibility.
>
> GLORIA E. ANZALDÚA, "NOW LET US SHIFT"

WE ARE LIVING THROUGH A pandemic, a global health crisis unparalleled in a century's time. We are also living amid white supremacy and its foundational anti-Blackness. For the first three months of this pandemic I saw only two people, only twice, until suddenly I was in the streets in protest with thousands. It is clear to most of us that a pandemic is a public health crisis. So too, though, is racism.

I am trained as a therapist and in training as a social work scholar. Before these trainings, my work was in arts activism and community support for people impacted by sexual and intimate violence. This work centered the experiences of survivors of color and queer survivors, margins of margins; of course, it is not always acknowledged that there is much space and love there, in the liminality. Here I write into spaces of liminality in my own heart and mind. The liminalities where I operate as a mixed-race woman, where I traverse the intersections of connections to ancestral Buddhism, training in decolonial herbalism in what is now called North America, and training as a therapist in doctoral study. Graciously, Gloria Anzaldúa offers a map to live and speak fervently from these borderlands. An arrebato creates a rupture; to exist in liminality may be to make a home in that space.

Anzaldúa writes of the arrebato, the earthquake, that splits us so we are no longer before and not yet what is to come, the dropped heartbeat as time continues. Through the arrebato, we embody the elongated moments of transition. Of course, we are always here in the long present moment of change, really, as in the Buddhist teachings referred to these days, in mental health fields and beyond, by the whitened and studied name *mindfulness*. Buddhism teaches "this moment, only moment." Yet, though the quiet possibilities of the present moment are always around us as a collective, the arrebato can create a conscious rupture in our ideas of linear time and sense. To attend to this rupture's transition offers opportunity to attend to change and to growth. What comes after these arrebatos? The arrebato of all the peoples in the streets for the mattering and thriving and brilliance of Black lives? The arrebato of the pandemic roiling in these early summer months?

I want to imagine a therapeutic arrebato. To imagine, as in, to work toward possible futures. Therapists are trained in a form of healing and, too often, to believe that it is the only form of healing. We learn clinical modalities, filtered through various systems of raced, gendered, and classed power that inscribe in the discipline theories of humanity, normalcy, pathology, health, and illness. Maybe we are trained to think psychodynamically, rooting into the impacts of a client's early days as we attune to life patterns. Or maybe we think cognitive-behaviorally, in that modality most presently funded and studied for its successful replicability in research settings, which links thoughts to feelings to behaviors. If we intervene in the thinking, cognitive behavioral therapy suggests, we can make changes in distorted cognitive-behavioral-emotional cycles.

Central to these clinical models is the notion of pathology, that something is wrong with someone. To focus on pathology is also often to focus on the individual, as a being alone, suspended outside of history and relationality, and their specific behavior or personal past. Critiques of pathology as a clinical framework, circulated at the periphery of the discipline, focus powerfully and impactfully on the gendered and racialized complexion of the concept, as well as on its generally dehumanizing impacts on the provision of therapeutic care. Focus on the individual, though, does not just occur in traditional clinical ideas of pathology. Individualization also occurs in clinical conceptions of healing itself and, relatedly and foundationally, in our theories of being and selfhood. Central to many ideas of clinical health and well-being is individuation, the process of being alone for oneself, of enacting freedom from enmeshment with other forms of life, also individuated.

Enmeshment is a clinical term to describe fusions in identities that can happen in family and relationship systems (Minuchin 1974), and what an evocative term it is. Enmeshment: as in, netted together; as in, entrapped with one another in a shifting relational tapestry; as in, tangled together. Influential theories in the discipline of human development suggest that individuation is a key task of healthy human growth (Minuchin 1974). In order to be healthful and whole, we are not to be enmeshed.

Of course, theories intend to reflect and provide frameworks of understanding for an expansive and multidimensional reality that is impossible to contain. Theories also reflect the social moments and embodiments within which they are formulated, and individuation as an essential expression of healthfulness speaks to us from a gendered and raced home. Indeed, the insistence on the individual as the site of both harm and of healing is not only or even primarily a clinical operation so much as it is a clinical expression of a broader political, economic, and social orientation. This is an orientation, both ideological and institutional, that enforces social alienation rooted in patriarchal, racial, and capitalist beliefs.

Living through this pandemic, we are experiencing a kind of exaggerated, if only apparent, break from the daily expressions of our enmeshment with one another. Many of us suddenly feel, in some or several ways, alone. Also, many of us are newly, in some or several ways, unwell. The pandemic can be a kind of arrebato to the narratives of healing that call for, practice, and enforce frameworks of individuality as wellness. So, if we are to embrace the opportunity of the arrebato and break down the operations of living, shifting, and interpersonal and structural violence, clinicians must shift their thinking and practices beyond the individual, beyond the pathologization of identities, traumas, and symptoms. In this break, I want us to also imagine, What would it mean for clinicians to fundamentally shift an understanding of healing itself to consider our interrelatedness?

Potawatomi scientist Robin Wall Kimmerer engages sciences native to North America to call us back to our relationality, not just with each other, as humans, but to the earth. The relationship she calls us to is one of reciprocity and interdependence. She writes of the interrelationship between bean, squash, and corn, "Of all the wise teachers who have come into my life, none are more eloquent than these, who wordlessly in leaf and vine embody the knowledge of relationship. . . . The gifts of each are more fully expressed when they are nurtured together than alone. In ripe ears and swelling fruit, they counsel us that all gifts are multiplied in relationship. This is how the world keeps going" (Kimmerer 2013, 273). Humans, too, are a part of this world of reciprocity. Here, the plants, as ancient teachers, remind us that our health, healing, and being are interrelated not just in the human and social realms, but in reciprocal relation to the earth. When we grow together, we amplify the generative, healthful, and expansive possibilities of our growth.

Relatedly, our interdependence does not just support our growth; it is the foundation of it. It is how the world keeps going. Healing, as we undertake it, must be a relational and iterative effort within our inescapable enmeshment with one another and with the world that offers our life and our home. Vietnamese Buddhist monk Thích Nhất Hạnh (2017) describes this fundamental condition of interdependence as interbeing: In all of us is all of us. We, meaning humans, animals, plants, minerals, cosmos, exist with and in relation to one another, so intimately and so cyclically that we are not fixed separate selves.

If we are interdependent and reciprocally interrelated, we must begin to incline our praxis of healing in the direction of this recognition. Such change, though, does not always feel easy. While Anzaldúa offers the arrebato as a seed of change, artist and activist adrienne maree brown transmits a valuable account of how such a seed might grow. On her theory of emergence as change process, she writes, "The whole is a mirror of the parts. Existence is fractal—the health of the cell is the health of the species and the planet" (brown 2017, 13). Here, too, health and healing relate intimately between all of us. What's more, our interrelatedness can be, or must be, the soil in which to cultivate not only our healing but also our capacities for change toward liberation. Change through emergence involves understanding and engaging these interrelationships; leveraging the awareness that the simple makes the complex; and recognizing that change is always afoot, and that emergence is a matter of seeing it and moving with change toward collective vision and liberation (brown 2017; Butler 1993). Small changes can reflect fractally into the systems they make up. Complexity is always made up of simplicities bound together. We can begin change, may always be beginning change, right now.

Of course, if we are connected in these ways, we are faced with the troubling realities of our own capacities for harm. We, all living beings, are enmeshed not only in our healing but in our history and present, in the active legacies of harm upon Black peoples, Indigenous peoples around the world, and other peoples of color. We are all tangled up in our well-being with the reality of ongoing harm to queer, trans, femme, and differently abled peoples. And we are connected not only with the earth as it is but also with the earth in the harm that has been done to it. Grappling with the question of how to make the most of this enmeshment, feminist biologist Donna Haraway writes, "The task is to make kin in lines of inventive connection as a practice of learning to live and die well with each other in a thick present" (2016, 1). We are tasked not only with recognizing our interrelatedness, but with making and remaking it in the face of difference, love, harm, and healing. To begin to recognize interrelatedness in clinical thought is not to collapse difference or to deny the embodied signs and shapes of historical and ongoing violence. It is, instead, to embrace the lessons offered by liminality, to make ourselves expansive enough to hold complex and even opposing truths together in the very same moment. It is to recognize and account for active legacies of harm *and* to recognize, imagine, and heal our interdependences. It is to allow and cultivate critical interdependence as a site of healing.

The pandemic is an arrebato, a kind of elongated liminal moment that, if we can see it and stay with it, invites us to healing even as it demands change. I imagine and I write with the vision that the pandemic can teach us the importance of our connections with others as we endure their painful daily absence. Also, I believe the pandemic can teach us that even when we are alone, we are connected to each other, that our health is not only, or even mainly, in our own hands, but in the choices of our community and the related movements of our very earth. I hope that this difficult arrebato can offer to my field, to social work thought and practice, the revelation that we *are* enmeshed. Beautifully, painfully, powerfully entangled. In fact, this entanglement may be the site of our healing. Staying awake to moments of great change can help us awaken to the possibilities and realities of change around us always. Beyond change, we are around us always. Ultimately, we heal with each other because we have to.

Bibliography

Anzaldúa, Gloria E. *Borderlands/La Frontera: The New Mestiza*. Aunt Lute Books, 1987.
brown, adrienne maree. *Emergent Strategy: Shaping Change, Changing Worlds*. AK Press, 2017.
Butler, Octavia E. *Parable of the Sower*. Four Walls Eight Windows, 1993.
Haraway, Donna J. *Staying with the Trouble: Making Kin in the Chthulucene*. Duke University Press, 2016.
Kimmerer, Robin W. *Braiding Sweetgrass: Indigenous Wisdom, Scientific Knowledge, and the Teachings of Plants*. Milkweed Editions, 2013.
Minuchin, Salvador. *Families and Family Therapy*. Harvard University Press, 1974.
Nhất Hạnh, Thích. *The Other Shore: A New Translation of the Heart Sutra with Commentaries*. Parallax Press, 2017.

31 • SHIFTING TOWARD THE SACREDNESS OF LIFE

Nathalia P. Hernández Ochoa

¿Achike nab'ij pa awanima wakamin?
Matyöx loq'oläj k'aslelm

What does your spirit say right now?
Thank you sacred life

Matyöx roma
Loq'oläj ak'u'x
Loq'oläj nuk'u'x
Loq'oläj qanima qonojel

Thank you for
The sacredness of your heart
The sacredness of my heart
The sacredness of our spirits

Ronojel ri loq'oläj man k'o ta rajil

RUK'U'X RI LOQ'OLÄJ

Everything that is truly sacred does not have a price.

THE ESSENCE OF SACREDNESS

This is an excerpt of a poem I wrote in the Maya Kaqchikel language amid the COVID-19 pandemic, in March 2020. As I look at it, right now, I realize that these words have such deep meaning to me, and they are not even written in my first language, Spanish. I interpret this skill as a gift that allows me to navigate different worlds. How did I get here? My educational path has led me to learn both languages (English and Maya Kaqchikel), and this is *no coincidence*. I was born in San Francisco to immigrant parents in the late 1980s, but I grew up in El Salvador and did not learn the English language until I moved back to the US, when I was seventeen years old. Considering my family genealogy a bit further, it could seem ironic that as a graduate student, sponsored by US-based academic institutions and resources, I would be able to learn an Indigenous language from my ancestral territories. My great-grandmother, Mamá Chenta, was a Maya woman from Guatemala who migrated to El Salvador. In order to survive, she stopped speaking her native language and dressing in her traditional clothing (huipil and corte). This is my connection to the Maya Kaqchikel language.

Even though I will never know the ethnic group my great-grandmother was from, learning a Maya language from Guatemala is a way to revendicate and honor her memory and my ancestral roots. Some might call this destiny or faith, but I understand it as spirit guiding my path to purpose. The sacredness of life.

I am currently conducting fieldwork in Guatemala, where I have been collaborating with and learning from Maya Kaqchikel women who use theater and performance as a tool to eradicate multiple forms of violence while simultaneously working toward healing and liberation. In addition, I am learning the Maya Kaqchikel language with the Foreign Language and Areas Studies (FLAS) grant. My fieldwork was disrupted by the COVID-19 security measures taken by the Guatemalan government, but I have been fortunate to continue my language-learning process online. I felt as if my work had been cut in half and all my research plans were destroyed. However, now that I have had more time to rest, think, and absorb, I was able to shift my perspective on what working with purpose and spirit might look like.

On this particular week, my Kaqchikel tutor taught me a new word, *loq'oläj*, and I immediately knew this word had power. He explained to me that the word meant "sacred," in a literal way. It can also mean the heart or the essence of something. I do not know if that day I was extra sensitive, vulnerable, or excited to learn, but this word became a key referent to the ways in which I came to understand, feel, and live through this pandemic: I thought of *the sacredness of life itself*. Throughout this journey, I have come to think of three key concepts that guide this reflection on how the COVID-19 pandemic might allow us to make a shift toward the sacredness of life. The first one is the concept of the tower moment (based on the tarot deck meaning), followed by el arrebato (borrowed from Gloria Anzaldúa), which leads to the final reflection on how we might build a world with spirit, honoring and respecting the sacredness of life itself. Each of the following sections explores these three main concepts as an invitation for personal and collective reflections.

A Tower Moment

We are in a moment known as "the tower." In the tarot deck, the tower symbolizes the destruction of worlds, internal turmoil, sudden changes, and revelations that announce transformation processes in our lives. I reflect on what the COVID-19 pandemic has brought into our lives and interpret it as one of these moments where the tower collapses. How can the destruction of worlds be interpreted as something positive? Because the tower in the tarot is precisely built and erected on false premises. So, when the tower falls apart, it opens spaces to create new worlds more aligned with our true essence, to our frequencies, to our life purposes. Thus, the foundations of these worlds are solid, sustainable, and a better fit within our paths to divinity. Therefore, I agree with the popular statement that has risen from this situation: "We don't want things to go back to normal." Things were never great for many of us in a world that has been built on the rape, exploitation, and extermination of Black, Indigenous, and immigrant bodies. A world that has been the product of colonialism, imperialism, and Eurocentrism, where thousands of cultures, languages, and peoples have perished at their hands. A world where misogyny and patriarchy have taken so many sisters' lives. A world where capitalism and imperialism have used corrupt politics and economic power to gatekeep all areas of life and basic services, such as education, healthcare, and socioeconomic wealth. The coronavirus pandemic did not come to destroy our ways of life; they were already rotted and destined to irrevocable damnation. I could talk about the countless lives that we have lost due to the pandemic or about the ways it has affected women and children trapped in violent homes. Perhaps about the economic impact that it has had in the lower and middle classes, or about the ineptitude of the US, Mexican, and Brazilian governments (just to mention the worst of the worst).

I will not expand on all the negative outcomes and human suffering this pandemic brought to us globally. There are experts on these subjects who can give better assessments and critical analysis about these important matters. However, what I bring here to you is *una ofrenda para el espíritu*, an offering to spirit, so that we may return to the sacredness of life itself. This tower moment can help us make sense of the following questions: What sorts of transformed worlds might we hope for (during and after this pandemic)? What sorts of loving labor might it take to get us there?

El Arrebato

This academic pause forced me to go back to the basics, my feminist roots, where I find comfort, joy, and purpose. I revisited bell hooks's *All About Love* and Gloria Anzaldúa's "Now let us shift . . . the path of conocimiento . . . inner works, public acts" as I was trying to grapple with spirit and our return to the sacredness of life. The first concept I want to explore is Anzaldúa's notion of el arrebato—the snatching—which can be broadly described as a violent attack that shakes you and removes you from the familiar, forcing you out of your comfort zone: "Cada arrebato (snatching) turns your world upside down and cracks the walls of your reality, resulting in a great sense of loss, grief, and emptiness, leaving behind dreams, hopes, and goals. You are no longer who you used to be" (546–547).

Therefore, the tower moment might be interpreted as a collective arrebato. This pandemic has forced us to confront things about ourselves and our lifestyles that can provide insights into what we (individually and collectively) need to work on to improve our lives. The answers about how to envision and create a new world won't come from outside, but rather from within. I do not mean this as a selfish self-improvement task that is detached from our social and collective responsibilities. Here is where bell hooks's work on spirituality and divine love is crucial. She makes clear that "spiritual life is first and foremost about commitment to a way of thinking and behaving that honors principles of inter-being and interconnectedness" (77).

We need to look inside ourselves and see how we are oppressed and benefit from the multiple systems of oppression we have either internalized or seek to dismantle. We must be honest and brave to reflect and understand who we are within the persisting colonial, capitalist, racist, patriarchal, heteronormative, and imperialist systems. We must acknowledge our complicity and comfort within these systems because we have lived in an inherited world without love for too long. Internalizing and reproducing forms of oppression is something I, too, had been complicit in throughout my life and within my own flesh. As a middle-class heterosexual and cisgender mestiza who grew up in El Salvador, I have done an enormous amount of labor to reflect on the ways in which I am the product of and have continued to reproduce racist, classist, and patriarchal beliefs imposed by sociocultural practices within different contexts. I have often failed to accept and love parts of my body, felt ashamed of my ancestors, and bought into Western standards of beauty, knowledge production, and capitalist consumption (to mention a few). These are all part of the world I have inherited through complex historical processes of colonialism, imperialism, racist genocidal states, military authoritarianism, exploitative global capitalism, and patriarchal violence across the American continent. These are all expressions of a deeply flawed world that does not honor the sacredness of life. "A culture that is dead to love can only be resurrected by spiritual awakening," hooks argues (71). Search inside your own life: Where do you find love? Within yourself? Within your family? At home? At work? In your thoughts, visions, and dreams? How do you love others? Is there love in our educational system? Is there love in our health systems? Is there love in our governments? Are these systems truly what we deserve? Are we true to the sacredness of life? These questions are not easy, but they are the work of spirit. People who embark on spiritual journeys do so because they are wounded; they have experienced different forms of trauma, loss, and pain. There are many who do not work on their spirituality for different reasons, but the traumas remain in the subconscious. If they are not addressed, we cannot grow, we cannot learn, we cannot evolve as people. We remain stuck, and this often calls negativity, frustration, and unhappiness to our lives. The dysfunctional cycles continue to reproduce. Likewise, our collective consciousness works in similar ways. If we do not do the work of confronting the ways in which structural inequalities are institutional and simultaneously internalized in our bodies, minds, and actions, we are doomed to continue to reproduce them, consciously or unconsciously.

On Building a World with Spirit

I believe spiritual work, at the personal and collective levels, is a labor of love. We need more love within ourselves, in our interactions with each other, in our institutions, in our societies, and in our worlds. "When we make a commitment to staying in touch with divine forces that inform our inner and outer world, we are choosing to lead a life in the spirit." (hooks 2001, 81). This is the world I would like to build, a world with spirit.

Anzaldúa often theorizes about el arrebato, ruptures, wounds, endings, and deaths, but she does it in a hopeful way. She was able to see magic where there was pain, destruction, and violence. I think this is a wonderful legacy she left us, the assurance that the sun will come up and we will get a new beginning. We are at that middle ground, in nepantla, in that transitional yet crucial moment. My hope is that in the midst of this pandemic, we can pause, look inside, and let ourselves shift into the sacredness of life. And what other than love can be the sacredness of life? There is not a single path or formula for us to identify what love and the sacredness of life itself means to us, but rather it invites us to reflect on these important questions. Also, it is an invitation to realize that there will be a diversity of meanings and responses, but we all have an important role to play in it. bell hooks offers a possibility to us: All awakening to love is spiritual awakening (83). In the Kaqchikel language the word *loq'oläj* is used to describe the sacredness of all living beings in the world: places, plants, animals, elements, and people. In sum, everything that has spirit is sacred. I am thankful for this reminder as a building block to work for a world where we can truly live in *Ruk'u'x ri loq'oläj*.

Ruk'u'x ri loq'oläj

Matyöx roma ri loq'oläj	I am grateful for the sacredness of life
Po	But
¿Akuchi k'o ri loq'oläj?	Where is the sacred?
Loq'oläj kaq'iq'	Sacred is the wind
Loq'oläj ri q'aq'	Sacred is the fire
Loq'oläj ri ya'	Sacred is the water
Loq'oläj ri ruwäch ulew	Sacred is the earth
Loq'oläj qatit qamama'	Sacred are the ancestors
Loq'oläj qach'alal	Sacred is the family
Loq'oläj qochoch	Sacred is the home
Loq'oläj qaway	Sacred is the food
Loq'oläj rajawal q'ij	Sacred are the nawales [energies of the day]
Loq'oläj ruk'u'x kaj	Sacred is the heart of heaven
Loq'oläj ruk'u'x ulew	Sacred is the heart of the earth
Loq'oläj winaqi' kanima	Sacred are our spirits
Loq'oläj ri q'ij	Sacred is the sun
Loq'oläj ri ik'	Sacred is the moon
Loq'oläj ri ramaj	Sacred is time
Loq'oläj chikopi'	Sacred are the animals
Loq'oläj raxnaqïl	Sacred is health
Loq'oläj ajowab'al	Sacred is love
Loq'oläj kikotem	Sacred is joy
Loq'oläj qachik'	Sacred are our dreams
¿Achike n'abij awanima wakamin?	What does the spirit tell you now?
Matyöx loq'oläj k'aslem	Thank you, holy life
Matyöx roma	Thank you because:
Loq'oläj ak'u'x	Sacred is your essence
Loq'oläj nuk'u'x	Sacred is my essence
Loq'oläj qanima qonojel	Sacred is everyone's essence
Ronojel ri loq'oläj man k'o ta rajil.	Because everything sacred in this life is priceless.

Note

The complete poem, "Ruk'u'x ri loq'oläj / La esencia de lo sagrado / The Essence of Sacredness," was featured in the poetry podcast *Jazz Ready*, episode 135, August 7, 2020. Available at https://creators.spotify.com/pod/show /magdalena-gomez/episodes/Episode-135—S2—Nathalia-Hernndez-Ochoa —Poet—Doctoral-Candidate-Reads-in-Kaqchikel-Spanish-and-English-ehr615 /a-a1pvrl.

Bibliography

Anzaldúa, Gloria, and AnaLouise Keating, eds. *This Bridge We Call Home: Radical Visions for Transformation*. Routledge, 2013.
hooks, bell. *All About Love: New Visions*. Harper Perennial, 2001.

32 • RADICAL LOVE IN NEPANTLA

Latina PhD Holistic Support, Validation, Community Building, and Organizing

The Latina PhDs at USC: Cassandra Flores-Montaño, Olivia González, Mabel E. Hernandez, Theresa E. Hernandez, Divana Olivas, Blanca A. Ramirez, Karina Santellano, and Cynthia D. Villarreal

LATINAPHDS@USC BEGAN IN 2018 AS a chat (the Chat) in a mobile group messaging application between a small group of friends in different departments who sought a space to connect with other Latinas pursuing doctoral degrees at the University of Southern California (USC). The low number of Latinas accepted into any given doctoral program challenges our ability to form a critical mass. We drew on our networks to build *comunidad* across the many academic borders that might silo us. By fall 2019, we formalized our group with university recognition that enabled us access to institutional resources. We had coalesced and were developing our group identity, a mosaic held together by our Latinidad. Now that we have over fifty members, this essay serves as a reflection on our growth and desires for our collective's future.

We, the authors, are a subset of this collective. The ways we express our Latina identities are informed by our hometowns, proximity to the immigrant experience, sexual orientations and gender identities, and class backgrounds. El Paso, San Diego, Albuquerque, and Santa Cruz are just a few of the cities we call home, but other members hail from the East Coast of the United States and beyond. While most of us come from Mexican American/Chicanx backgrounds, our group harnesses a greater representation of the Latin American diaspora. A strong contingent of us come from working-class backgrounds, but not all. We are queer and hetero. Many of us are the first in our families to earn a bachelor's and/or pursue a doctoral degree. While none of the authors identify as white, some of us benefit from white privilege due to our skin tone. Some of our group members are Afro-Latina, but they are not among the authors who volunteered in the Chat to collaborate on this essay. We recognize the importance of supporting and uplifting Black women and Afro-Latinas through our organization. We are not a monolithic Latina doctoral collective, and we do not represent the full intersectionality of the Latina PhDs at USC group, nor do we want to imply that we can.

The multiplicity of our lives is reflected in the Chat; we share funding applications, celebrate each other's milestones from birthdays and births to presentations and publications, send Zoom links for writing sessions, and offer research advice alongside memes and GIFs. The Chat connects us informally, intimately, and it provides us with a nepantla, a liminal space for navigating a predominantly white and white-serving academia as our whole selves. Anzaldúa (2013) describes nepantla as "the site of transformation" and a "zone between changes" that functions as a "transition space" that anchors the evocative process of conocimiento. As a site, zone, and space, nepantla is spatial. We use the digital space of the Chat to create something new, a digital rasquachismo that cobbles together text messages, conversation threads, direct messaging, hashtags, GIFs, memes, and emojis to forge interconnectivity.[1] In the Chat we disrupt academia by offering each other support and validation in addition to demonstrating feminist and anti-racist praxis.

In 2020, COVID-19 changed everything. The Chat, our virtual nepantla, became our gathering place to process and grieve ongoing academic and societal traumas. In this essay, we present themes from a curated conversation where we discussed how we coped with the realities of a pandemic, structural anti-Blackness, and the unique challenges we faced as Latinas, researchers, students, mothers, daughters, sisters, wives, and partners. Below, we share how we used the Chat as a technology for supporting, validating, community building, and organizing in nepantla.

Support to Overcome Personal and Academic Challenges

The LatinaPhDs@USC group has worked to build a sustainable and socially just community one check-in at a time. In the times of a global pandemic, increasing civil unrest, government corruption, growing neo-Nazi movements, and the haunting specter of climate catastrophe, intense grief was expected. Our commitment to one another has taken shape through our virtual world. By intentionally dedicating time to checking in with each other, we have built a strong sense of camaraderie, *y comadre*ship.

In the Chat, we lay bare our social, emotional, and mental challenges and provide a space to center our wellness. Given challenges that surfaced due to California's stay-at-home orders, Jessica shared, "I was struggling with not only the anxiety of the situation, but also the stress and pressure of meeting deadlines." Through weekly writing sessions, we offered members an opportunity to work in a collaborative online environment. Olivia said, "I found opportunities for writing accountability and support, for expressing and processing my anxiety, grief, fears, and frustration." Our support for each other reflects one reason why our group began: to provide community and challenge the individualism that academia upholds.

The Chat is a space where Latina PhD students across a range of disciplines come together to imagine a radical future. Divana noted, "It's the only place where I connect with students outside of my bubble, and I think it's made me a better scholar, because I've had to explain and talk through my work and ideas with people from distinct fields." For this reason, we are, as Theresa emphasized, "not just siloed in our schools and fields, but bringing together our hearts and skills to make real shit happen." We supported one another in achieving our goals and maintaining our health through organizing virtual writing groups, coworking sessions, and wellness workshops. The Chat provided a channel for communicating about these opportunities, as well as for members of our group to offer or ask for support.

Our community of support spans across generations of Latina scholars as well. Cassandra shared, "I have appreciated the ways in which our strength as a group has attracted positive attention and mentorship from Latina professors at USC." However, the inequitable challenges of neoliberal higher education have meant that our relationships with those who wield power over us are complex, even when they involve those who share our identities. Rocío was particularly struck by a discussion in which we decided to make our own statement after collectively processing antiblack violence on a Zoom call with Latina faculty:

> I appreciated the honesty in the conversation as well as one of my colleagues saying, "We are in solidarity with each other first." This decision was not to displace our relationships with faculty or allies but to recognize the power dynamics that we are working under as graduate students and affirm this group as a space that can

validate and help us work through the harm that we have faced in academia.

This led us to prioritize supporting each other.

Validating Our Whole Selves

The Latina PhD group has been a space for us to recognize and validate each other as our whole selves and intersecting identities. Our community counters academia as it limits our ability to bring our full selves to our praxis. We emphasize bringing in the pieces of us that are broadly disregarded, unwelcomed, or undervalued on our campus and academia. Understanding our role as nepantleras, we created a wellness director position to intentionally cultivate a culture of wellness, joy, love, and care within our organization. Before each event we engage in meditation or stretching to show love to our bodies. Because of the recognition and validation that we provide each other, we have cultivated a sense of belonging that commonly eludes Latina PhD candidates in academia. Through the Chat, with the use of emojis, GIFs, and likes, we vividly express our humor, insecurity, sarcasm, outrage, support, and love.

Our community cultivates a nepantla where members can be unapologetic and uncompromising while validating each of our differences. Mabel noted that our community "is the place and people that I can be most myself with. I can embrace my identity fully and unapologetically! We can cry, we can laugh, we can encourage each other, we support each other, and we collaborate on things that we feel passionate about and will make a practical difference." Theresa colorfully expressed how important multiple forms of coming together fostered the sense of community that has developed in our group:

> I'm so grateful to be getting to know more mujeres getting their PhDs across disciplines, through the 🍷 🌮 HH, 📃 📱 💻 co-working spaces, check-ins, and 🐚 activism 🖤 🤍 🤎 🖤 🤎 🖤 🤍 🖤.

In addition to capturing gratitude in the validation of our community, Karina shifted the dialogue to a forward-thinking orientation: "I hope the future of the group is community focused, open to growth (bc I am open to working with folks who are doing their homework/doing deep reflection/learning), and dedicated to fighting oppressive systems."

One instance of recognition that stood out among our group involved our founding president, who has been a strong and loving source of support for all of us. Knowing the doctoral hooding and graduation would be cancelled due to the pandemic, several members organized to celebrate Cynthia, a new mother, when she earned her doctorate. Her response warmed all our hearts:

> I also will be eternally grateful to the women of this group for celebrating me as a graduate of 2020. I didn't get the chance to feel like a graduate because my hooding ceremony was cancelled BUT the women of this group came together and sent me hecho a mano graduation gifts for me and my daughter <3 The fact that you thought of my daughter too is just something I will never forget.

For us, feeling like a family of aspiring *doctoras* while celebrating and honoring our roles in our home lives is vital to feeling validated in our journey. Through the Chat, many of us feel the freedom to openly express ourselves and support each other in ways that academia does not.

Community Building: Celebrations and Condolences

As we navigated the COVID-19 crisis together, we achieved and collectively celebrated professional and personal milestones. Some members of our collective defended their dissertations, graduated, and met each other for the first time in person—donning masks and ruby red doctoral tams— at USC's 2021 commencement ceremonies. These joyous moments— memorialized in selfies and group photographs—were shared with our collective via the Chat. Other members of our group completed qualifying exams; earned master's degrees; obtained grants and fellowships (e.g., the Ford Dissertation Fellowship, the Haynes Lindley Doctoral Dissertation Fellowship, and the Smithsonian's Latino Museum Studies Program Fellowship); presented work at virtual conferences, webinars, panels, and *encuentros*; published research and writing; taught courses; received awards for our scholarship; and began jobs as *profesoras* and postdocs. Members also got engaged or married, mothered children, started new hobbies, ran new distances, tried and perfected recipes, and started or continued therapy.

Over the course of the pandemic, members shared successes and milestones through the Chat, where our collective celebrated and came up with additional ways to honor them. For example, in December 2020, we organized a virtual end-of-semester celebration during which we reflected on the fall semester—holding space for both joy and grief. We also shared accomplishments via our collective and individual social media. In June 2021, we again organized a virtual graduation celebration, during which we commemorated each of our graduates. This celebration was held in English and Spanish and open to graduates' families, who were invited— alongside members of our collective—to share testimonios about our newest doctoras.

In addition to being a space for collectively celebrating each other's achievements, the Chat also became a space for sharing prayers and condolences with members who themselves and whose family members were fighting COVID-19. Our virtual nepantla provided opportunities for recognizing our perseverance and successes, *and* for being compassionate with each other and ourselves as we navigated illness and loss. Through care packages and financial assistance with health-related costs, we offered crowdsourced material support and love to our fellow members who were directly impacted by COVID-19. Through this space we practiced healing and coping with the COVID-19 crisis amid the toxicity and individualism of academia. The Chat, and all that we organized through it, exemplified our efforts to carve out a distinctive, Latina feminist space for ourselves in our university.

Organizing Around Feminist and Anti-Racist Praxis

We believe that academics should pursue revolutionary goals that extend beyond publishing in paywalled journals, presenting at conferences that privilege whiteness, and engaging in individualistic behaviors that reflect and reinforce false meritocratic ideologies. Feminist and anti-racist interventions in pandemic and post-pandemic worlds must challenge these norms within academia and actively encourage praxis that is not limited to the university setting.

After a virtual check-in, a member discovered that the USC Black Student Assembly was hosting a march for Black lives the following Saturday. We saw this march as a way to support the global movement for Black liberation and the Black community in and around USC. Given the summer heat and health concerns associated with protesting during a pandemic, we decided to make two hundred protester care kits, which included snacks, water, a mask, and a bilingual "Know Your Rights" information sheet. Latina PhD members split into teams to manage logistics, obtain and develop the materials, and distribute kits at marches around USC's campus and downtown Los Angeles.

Through creating and distributing the kits, we strengthened our connections as a community and found an opportunity to put our feminist and anti-racist politics and hopes for the future into practice. Cassandra shared,

> I was also amazed by how quickly we mobilized to fundraise for, assemble, and distribute supply kits to protestors in support of Black Lives Matter in Los Angeles. That entire process made me feel more connected to everyone who participated and also gave me another tangible way to support this global movement for Black lives. I have cherished these experiences.

Additionally, Tisha stated, "Helping to assemble supplies for protest care kits alleviated the feeling of helplessness that has interfered with my ability to complete doctoral work this summer." Our hands-on efforts beyond the confines of our classrooms and computers thus shaped our individual and collective coping—a means through which we sought and found hope and healing. By activating our skills and harnessing our resources, our group channeled feelings of anger and frustration into mutual aid.

To follow up on these efforts, we wrote and published a statement in support of Black Lives Matter and discussed approaches for keeping ourselves, our organization, and our families, friends, and university accountable. For example, Jessica claimed,

> [These discussions] challenged me to examine my own understanding of what my resistance looks like during the season #AudreLorde and forced myself to be more conscientious of any ways I have been complicit regarding anti-Blackness in my life #LasVidasNegrasImportan @Divana and how I can make sure that this does not happen in my classroom, w my fam, in my research, w my friends and colleagues, etc.

Similarly, Johanna shared, "I want to continue learning about these issues and be more inclusive both in the classroom and in my own research with the implicit biases that I may have deeply rooted in me and I would love for the group to be inclusive of the Afro-Latina womyn that may not know about this group." As these quotes illustrate, during this period of tremendous change and uncertainty, members of our group came to reflect on the importance of radical and meaningful praxis in community building within and beyond academia.

The Latina PhD group unified us under a shared but heterogeneous ethnic identity. Moving forward as a group revealed the frictions and tensions in how we understood Latinidad and the complicated racial and ethnic landscape that we collectively navigate. The reality is that not everyone in the group is trained to study racism and the function of race and ethnicity in the US. In an effort to call people into the conversation, our group led a virtual event, Latinas and Race: The Intersections of Race and Latinidad, during which we addressed questions like "What is Latinidad? How does my Latinx identity inform how I build community?" We plan to hold a similar event interrogating the intersections of Latinidad, gender, and sexuality. Creating and nurturing our collective prompted a shift in consciousness, which continues to spur curiosity, learning, and growth.

Radical Love in Nepantla

The movements in response to racial injustice toward Black, Indigenous, and Asian communities encourage us to continue examining how our communities are complicit and perpetuate inequity. Through engaging in collective praxis, group members are thinking more deeply about and strengthening commitments to challenging anti-Blackness in our communities and classrooms. We recognize that many of our communities center and elevate whiteness, and that to create radical change we need to commit to continual learning about and enacting of Latinidad that recognizes, celebrates, and defends Blackness and Indigeneity within and beyond our communities. We use our varying expertise and skill sets in an interdisciplinary praxis to collectively engage in both the theoretical and tangible work required to reimagine academia and the future.

In our individual and collective processes of conocimiento, the Latina PhDs are creating shared identity around radical love and community care. Our spiritual activism leads us to think of *la otra* in a compassionate way, through respectful reflective dialogues intent on fostering the empowerment of all (*nos/otras*) (Anzaldúa 2013, 572). We collectively dedicate ourselves to community building among not only ourselves but also a justice-oriented and liberatory community. We center spirituality, recognizing that not all of us practice religious spirituality. We continue to show each other radical love and support beyond what we have been told is possible in academia. Divana's remarks embody our values of collectivism, care, and interdependence:

> As the world continues to burn . . . I know at least one thing: we
> need each other. I do better when I am taking care of [others],

and being taken care of [by my community]. Our acts of mutual compassion have sustained me. I hope that this group finds solace in unapologetic solidarity, to choose camaraderie over a career, and to fiercely protect our communities.

This is how we conceive of making a feminist, anti-racist world during these pandemic times. Our radical love is our legacy and how we create our own world in nepantla.

Note

1. *Rasquachismo* is a term that originated to describe a Chicano/Chicana art style that uses available resources to make art that embodies hybridization and juxtaposition. Tomás Ybarra-Frausto (2019) described it as a barrio attitude and sensibility that exhibits an improvisational attitude of making something out of little.

Bibliography

Anzaldúa, Gloria. "Now let us shift . . . the path of conocimiento . . . inner works, public acts." In *This Bridge We Call Home*. Routledge, 2013.
Ybarra-Frausto, Tomás. "Rasquachismo: A Chicano Sensibility." In *Chicano and Chicana Art: A Critical Anthology*, edited by Jennifer A. González, C. Ondine Chavoya, Chon Noriega, and Terezita Romo. Duke University Press, 2019.

33 • THE LANGUAGE OF LOVE

Wesley Stevens

Best Beloved,

My body has been stretched so thin I feel it is going to snap. In every direction, ceaselessly they pull, begging me to be a source of clarity amid this economic and political upheaval. We don't know what "systemic" means; please tell us! We need to be educated on privilege; please lecture our groups! We need a nuanced reading of how COVID-19 has affected the Black community; please provide it! We need your insight as a Black woman; please share it! Your identity affords you the ability to speak in ways that we cannot possibly understand; please do so!

Is this the language of love?

I have spoken and you have not listened. My voice was never a priority before—seldom have you asked to hear it outside of Black strife. I have shared my insight time and time again. I have coached you on the tools it takes to be an ally and how to recognize when to use them. Did you not listen? Did you not care? And when has my voice ever afforded me anything that yours could not? You need me to be the Black person now.

Is this the language of love?

Never have I felt so naked, so vulnerable, so alienated. I am simultaneously hailed and othered in their demand for my energy. In the struggle to protect my mental and emotional well-being, a cold, creeping feeling twists down my spine and settles in my gut. Have I forfeited my responsibility as a scholar, as an educator, as a Black woman? In taking space for myself, am I necessarily hindering the discourse with my absence? To what extent should I make myself available to educate? In the back of my mind, I wonder:

Is this the language of love?

My greatest fear is losing myself to the Cause. Each time I refuse to drive myself into the earth and choose to assert my needs at the expense of activism and education, I loathe myself a little more. Now, more than ever, drawing inward to care for myself feels like an excuse. Is it possible to love myself and do the work that needs to be done? Their incessant calls, messages, and inquiries dictate otherwise.

My teaching is an intervention. My research is an intervention. The ethical and pedagogical principles on which I base and choose my words are, in themselves, an intervention.

But what am I? Where do I fit among the pieces? Is my purpose, my personality, my very being, subsumed by the work I do for my brothers and sisters? What a beautiful, sorrowful thing.

What is the language of love?

I cannot keep showing up to be the Black voice in the room. I will not rip myself from the tears, the treatment, or the respite for the sake of doing the brave and noble thing of speaking when called upon to do so. I will not be held hostage by the will of others who point toward their privilege, White or otherwise, as proof of being ill-equipped to educate themselves and their communities. I will not be the Black voice that soothes their White guilt and exonerates their ignorance.

My voice is not yours to conjure or manipulate to better fit the vision of a reasonable, articulate, and well-educated Black person. I will not be your smiling bronze trophy.

This is not the language of love.

But I will show you what is.

When I can no longer withstand the strain of discussing my fallen brethren, mention my unyielding affection for *The Dark Crystal* or show me a *Golden Girls* meme. When I am talking about an African-inspired fantasy novel that addresses systemic racism and provides me the imaginative relief I crave, ask about my favorite character. When I mention my own in-progress book draft inspired by my near compulsory maladaptive daydreaming, 113 pages strong, read part of it. When I recommend Amalgam Comics in Philly for your racially diverse and gender-inclusive superhero needs, check out their website and buy something. When I find a new recipe for Thai noodle bowls, let's make them together. When I mention struggling to find the motivation to do my hair routine, let's video chat while I tease apart my long-ignored coils.

Creativity has brought me solace, and I would love to share it with you.

Rather than demanding my voice, my body, my presence, and what you imagine they represent, greet me with love. Rather than asking me to perform at your beck and call for the sake of the Cause, relish in the intimacy of our friendship. Rather than asking me to explain the "problem of race" in purely institutionalized, academic jargon, let me speak about it freely in my own words. Rather than asking me to recount my worst experiences as a Black woman, ask me what I like about it. Rather than using my traumatic experiences as a segue to discuss Black violence, still yourself for a moment and give me the space to say what I want to say about it.

The world needs to feel the fire of change, but do not discount the necessity of gentleness. Amid the protests, political interventions, and rallying on social media, remember to listen. Remember that we can find both support and delight in creative Black media and literature. Remember to vibe with your friends of color and share in a well-deserved break from the wave of misfortune slamming their daily lives. A bout of playful wrestling and side-splitting laughter always does me a world of good. Remember the Black people who speak truth to power in their creative endeavors and their day-to-day successes.

Let our happiness be a fuel for the fire, rather than our tragedy.

And herein lies my radical solution: Amid the turmoil, let's remember to love each other. Amid the social and political upheaval, let's create spaces where we can enjoy one another. Even in physical isolation, let's remember to connect. In the face of it all, we can still laugh until the tears roll and love with incalculable ferocity. Let's appreciate ourselves, seek refuge in friendship, and share those beautiful, not-so-fleeting moments of light and joy.

This is the language of love. Will you speak it with me?

Signed,

Wesley E. Stevens

An angry, tired, but no less loving and optimistic Black woman

34 • A WORLD WHERE MANY WORLDS FIT

Don't Let the Future Be Written for You

Gizem N. Iscan

What are the words you do not yet have? What do you need to say? What are the tyrannies you swallow day by day and attempt to make your own, until you will sicken and die of them, still in silence?

AUDRE LORDE, *SISTER OUTSIDER: ESSAYS AND SPEECHES*

A Feminist Call

Gloria Anzaldúa and Judith Butler offer possibilities to "democratize democracy" but also give the tools to reconstruct and heal the "open wounds" we are living in and with during this global crisis. Anzaldúa describes "memory" as both a problem and promise to heal and reclaim our individual and collective identities, experiences, and histories. Unclaimed traumas and ambiguous losses throughout the pandemic have complicated the notions of remembering, forgetting, and grievable and ungrievable lives. However, witnessing and experiencing these traumatic experiences connect the past to the present, offering possible spaces of mourning, collectivity, and hope. This feminist call centers "collectivity, grieving, and healing," and uses poetry and prose to mend the multiple borders that separate humanity on many levels, in addition to the borders we carry within ourselves toward individuals, groups, and the world during a global pandemic. What do an "open wound" and "grievability" stand for in a time of global crisis, and what do they mean for our past, present, and future? Open wounds, history, memory, trauma, identity, and poetry-as-healing are more than isolated concepts or ideas during pandemic times; they become intricately interwoven as we collectively claim our humanity.

A World Where Many Worlds Fit: Living in and with "Open Wounds"

In the face of fragile democracies, global conflicts, wars, pandemics, structural powers, hegemonic discourses, gender oppressions, growing injustices, inequalities, and death, a feminist call toward grievability and healing has become more significant than ever. Audre Lorde writes in her poem "A Litany for Survival," "we were never meant to survive." Cherríe Moraga and Gloria Anzaldúa paint this survival in the feminist anthology *This Bridge Called My Back: Writings by Radical Women of Color*. With the bridge metaphor the goal is to come together against existing systems of oppression that threaten to discriminate and extinguish women of color feminists' lives and discourses. I extend and expand on this goal of coming together during the global pandemic and use Anzaldúa's "open wound" metaphor and Judith Butler's "grievability" concept to offer a feminist call of collectivity, grieving, and healing.

Within this context, Anzaldúa asserts that the border is an "open wound where the Third World grates against the first and bleeds. And before a scab forms it hemorrhages again, the lifeblood of two worlds merging to form a third country—a border culture" (25). On this basis, the pandemic constructed physical, virtual, and psychological borders for my personal life and family, and within my communities. This global crisis functioned as an open wound, creating spaces of individual and collective trauma and memory, breaking down bodies, families, and futures. However, in these contested spaces of trauma, grieving, mourning, and witnessing the open wound can offer a possibility of reconstruction and a process of healing.

In this global pandemic, the bodily experiences of individuals and groups that go through multiple versions of violence and trauma stand as symbols reflecting the difficult human condition under forces of power, oppression, and domination; and reveal the devaluation of human bodies and lives. The body becomes involved in this political field, where "power relations have an immediate hold on it, torture it, force it to carry out tasks, to perform ceremonies, to emit signs" (Rabinow 1987, 173). My biggest fear is the human body becoming an ungrievable life and site where different forms of political power, racism, classism, sexism, violence, authority, and sovereignty are exercised. Within this reference, the pandemic not only revealed the multiple violence(s) women and children experience on a daily basis, but also opened a dialogue for lives, stories, and bodies to become publicly grievable and memorable. With the start of and throughout the pandemic, many individuals and groups were not able to grieve and mourn the lives and bodies of their loved ones. Given the stressful and political atmosphere of the election, and the Trump administration's take on the pandemic, grieving has become a mode of feminist intervention, interruption, and witnessing where social recognition creates a possibility of healing.

Within this context, Gloria Anzaldúa's open wound metaphor and Judith Butler's grievability concept can offer an alternative post-pandemic future. Butler argues for the social and political rights of protection regarding individuals and groups, and rethinks concepts of precariousness, vulnerability, injurability, interdependency, exposure, bodily persistence, desire, work, and the claims of language and social belonging (2). For Butler, grief is tied to life that has already been lived, and life as having ended; however, without grievability, there is no life, or, rather, there is something living that is other than life. Instead, "there is a life that will never have been lived," sustained by no regard, no testimony, and ungrieved when lost (15).

In light of Butler's concepts of "grievability and grievable life," many individuals and groups have not been and still are not mourned in this global pandemic. Their lives are not seen as grievable by the governmental, societal, and patriarchal systems. To maintain their power, their ideal, and their interests, these hegemonic forces value only the lives of "their own individuals and communities," creating a division of grievable and ungrievable lives in a liminal space. As Butler indicates, "An ungrievable life is one that cannot be mourned because it has never lived, that is, it has never counted as a life at all" (38). These hegemonic forces in power do not want to openly grieve and face inequalities and injustices because it creates resistance and political potential to disrupt the order and hierarchy of political authority.

In this framework, Anzaldúa's *Borderlands/La Frontera* offers and provides a model to live in a society that acknowledges and defines hybridity, multiplicity, and difference. Considering that the past is a part of us, Anzaldúa's open wound is about confronting violence, oppression, domination, pain, and traumatic experiences to reconnect our multiple selves, individuals, and cultures. The open wound encompasses notions of knowledge and non-knowledge, here and there, past and present, life and death, being and non-being. During this global crisis, recognizing, mourning, grieving, and accepting memories as well as the ambiguous losses that give one psychological, physical, spiritual, and sensory pain become possibilities toward healing.

"We" Recognize the Open Wounds "We" Refuse

During this global pandemic, individually and collectively, our stories, our lives, our traumas, our bodies, our time, our labor, our minds, our power, and our open wounds have been and are still being written for us. We need to write our own future. We have the knowledge to survive, and to ensure survival. We need to keep exploring, keep searching, and keep moving. We, as in every individual, are not recognizing each other as humans. If we do so, we also change the perceptions of ourselves. We come to see that we have been a part of the problem. We accept that we have not listened, acted, or been reflexive toward one another.

By recognizing our wounds, we also recognize past traumatic histories that have been unrecognized. The change and the possibility of healing from our open wounds are bound to recognizing the past, both individually and collectively. In this global pandemic, it has become evident more than ever that we are all connected to each other through history, trauma, and memory. We need to participate in recognizing violences of the past and present, and we need to take responsibility as witnesses of history. A significant question arises from this context. How do we recognize, participate in, and witness the horrors we are living through now, and what can it mean for feminism and the future?

In recognizing the violences of the past and present, we participate in establishing a future of survival for all of us, one that paves the way for healing. Healing is a process, a constant attempt to balance the histories of silence, fear, and bearing witness to a violent history. Healing is also accepting pain, recognizing open wounds and the possibilities they bring about. In these hard times, there is one more significant component that we need to recognize: memory. Memories are complicated; they forge discoveries but also problems. We need to recognize the dual nature of memories to connect to the past and present. Memories are records of dreams, pains, silences, and individual and collective lived experiences, and to solve the problematic nature of memory, we need to recognize the wounds we refuse. Only then can we achieve collectivity. Only then can we reconstruct a world where many worlds fit. And only then can we really work together to build a future equally written by all of us.

We Heal from Our Open Wounds

In the last section of the feminist call, I have included poems that are connected to lives, stories, and identities going through traumatic experiences due to the pandemic. I have been trying to cope with the pandemic by writing poetry. I process trauma and memory, heal from my own wounds, and become more reflexive. I look through life with the lens of poetry and prose, which helps me build new frames for a useful and meaningful life, and for an autonomous future. Poetry is a vision of "individuality and collectivity" that gives voice to multiple and diverse experiences. It is a form that raises consciousness and resistance, and encourages political activity, offering an individual and collective space for healing, survival, and change. The following poems depict confusion, sorrow, vulnerability, desperation, inequalities, and injustices becoming more visible in the world during a global crisis. However, each poem gradually captures a corner of hope and offers grieving as a way of healing from our open wounds and ambiguous losses.

The Fraying Edges of the Lockdown

I am inside my own prison,
in a certain stillness,
and maddening silence.
There is no warmth,
light
and summer.
I cleanse the sorrows within
my body, mind, and soul,
I don't know
which one is further now?
my dreams,
my freedom,
the stars,
or hope?

A Moment of Grieving

One day I broke out
of my cold iron cage
and walked
furthermore;
to unhomely homes
and forgotten places
thinking

what I left behind.
I listened to the frozen landscapes
and ran
in and with my open wounds
mourning for the world
furthermore
and
furthermore . . .

Departures

Darkness surrounds my home
as I lay stuck
with hunger, desperation, and pain.

Grievances pour on my body and mind
something inside and outside of me
so fragile
unknown
and broken
departs . . .
I am on a quest for survival
where death awaits me
in pitch-black space.
even the sorrows of yesterday are tired
standing
to be mourned and healed
maybe today (?)

On Remembrances

I navigate through,
spaces, places, and people
only to find home
within me.
I wander through
the past, present, and future
only to realize
that I am
trapped in time.

I carry the weight
of shattered lives
and stolen labor
only for centuries
with heavy
but
hopeful eyes.

Ode to Collectivity

We are different rivers running together
displaced and disremembered
lost in trauma and violence.
We are sentenced to life
through the echoes of death
and plagued by open wounds . . .
reality hits our cheeks
illusions crush
we remember
how it all begins and
we forget
how it all ends.
Then . . .
I pour my memories onto yours
and piece the remnants of yesterday.
You pour your memories onto mine
and mend the silences of today.
That is how
"WE" heal
become whole
and the future.

Bibliography

Anzaldúa, Gloria. *Borderlands/La Frontera: The New Mestiza*. Aunt Lute Books, 2012.

Basu, Amrita. "Globalization of the Local/Localization of the Global: Mapping Transnational Women's Movements." *Meridians* 1, no. 1 (2000): 68–84.

Butler, Judith. *Frames of War: When Is Life Grievable?* Verso, 2010.

Caruth, Cathy. *Unclaimed Experience: Trauma, Narrative, and History*. Johns Hopkins University Press, 1996.

Culbertson, Roberta. "Embodied Memory, Transcendence, and Telling: Recounting Trauma, Reestablishing the Self." *New Literary History* 26, no. 1 (1995): 169–195.

Harraway, Donna. "Situated Knowledges: The Science Question in Feminism and the Privilege of Partial Perspective." *Feminist Studies* 14, no. 3 (1988): 575–599.

Kandiyoti, Deniz. "Bargaining with Patriarchy." *Gender & Society* 2, no. 3 (1988): 274–290.

Moraga, Cherríe, and Gloria Anzaldúa, eds. *This Bridge Called My Back: Writings by Radical Women of Color*. Persephone Press, 1981.

Rabinow, Paul. *The Foucault Reader*. Peregine Books, 1987.

Reed, T. V. "The Poetical Is the Political: Feminist Poetry and the Poetics of Women's Rights." In *Feminist Theory Reader: Local and Global Perspectives*, edited by Carole McCann and Seung-Kyung Kim. 4th ed. Routledge, 2016.

Yuval-Davis, Nira. *The Politics of Belonging: Intersectional Contestations*. Sage, 2011.

PART VII · UTOPIA

"The Language of Love . . . Will You Speak It with Me?"

7. shifting realities . . . acting out the vision or spiritual activism

For you writing is an archetypal journey home to the self, un proceso de crear puentes (bridges) to the next phase, next place, next culture, next reality. The thrust toward spiritual realization, health, freedom, and justice propels you to help rebuild the bridge to the world when you return "home." You realize that "home" is that bridge, the in-between place of nepantla and constant transition, the most unsafe of all spaces. You remove the old bridge from your back, and though afraid, allow diverse groups to collectively rebuild it, to buttress it with new steel plates, girders, cable bracing, and trusses. You distend this more inclusive puente to unknown comers—you don't build bridges to safe and familiar territories, you have to risk making mundo nuevo, have to risk the uncertainty of change. And nepantla is the only space where change happens. Change requires more than words on a page—it takes perseverance, creative ingenuity, and acts of love. In gratitude and in the spirit of your Mamagrande Ramona y Mamagrande Locha, despachas éstas palabras y imágenes as giveaways to the cosmos.

"NOW LET US SHIFT," 574

35 • FEMINIST INTERVENTION

Black Children for "Alternate Nows" and Futures

Nnenna Odim

THINKING ABOUT THE UPRISINGS IN a pandemic of many pandemics, I look to children, Black children, as testimony, as visions of clarity, in next steps through this labyrinth of anti-Blackness. Leaning into Christina Sharpe's (2016) notion of "beyond the precarity," I listen to Black children as testimonies of life in solidarity, specifically during times of protest. Grounded in the work of Black feminism (Combahee River Collective 1977; Davis 1981; Collins 1989; Crenshaw 1991) and Black mothering (Gumbs 2016; McClain 2019), I think with visuals of Black children present in the streets during recent uprisings to reclaim justice and honor the lives of Breonna Taylor, Tony McDade, George Floyd, and so many Black lives stolen by a murderous police force backed by a systemic attack on the Black family. In this feminist intervention, I propose we gather to listen to how visuals of Black children speak about the uprisings. I join critical work focusing on Black children (Muhammad and Haddix 2016; Dumas and Nelson 2016; Butler 2018) to imagine young Black children as *guías* of engaging "alternate nows" (Elliot and Tuck, 2017) and futures filled with examinations of power beyond a life of precarity.

Life "Beyond the Precarity"

In the Wake: On Blackness and Being (2016), by Christina Sharpe, calls for us to look for the details in the archive of Black being in order to shine light on life "beyond the precarity." Within this perspective, we think with the details of Black joy, Black care, Black community, and Black power. I lean into Sharpe's method to look through the systems of inequity that ravage our communities with an intent to destroy and bring focus to the ways our Black lives engage humanity. In her beautifully crafted examination, Sharpe focuses on a photo of a young girl during the traumatic response to support the Haitian people after experiencing the destructive earthquake of 2010. Focusing on a detail in the image, Sharpe describes that a "leaf is stuck in her still neat braids. Somebody braided her hair before that earthquake hit" (120). Sharpe archives a public truth of care where a young girl was cared for by a person who plaited her hair neatly. In this way, Sharpe expands the gaze of this photo to include moments of attention and care. She mentions a leaf in her hair, showing this young girl's relationship with beings that were more than human. She was not alone. Sharpe describes her life in context with this photo to archive this beautiful Black child's life "beyond the precarity" and show her continued partnership with family, nature, and care. Sharpe's intervention holds Black life before and during this photo as part of the archive. As I learned more about her moments in this photo, I thought about how her life after this photo is held in close relationship also.

I follow Christina Sharpe as a guide in engaging this feminist intervention of care for Black children. I take care to notice and listen to the details in photos of Black children with their communities. Each photo was taken during the recent uprising to claim justice for Black lives stolen by an unjust and targeted attack on Black families. This intervention situates Black children in an expanding archive of solidarity and ever-present testimony of life in solidarity, especially during times of reclaiming justice.

I offer details of visuals I found during the recent 2020 uprising to claim justice for Black lives stolen by an unjust and targeted attack on Black people taking place in late May, June, and July, a few months after the COVID-19 pandemic shook Turtle Island, currently known as the United States. Post-it notes give life to a visual archive, which includes one actual photo.

Post-it #1: Black girl power

A visit to the @blackwomxnfor Instagram account post from #Blackmamasmarch on June 27, 2020.

Image description: little girl walking in a pink and yellow tutu, sunglasses on face, hair braided with pink, white, and clear beads, holding tight to a snack bag, marching the streets with family. "Lightly melanated hella black" printed in white letters on a black shirt.

Caption reads: Let the babies lead—we gon be alright.

Black Children Are Protest for "Alternate Nows" and Futures

Living within the COVID-19 global health pandemic among a racial pandemic, I think of the world in moments, in flashes that signal shifts and dramatic changes calling for something different. I look to the visuals of young children claiming their "alternate nows" by taking to the streets to show another world is here and possible. I am grounded in the work of Alicia Elliot and the *Henceforward* podcast (2017), where imaginations of changed ways of being in the present are "alternate nows." Young children are part of how we know these changed ways of being are possible.

Young person, your fist in the air, mouth open. You signal a change. Knowing your strength and claiming your voice. What did you want us to hear as we listened to the car horns, city buses, and rustling of the city? This photo taken by Kenny Cousins from FlatTopPhotography shows your need to share and be included in this movement for change.

We're Black & We're Proud. *Courtesy of Kenny Cousins @Flat-TopPhotography.*

Black Mothering

Mothering and nurturing a growing human connects deeply to hope because we, "the larger ones" (Gumbs 2016), cultivate space for others to think in community as they care for a new being. In *We Live for the We* (2019), Dani McClain talks about Black moms and the amount of hope they must hold to bring up a Black child in this world currently guided by antiblack polices. Black mothering is an act of revolution because despite seeing and hearing atrocious and life-sucking examples of anti-Blackness in the numbers of school suspensions or police brutality of young Black people, HOPE. Is. Held! Black mothering is a hope that the world will adapt and cultivate space for this beautiful Black being as a mother would, and want to take care of, nurture, protect, and listen to Black children.

Post-it #2: Black mothering

A visit to @TheRoot Instagram account post from June 4, 2020, a photo taken by @uluvmylovefaces.

Image description: a Black mom, mask on, arms up, holding a sign saying, "We are NOT carrying for 9 months, then struggling during labor for 9 hours, just for you to kneel on their neck for 9 minutes!! BLACK LIVES *MATTER*."

Standing in front of the Capitol, beautiful belly on display.

In this way, Black mothering is the act of "alternate nows" and futures of "radical hope and radical love" because you dream the world is better and cultivate in your body a person who can live in that life with you, who can push the world to change.

Children. Black Children.

We are called to listen to Black children in Roger Reeves' recent poem "For Black Children at the End of the World—and the Beginning." Their innocence and ability to read power while somehow knowing the power they hold. Roger Reeves described how he arrived at writing the poem: He was listening to two young beautiful Black boys, five and eight, who said, "I don't want the police to shoot me" (Reeves 2020). Later, while walking in an Austin protest for Black lives, one of the boys waved at a sniper in the hopes the overmilitarized policeman might not shoot him. In this young Black boy, I imagined kindness and fire, while meeting deep violations of humanity based in hatred. Roger Reeves's poem ends, "You are in a beautiful language. / You are what lies beyond this kingdom / And the next and the next and fire. Fire, Black Child."

Post-it #3: Fire, Black Child

A visit to the @NPR Instagram account post from July 10, 2020.

Image description: Young black child, kneeling on right knee, hand in the air with sign saying, "Black Lives Matter." Shirt with the words "We will fight." People behind, similar body posture, wearing masks and holding signs.

I saw this image and thought of the Black boys Roger had in mind in his poem. You, Black child, are power. Raising your fist in a sea of others, holding your Black Lives Matter sign. Following the adults and elders around you. I imagine you were listening to someone speak or sitting in silence, remembering the pain, agony, and fear that George Floyd might have experienced. Your arm casually resting on your knee, as though you are ready to wait as long as needed.

How does a person kneel on another person for eight minutes and forty-two seconds? This shows a particular absence of care. I think about the ways this display of abhorrent and casual dismissal of Black life was a catalyst for the world to shake out of a predatory fog. In these uprisings, I see support for funneling resources to community needs in place of militarizing police. Examples like organizing to send money to people who take care of young children, bail relief services for protesters, and sidewalk refrigerators for fresh food. How are these moments of solidarity connected to longer-term changes to support beautiful Black children in every space? You, beautiful Black boy, I see your arm resting casually and your comfortable walking shoes as a signal of your desire to put in the time to fight for change. Your face seems intent. Your eyes are watching, observing, and discerning. How can we continue to take note of your actions and take you seriously as a child of political activism and solidarity?

Listening to Black Children

In a podcast conversation with her sister, adrienne maree brown (2017) was reminded of the ways water holds the sounds of our majestic ancestors who jumped in the water during the Middle Passage. The memories of the ocean waves holding frantic calm as bodies jumped away from enslavement. Water holds these memories and our ancestral memories live in us. We hold those memories and stories. I think about the concrete that holds the memory of the feet and knees of young children who waved at snipers, kneeled while listening as they marched for our lives. The "hawk sky" (Reeves 2020) wind who carries these stories to others. The power in story protest. Stories in memories. How does a smaller body hold this physical demonstration of protest when your existence is protest? When your existence is joy? When your existence is a desire to thrive in the world?

Post-it #4: Innocence faces off with imposed trauma

A visit to the @Melanincode Instagram account post from June 1, 2020.

Image description: Young child comfortably sitting on the shoulders of an adult, dressed in a superhero costume with a snack in hand. A policeman with protective gear, standing next to two other police officers, aims a precision gun at them.

I listen to this image with Christina Sharpe's notion of life "beyond the precarity" (2016) as a feminist intervention to imagine the before. Your smile as this beautiful Black man picked you up to place you on their shoulders. You got to eat your snacks while sitting up higher. From there you could see the heads of people for blocks. You were closer to the sun and your legs could rest. That feeling of being tall is something you could have imagined, but now you were living it. Was that how you felt when you were putting on your clothes today? Deciding to let others know about your superpowers. Today. Is. The. Day. To. Let. Them. Know.

And then you arrive in this moment, where a white policeman is holding a gun to the face of a Black man you care about as you sit on their shoulders. Your blue suit reminds me to think about your superpower as a young Black child to hold anguish, fear, pain, joy, and solidarity in everyday moments. I am reminded to take seriously your life and the care in cultivating your environment. I am reminded of the hope, anger, and solidarity wrapped up in mothering a Black child. I lean into these emotions to guide my way through this moment, this now, to other moments where interactions with methods of policing community are seen as a protection of and relationship with Black and Brown lives, rather than a violence against life.

Black Life

There is a spectrum of experiences that culminate in the vibrant memories of a complicated existence as a Black person. Life with precarity and life beyond the precarity. Taking notice of each aspect to develop next steps to the future. I look deeply into these images of Black children to notice life "beyond the precarity" while actively fighting to change the material condition of systems that demean and ignore Black life. Engaging the stories in these images are my feminist intervention in imagining an expansive world, simultaneously uplifted and undermined by our histories. Young children joining, watching, and standing for solidarity. Watching the fire burn as we create something new. As we sustain community, as we hope, dream, and fight. This is why we, Black people, remain. Ancestors and descendants. Always. Because. Children.

A child with that mask that many of us have been wearing during the COVID-19 pandemic, standing in front of the fire, holds a sign: "Stop killing us." Photographer David Beard shared the image with the world in June 2020.

Our people are beautiful.

Bibliography

Brown, Autumn, and adrienne maree brown. *Let the Ancestors Speak: How to Survive the End of the World.* November 28, 2017. https://endoftheworldshow.org/episodes/let-the-ancestors-speak-742.

Butler, Tamara T. "Black Girl Cartography: Black Girlhood and Place-Making in Education Research." *Review of Research in Education* 42, no. 1 (2018): 28–45.

Collins, Patricia Hill. *Black Feminist Thought: Knowledge, Consciousness, and the Politics of Empowerment*. Routledge, 2002.

Combahee River Collective. *The Combahee River Collective Statement*. Library of Congress, 2015 (original 1977). https://www.loc.gov/item/lcwaN0028151/.

Crenshaw, Kimberle Williams. "Mapping the Margins: Intersectionality, Identity Politics, and Violence Against Women of Color." *Stanford Law Review* 43, no. 6 (1991): 1241–1299.

Davis, Angela Y. *Women, Race & Class*. First edition. New York: Random House, 1981.

Dumas, Michael J., and Joseph D. Nelson. "(Re)Imagining Black Boyhood: Toward a Critical Framework for Educational Research." *Harvard Educational Review* 86, no. 1 (2016): 27–47.

Elliot, Alicia, presenter, and Eve Tuck, producer. *Henceforward: Futurities with Alicia Elliot* (podcast). Episode 17, November 3, 2017. http://www.thehenceforward.com/episodes/2017/11/3/episode-17-futurities-with-alicia-elliot.

Gumbs, Alexis P., China Martens, and Mai'a Williams. *Revolutionary Mothering: Love on the Front Lines*. Between the Lines, 2016.

McClain, Dani. *We Live for the We: The Political Power of Black Motherhood*. Hachette Book Group, 2019.

Muhammad, Gholnecsar E., and Marcelle Haddix. "Centering Black Girls' Literacies: A Review of Literature on the Multiple Ways of Knowing of Black Girls." *English Education* 48, no. 4 (2016): 299–336.

Reeves, Roger. "For Black Children at the End of the World—and the Beginning." Academy of American Poets, June 16, 2020. https://poets.org/poem/black-children-end-world-and-beginning.

Sharpe, Christina. *In the Wake: On Blackness and Being*. Duke University Press, 2016.

Taylor, Keeanga Y., ed. *How We Get Free: Black Feminism and the Combahee River Collective*. Haymarket Books, 2017.

36 • THE SURVIVOR'S BREATH

Amira Yaem Trevino

I wonder,
My dear,
How did you wake up today?

How do you continue to push forward
While holding
Sorrow,
Fear,
And
Pain?
Exposed to the falling of
Those familiar,
Those close,
And
Those far

Fallen,
Like the taken
trees of the forest

Fallen conduits
For oxygen

Fallen connections
Between mother earth's breath
And our own

The mothers
Grandmothers

Caregivers
And lovers

Fallen . . .

How is it,
My dear,
That you continue to
Open your bedroom door
When later
It might be
Pushed in

How do you
Continue to open
Your eyes
When later
They may be
Exposed to
Overwhelming
Power
That freezes
You to
Submission

My dear,
How is it
That you continue
To use your breath
To support
Those you love
When
Later you may struggle
To find
Your own breath
To survive

When your eyes
Swell with
The tears of

Your heart
And
Your family
And
Your community

My dear,

I see
The reflection
Of myself

And in that reflection
I see my own
Heart
And
Family
And
Community

Together
We are connected
Through cellular linkages
Through the droplets
That collect
On the exposed roots
Of our sorrow

And it is
As I stand outside
Alone
And feel the breeze
Whip under my hair
And graze my neck

As I feel the gentle
And honest love
Of mother earth

And as I place my hand

On
The textured bark of a tree

I am reminded of you

Those who have been violated
Those who survived
Those who are being violated
Those who are surviving

Those who are kept up
At night
By the disturbance of
unrelenting tears
By the fear of
What the night
Or the morrow
will bring

I think of you

So tell me,
My dear,
Is it the size of your heart,
That allows you room
to
Continue to love?

Is it the strength
You've gained
From what you've carried
Thus far
And continue to carry
For yourself and
Others
That helps you
Take another step?

Is it the blood
Of your

Ancestors
That floods
To your limbs
In your
Fight to
Live?

Or is it the magic
That rests inside
That motivates
You
To continue
For the
The lives
Of those
You'll soon change?

Whatever it may be,
My dear,
I am captivated by you

I am captivated by
Your light
That flickers
and
sparkles
with every breath

Your light
that adds hope
to the dark sky
of abuse's void

Your light
That will not
Be smothered
Dimmed
Or
Snuffed

Your light
That will continue to
Pulsate
Far beyond
The boundaries
of flesh

It is to you,
My dear, that
I send my love

When you feel alone,
Feel the sensation of my warmth

When you feel helpless,
Feel the weight of my love

When you feel like you
Can't open your eyes
Can't take another step
Or
Can't keep pushing through

My dear,
Know that our
Roots are connected

Your reflection
Is in my eyes
As mine
Is in yours
And
Just as the trees that we are,
Your existence
Helps this world
To breathe

So keep breathing, my dear.

Summer 2021

As the virus swept the globe, I recall the fear of death also moving across continents. Doors were urged to shut, as though to keep the virus out. And yet, those same doors also contained what was within. No longer were the consequential marks of in-home violence seen by those outside. Abused children and partners were kept further out of reach from those who cared, those who saw, and those who reported. As someone who had worked with survivors of childhood abuse and sexual assault in the past, I found myself worried about the people I wouldn't see: the people who were kept caged in their abusive prisons.

In my imposed isolation, I fought the fall into despair by doing what I could to be active in community building. While I found service to be meaningful, I felt the subsequent dips fall sharper and deeper as the days went on. I knew that to sustain the work that I do, I needed to go within. I am a survivor, and reflective, meditative, and spiritual practices have been the cornerstone of my healing. Connecting with others who also knew love and suffering further offered glimmers of hope.

At the time of writing "The Survivor's Breath," I recognized that while my home was now safe, my body was still filled with fear. I often found myself wondering about those whose bodies *and* homes felt unsafe. Oh, how I wished I were there with them, to hold their hand and to let them know it was going to be okay. Thus, my own healing practices became a way to connect. My mindful walks turned into mindful cleanses. My sensory exercises became deliveries for energetic healing. My meditations became journeys of protection. While I was physically separated from those who share in pain, we remained spiritually and energetically connected.

As a woman of color, I believe that building sustainable, socially just communities requires engagement in our own healing practices, however that may look for us. Oppression's hammer often attempts to shatter us, and sometimes it succeeds, leaving us fragmented and bruised. Thus, we need to do the radical work of turning our intention, passion, and love toward ourselves. Rest your body. Love your body. Be in your body. *We need to line our edges with gold.* It is then that we can reconnect, reclaim, and resound our voices for change.

37 · QUEER COLLECTIVE CARE IN PANDEMIC TIMES

Jessennya Hernandez

GLORIA ANZALDÚA HAS ALWAYS BEEN an inspiration for me to analyze, accept, move with, and transform the chaos and complexities of nepantla as a queer Brown femme Xicana. Taking her cue, I draw on my journal entries from the beginning of the pandemic in 2020. I offer you my personal poems, each of which is followed with an analysis and reflection that I am now able to present to you, as I look at the past two years in retrospect. My hope is for you to use the poems as a guide to read, feel, and think through the reflections that follow. This essay is about queer collective care, an active practice of survival, healing, and transformation that has been essential for my own community, especially during—*but not limited to*—the pandemic. As part of my own practice of queer collective care, I offer this essay to you so that we may find connection and move together toward something informed and *transformed by* our shared pains and discomfort. It is nearly impossible to express the sadness, fear, joy, and peace I felt during the pandemic, but perhaps this essay will evoke something already familiar to you.

Queering Our Affective Traumas for a Radical and Feminist Future

Spring–Summer 2020
Inside the now unfamiliar childhood home she had to relive,
she was made to feel scared, burnt out, and anxious
and believe the colonial myth that she was   alone.

What she saw outside of this home seemed to confirm that,
with BIPOC communities dying,
sick while caged,
and put at risk every day.

But she found queer kinship and community
grounded
in unapologetic feminist energy, mutual aid,
abolition, and transformative justice.

Working through the violence and pain,
she shares her trauma and discomfort with her comrades.

Together they heal;
provide networks of safety, comfort, and security;
breathe deeply;
listen actively to support each other's needs;
connect to their ancestral past in the present;
and make the space to laugh and feel joy and pleasure again,
now and for the future.

Despite the perils of her childhood home
and the state's inability to protect her community during a pandemic,
her home, health, and safety lie within
the connection and care between her spirit
and her queer community.

That is,
collective care.

Fall 2022. I have come to realize uncertainty is ever-present. I feel uncertainty now during a pandemic, where the state and its institutions have revealed how little they care for us, especially as working-class BIPOC. But in connection with that, I have always felt uncertainty as a queer femme Brown grad student whose experiences with white supremacist heteropatriarchy often push me to want out. Yet I continue to learn how to strategize through a collective care that centers physical, mental, and spiritual health within and among trusted amigxs, queer kin, family, and comrades. Not just in academia, queer BIPOC communities *need* a collective—formed through caring practices—to transcend survival. As the pandemic further highlights the realities of colonialism and imperialism's legacies, many of us can no longer ignore the failures of the white supremacist neoliberal state and its institutions. For example, our people have been the first to die or fall into deeper poverty or houselessness because they're sick and cannot work. More and more I have witnessed those around me realize that the state and dominant society neglect, surveil, and erase us. Overall, I see that in the time of this pandemic, we are deeply feeling our colonial, imperial, racist, capitalist, and other systemic *traumas*.

But that is not the end of our story. Amid these experiences of chaos, violence, and death, there are spaces and moments where we find a collective and practice care with each other. Finding, caring for, and building the collective requires *queering* our affective discomforts, pains, and traumas that are rooted in and continue from our collective pasts. By *queering our traumas*, I refer to spoiling, uncovering, sitting with, and working through them. Queering our affective discomforts, pains, and traumas together is a healing practice and leads to what many might think of as an (im)possible feminist and radical future.

The possibilities for this queering have been imagined through the labors of love pushed forth by transnational Black, Brown, and Indigenous feminists and their knowledges. As we connect to our own lineages, Indigenous knowledges are with us—we *feel* them. They transcend time and space, speaking to us, directing us to an essential practice of collective care. That is, only if we listen. If we listen, we can practice healing our painful and traumatic histories. This pandemic is a moment in time that will imprint trauma and pain in our collective history, yet we emerge. As academics of color invested in a feminist and radical future, we can follow the blueprints of these BIPOC feminist knowledges and work to collectively queer the damage and traumas from our colonial and imperial pasts that have been catalyzed and have found new formations. My experiences of racial, heteropatriarchal, and COVID pandemics have shown me that collective care is essential for transformative change. Indeed, it has been a source of personal transformation and grounding during the last couple years of my academic and personal lives. Thus, while these pandemics uproot, they also further ground me in the people, spirits, and community around me.

Spring 2021. In the spring of 2019, before the pandemic began and due to financial limitations, I had to move back to my parents' home—where I grew up—to finish my data collection for my dissertation. Once the pandemic hit, I had to stay for longer than I planned. As the pandemic has retraumatized BIPOC communities with the ways in which it disproportionately affects us, the pandemic also highlighted the traumas hidden underneath the surface of my own family and personal life. And I found myself reliving what I am most afraid of: believing in the colonial myth that I am alone in my pain and cannot have hope for a just and safe future. I now know I shared this fear with so many BIPOC, especially my queer kin. A microcosm of generations of colonialism and imperialism, the pandemic made the collective, including myself, feel disconnected and hopeless.

But in this chaos of isolation and impending doom within and outside my home, I felt hope when seeking refuge with like-minded Black and Brown feminist comrades, primarily queer folks and women. Despite the fear, we coped and felt glimmers of relief when coming together virtually. We wanted to think about what we could do for the most vulnerable in our community. With intention, but humbly, we ended up forming a grassroots mutual aid collective based on abolitionist and transformative justice practice. We aim to build autonomy and self-determination that counters a state that was never made for us. Our understanding of mutual aid and collective care is distinct from white-dominant and charity-based frameworks of care. We move with traditions of mutual aid that working-class and poor BIPOC communities have always used to survive. Practicing collective care and love through mutual aid, we provide hygiene kits, bus passes, gift cards, and food to our houseless community members; fundraise for those dealing with emergencies; and read, study, and learn together as we attempt to build alternative networks and systems of care outside of the carceral state.

Little did I know that through these comrades, queer colleagues, and mentors, I would find the healing to break from the colonial myth and traumas that once made me believe I was alone. Because of these networks of collective care, I was able to work through my own housing, financial, and food insecurity; family rejection/betrayal; sickness; intergenerational trauma; and doctoral studies during a pandemic. I moved in with a comrade and began to feel safe again. The waves of nepantla calmed, even if it was just for a moment, and I could see the possibilities for hope in the future.

Practicing Collective Care

Fall 2021

They asked each other,
how can I show up for you?

They tended to the past
to transcend time and remembered
it was circular.

It hurts
to remember,
relive,
and heal
as queer brown women

They took care of each other and remembered
how to survive like they had in the past.

They began to heal their pasts
in the present.

They began to imagine
their futures.

in academic institutions,
and
it also feels good
to move
towards joy and peace
again.

Spring 2022. In my most recent seasons of life, I have had the privilege of practicing collective care more mindfully with my chosen family and mutual aid networks. Since 2020, I have been intentionally working to heal my heart and spirit in such a way that allows me to want more out of life than to just stay alive. In fact, I demand a present and future where my community and I have the ability to *feel* and *desire* hope for something more than the traumas we have been given. I want there to be more room for joy and pleasure in and outside of academia. My lived experiences have taught me to unapologetically move through and against what takes joy and life away from my communities and move toward what gives it. Collective care allows us to move through the pandemic, toward life and joy.

Witnessing my queer kin, comrades, and the BIPOC feminist and queer creatives whom I center in my research, collective care can also look like: healing and treating sickness and symptoms with holistic remedies passed down through generations rather than turning to the medical industrial complex; sharing resources, feelings of imposter syndrome, and tears with other queer BIPOC academics; creating art to raise funds for undocumented community members who do not get government relief; actively choosing to mend familial wounds even when it hurts; creating virtual spaces among BIPOC femmes and women across state borders to play their records, DJ together, dance, and experience joy; and QTBIPOC sharing intimate yet socially distanced space—*exclusively* for them—to express anger, fear, and hope for a future beyond a carceral imperial state. This is radical love.

Queering what is painful and uncomfortable is healing, and doing this in community is an example of collective care. It is how I (un)learn survival strategies—whether related to the pandemic or not—and move toward different horizons. It is part of how I learn to desire a future in which I feel connection and joy. Indeed, it is how those Black, Brown, and Indigenous communities before us—especially those femmes and women—learned and coped through colonial diseases and systemic violence. These knowledges have existed for centuries; we just need to recover, preserve, and nurture them as we practice collective care so that we can move toward finding community, joy, and relief. To be relieved is to have space and time to breathe and ground yourself in the present, making it possible to envision our liberation. As a final offering to you, I close this essay with a poem from spring 2022.

As we build networks with queer kin, feminist family, and loved ones across borders of time and nation-state, we can make space to continuously heal our shared pains and traumas.

As this ongoing physical, mental and spiritual healing happens in community, liberatory imaginations can be better built, embodied, and enacted.

We have no choice
    but to continue
      creating bridges
      and connections
between our spirts and selves
    if we want to create systems
        where we can
        autonomously
      take care of ourselves
  and our community needs and heal
    better than the current neoliberal
      and white supremacist state.

This system
of collective care
grounded
in spiritual
and material wellbeing
and built around knowledges
that use plants and herbs,
laughter,
queer politics,
and art
to heal collective trauma,
has and will continue
to bring radical love and hope.

Como Nepantleras
en el desorden y el engaño
de la familia, la enfermedad, las instituciones y el estado,
podemos cuidarnos como colectiva
para imaginar futuros (im)posibles
donde todos, especialmente la gente queer/cuir/joto, tienen vidas
de paz, seguridad, alegría y placer
al máximo.

As Nepantleras
in the chaos and betrayals
of home, disease, institutions, and the state,
we can queer collective care
to envision (im)possible futures
where we experience
peaceful, safe, joyous, and pleasurable
queer lives
at their greatest potential

38 • ABOLITION
A Joyous Rebirth from the Flames
Joseph Emil Tibiru

COVID-19 and the unjustified killing of innocent Black lives, including but not
limited to Breanna Taylor, Michael Brown, George Floyd, Michael Ramos,
and Ahmaud Arbery, and the eventual civil unrest and protests;
it is quite clear 2020 has been a liminal space, making it a transitional year.

People in positions of power are attempting to shift us back into a normalcy
that will never happen.
We currently exist in a pocket of time where extreme transformation is possible
and it would be detrimental to seek the normalcy of the past.
A normalcy that exacerbated these catastrophes in the first place;
a normalcy that places rich, white, cis-heterosexual and able-bodied men at the
forefront.

The only way to rise out of the ashes of these violent phenomena
is to deal with the repercussions; I posit that abolition is the politic we must adopt
and represents the joyous rebirth and revolution Black people need.

We currently exist in a liminal space fraught with disorder
in which we must make radical transformations for the betterment of our society.

The pandemic as well as the Black Lives Matter protests have assumed the role of
whistle blower by exposing our country's ill-equipped regime:
from the state-sanctioned murder of Black people at the hands of the police
to lack of access to treatment and healthcare,
to the scarcity of governmental support during a mandatory lockdown,
such as rent and bill assistance.

It is important that a transformation is facilitated
as it is more than evidenced
that our status quo has fostered the end of countless Black lives.

Great loss has occurred during this pandemic, most notably in the form of Black
lives.
Our intervention must be a radical transformation of this country's policies
regarding policing,
prisons, healthcare, social security, accommodations, and even wealth hoarding.

Do not forget:
Our normal is what exacerbated this crisis and set fire to our country in the first
place.

Abolition is the phoenix Black people need
because it is the furthest shift from the normalcy of this country.

Why do we continue to fund and invest in prisons and jails?
2020 has screamed at us: police officers mirror plantation overseers
and their duty is to desecrate the Black community; incarceration is a public
health concern, as it creates reservoirs of disease which facilitated the spread of
COVID-19.

Truly, a return to normal is only digging this country's grave;
a grave that will be populated mainly by those deemed subhuman.

The crises of 2020 exhibit an epistemological break and we must take action
and seek our liberation through radical reinvention and transformation.
We cannot keep allocating resources to the police force
while people are unable to feed themselves;
we cannot continue to fund punitive methods such as incarceration
while those funds could be used to put a dent in our homeless crisis.

Our pillars of society have to be violently broken down and rebuilt
and we must realize how these structures of inequality aided and intensified the
horrors of 2020. Black death at the hands of the police and COVID-19
is tied to a whole slew of historical issues that tie back to colonialism,
enslavement, the lack of access to proper healthcare, and economic disparities.

We must look at abolition as a cleansing force: the ultimate decolonial project.

Instead of yearning for what was in the past,
we must make changes to ensure that we have an infrastructure rooted in justice
and healing,
one that does not promote Black death.
Black people are constantly in a collective state of post-traumatic stress.
The stories of Black death are many; we hear and see them every day.
We are always in mourning.
2020 was no different.

We must begin to question this reality and ask ourselves what constitutes humanity.
Blackness is the antithesis of whiteness, which is synonymous with human,
thus rendering Blackness subhuman. This is why we are dying at such alarming
rates.

As we continue unpacking what it means to be Black
in a society that has denied us humanity,
we must look at the collective stories of Black death
for exactly what they are: genocide.
Emancipation was a failure;
slavery has now transformed into the carceral system.
I vehemently believe: abolition is our only access to freedom.

This reflection is my attempt to make sense of 2020 in relation to the state of
Blackness.
I am grateful for the theories granted to us by our inspiring intellectual ancestors:
Angela Davis, Ruth Gilmore, Frantz Fanon, and Carole Boyce Davies come to
mind.
They allow me to think through abolition as an exhaustive solution
focused on the root of the issue rather than solutions that are akin to flogging a
dead horse.

Without an in-depth metamorphosis,
Black people will always bear the brunt
of that death through our own mortality.

39 • IMMEASURABLE
Kiana T. Murphy

5.26.2020 Flashes from Alexis Pauline Gumbs on Making Ourselves Anew

Sylvia Wynter teaches us about sociopoetics, which in my mind sounds like a process of becoming deemed impossible or illegitimate, or, more simply, a matter of being within a logic of life that does not allow us to be in relation to each other because of capitalism.[1] Wynter asks: "What constitutes the 'we' of self-making? What are the particular historical coordinates of that we?"

When I first read the term in graduate school, I found poetics to be defiantly malleable. To be poetic or to craft poetics is to be experimental, to bend life and humanity into a new order that allows us all to breathe, especially those who have not been breathing all this time. The poetic signals a double paradox of being made: the violence of dispossession alongside the plenitude of invention. There are some things that are immeasurably plentiful, like breath, and there are steps that can be made to unlearn the lie of scarcity. Others are immeasurable because we are fooled into the idea of ownership over all things, even life, even breath. Alexis Pauline Gumbs taught me this. And you can unlearn scarcity and relearn abundance. Toni Cade Bambara tells us that everything is here. We can extend gratitude and redistribute resources, like breath, like rest, like food, like water. We can do these things. We can unlearn scarcity and find ourselves immeasurable.

The first step is knowing we are not alone and practicing this as truth.

6.6.2020 Journeying with Sharon Bridgforth (A Workshop and Conversation with the Ancestors)

Q: What are you holding that you are being asked to release?
A: I do not know what I am holding sometimes, but I always feel it holding

me like it is not my own. Some days it is my body and other days it is fear. Some days it is perfection and other days it is comfort. Some days it is exhaustion and other days it is all I cannot see.

Q: What do you know you know but don't know why?
A: My mother's sadness. My father's weariness. That bodies are a vessel, and gender is a tool. That what I know is not all mine. Black people are in many different kinds of heaven. Angels walk the earth. Intuition is a love language. Systemic oppression changes the body. That love looks like me.

Q: What are treasures that you want to circulate?
A: That you are here and you matter. That the light inside you is the only one we will ever have in this lifetime. That the universe will shift without it.

6.14.2020 A Meditation of Sorts, or Why I Can't Stop Thinking about Breonna Taylor

I am thinking about Black girls and women as I always am
about shapeshifting and adaptation
about resistance as a kind of awareness necessarily
as in we, Black girls and women,
often come into resistance
prematurely
"Existence as resistance" a student says to me
and I wonder
how to account for this structural fact
and when to determine whether it's a choice one can even have
I am thinking of Black girls and women for this reason
how we are shaped into resistance as a fact of life

has resistance become a map to find us?

Note

1. This is a version of a definition I remember meditating on in graduate school between coursework and creative workshops. To read more from the actual essay, see Sylvia Wynter, "Ethno, or Socio Poetics," *Alcheringa/Ethnopoetics* 2, no. 2 (1976): pp. 78–94.

40 • ASCENDANCE

Sara Rezvi

There is something ascendant inside of me
And in all the beautiful women in my life
Who tend to broken things with kindness ~
The shoreline that I have been walking has been rocky, full of wounds and
    debris.
The stars are coming out tonight
They reflect the dark and powerful wave rising inside all of us
Blood moon, powerful spirit, ancestors. I see all of you
It is time to meet these waves
It is time to embrace my own glory
We are magic // blood and bond // We are centuries in the making
We are thunder and grace, lightning on moonlit path, tree bursting in half
    at the seams // to reveal the glowing amber hidden within
We who always tend to others before ourselves // no more
We have always been who we needed
We have always been our own best gardeners.
Together we rise, together our roots interlace
Today and everyday
we start something different the world has never seen
Let us begin ~

POSTLUDE

Christen A. Smith, Gloria González-López, and Sharmila Rudrappa

What is the calculus of human loss? Where does death begin and where does it end? This project emerged from a wave of uncertain death and confinement—a period when despair was ubiquitous, and our future was uncertain. For many of us, feminist community became the only path for potential survival in these uncertain times. Out of pain and a sense of loss and isolation, Gloria González-López and Pavithra Vasudevan started the Feminist Writing Salon at the Center for Women's and Gender Studies at UT Austin—a space of respite and community where a small group of us gathered weekly to write through the pain of all that we were going through. We wrote in silence, pouring our feelings out onto the page following prompts brought by our two facilitators; Nnenna Odim joined as co-facilitator in summer 2020. What we wrote was spontaneous and healing . . . at times prose, and at times poetry, but always a mirror into the depths of feeling that we otherwise found difficult to put into words. We found feminist community in that space online, via Zoom, among friends. Slowly but surely, lockdown lifted, and it seemed, if only falsely, that things had gotten back to "normal" (whatever that is). The salon ended, but its impact continued. Death had not left us, however; it was only in hiding and changing form. When it seemed that the pandemic was fading to the background, October 7, 2023, happened. Bombs, starvation, unimaginable loss, entire family lines destroyed in an instant. Dreams and hopes buried in silenced screams. The world was crumbling again. The unimaginable calculus of death was indeed chaos theory—shifting, predictably unpredictable, like the anonymous poem "#GenocideMath, Problem Set 1."[1] Somehow, the collective death that made us feel equal to one another transliterated into an unspeakable genocide that divided the world. For many of us, writing is the only way to heal in the face of what cannot be imagined, understood, or spoken. The feminist healing that we learned in our 2020 salon continued to be a refuge, and we wrote. It feels apropos to end this volume with the poetry of Pavithra Vasudevan, a passionate feminist who shepherded us through the pandemic with her writing and reflections and now, after spending months fighting to end the genocide against Palestinian people, turns again to the page for healing. We can think of no better way to end this volume than with her words from "There Are So Many Lessons I Would Have Rather Learned," a poem/reflection she prepared for a teach-in during the student protests against the genocide in Palestine. At first it may seem as though a poem about Palestine has no place in a volume on the pandemic. But our collective decision to end this book with Vasudevan's poem was made to acknowledge the continuing need for us as feminists to write to heal, even when it feels as if the world is ending.

What we began back in 2020 has now bloomed into writing beyond the pandemic—and indeed this is the theme that we choose to close this book.

We must write to survive.

We must build feminist community to find our way out of despair.

The calculus of death was not isolated to the pandemic.

Death continues; therefore we must also continue, so we write.

Note

1. Anonymous, "#GenocideMath, Problem Set 1," *Journal for Theoretical & Marginal Mathematics Education* 3, no. 1 (2024), https://doi.org/10.5281/zenodo.14057410.

THERE ARE SO MANY LESSONS I WOULD HAVE RATHER LEARNED

Pavithra Vasudevan

For a teach-in on Gaza, April 24, 2024

Heba Zagout who painted like
a poet, meditated upon suffering
so long the world turned into a painting.

If I met Heba, I would ask to see her prints,
the ones she captioned, "The sea, the sky
and the beautiful colors are looking for happy
dreams, clinging to life, love and hope."

I would ask her, "Did you find the sea and sky their happy dreams?"

We could have been learning from Mahmoud Darwish
every day for 200 days; we could have
considered what he meant by:

I am the shadow that walks on water
I am the witness and the scene
I am the worshipper and the temple
in the land of my siege and yours[1]

Today is 201.

Gaza is the beautiful land that created
the delicate lacy material that saves lives.
Gaza today does not have enough gauze

to bandage the wounds of the 70,000
human lives taken in 200 days.

Here, "free speech weeks" are followed
by executive orders
banning words like
books to be removed
from our shelves,
our tongues,
our bodies.

Did you also receive the lesson
on faith? On what it must take to
accept the death of your entire
family and still believe in your
God, yourself, your land.

Khaled Nabhan, whom we all, all over
the internet watched mourning
his granddaughter Reem
and her brother Tarek,
one month after Heba and her sons
Mahmoud and Adam were martyred.
"Soul of my soul," he called Reem.
Uncle Khaled, whom we all, all over
the internet watch, still caring
for the forgotten,
the orphaned
cats of Gaza.[2]

And what of the lesson on injustice:
on how absolute devastation can produce
so much poetry? And so many poets gone.

If I must die, Refaat Alareer had said,
you must tell my story
so we read his poem, in english
and arabic, and stand for an hour
in the heat of the midday sun
crying in our robes for all the

poets gone, crying because our
jobs now include standing between
students and state troopers.

I wear my keffiyeh like armor these days, or a talisman,
willing it to give me the courage again to call them liars.
It is still soft, twenty-three years of occupation later.
The first time I wore my keffiyeh it was
International Day at University Inc.™
No table for Palestine;
under colonialism not everyone gets to play.
Gaza had just been bombed again,
but the interminable "war on terror" had not yet begun.
We marched, two rows of students,
twenty years old, carrying one of our own
draped in a Palestinian flag through
the rows of college students tabling
for failed nation-states, across
the campus commons, past
the troops of investor parents, up
the chapel steps where we mourned.
That day, we understood—
we are all Palestinian.

We might have talked about
what solidarity means—and why
so many Jewish people are refusing
faith forged in artillery, refusing
the colonizer's gift of birthright.
Worlds destroyed by the same
bombs share kinship of a kind.

What if we had taught our students
that yes, genocide is contested,
not because we are not sure
how many tens of thousands
of Palestinians killed is sufficient
proof but rather, because of those
who build the bombs, and those
who mine the cobalt, and those

who want the oil, and those
who want more oil . . .

"WCNSF: Wounded child, no surviving family."
I listen to Hind Rajab, 6 years old, and trapped
in a car with her dead relatives, calling
for help, somehow incredibly getting through.
I want to believe she did have a chance, even if
every hospital and healthcare facility destroyed
is not a statistic that inspires hope.
The two paramedics, Yusuf Zeino and Ahmed al-Madhoun
who drove into the siege in search of Hind—
their van would be found feet away, melted into road;
they believed they might have
saved her, *and what if they had,*
and what if

But there is no lesson to be learned from 34,000 deaths, beyond our capacity
for cruelty.

Who have we become in forgetting how to be human?

Who may we become in mourning who we've lost?

Today is _____.
There is not enough gauze to bandage the wounds of the
_____ lives taken.

Notes

The poem presented here is an edited version of the original, first published in *LeftVoice* magazine on October 7, 2024. https://www.leftvoice.org/there-are-so-many-lessons-i-would-have-rather-learned/.

1. Mahmoud Darwish, "The Death of the Phoenix," in *Why Did You Leave the Horse Alone?*, trans. Jeffrey Sacks (Archipelago Books, 2006).

2. Khaled Nabhan was killed on December 16, 2024, by an Israeli air strike on the Nuseirat refugee camp.

ACKNOWLEDGMENTS

FIRST AND FOREMOST, WE WOULD like to express our heartfelt gratitude to the University of Texas Press for their trust and support from day one. We are especially grateful to Dawn Durante, who was the editor in chief at the University of Texas Press back in February 2022, when we had our very first conversations about this book project. Thank you, Dawn, for your kindness, warmth, and trust, and for introducing us to Kerry Webb, senior acquisitions editor at the University of Texas Press. Thank you, Kerry, for supporting this project with that same kindness, warmth, and trust throughout the process of making a dream come true. Our special gratitude also goes to Christina Vargas, Anahi Molina, Lynne Ferguson, the copyeditor Sarah Hudgens, and the proofreader Regina Fuentes, for their professional support, patience, and guidance during the process. And to all the other professionals at the University of Texas Press who have been supportive of this project, people we have not had the pleasure of meeting yet, thank you. In addition, we are grateful to Brianna Pippens for the beautiful image she created exclusively for the cover of this book.

We are deeply grateful to all the authors who submitted their contributions when we circulated the call for papers right after the COVID-19 pandemic hit our world, back in spring 2020. Our heartfelt gratitude goes to each one of the people who responded to that call and gave life to this anthology. Thank you for staying loyal to the project, thank you for your trust, thank you for your sustained motivation and enthusiasm, thank you for your incredible patience, thank you especially for not giving up on us—*gracias de corazón*. And thank you, Nathalia Hernández-Ochoa and Adriana Quiroga, for your support with various tasks at different stages of the project.

As coeditors, we honor the presence, love, and support of our respective families, loved ones, and friends, special people in our lives, for their invaluable support as we navigated the pandemic individually and collectively. And we are especially grateful to you, dear reader, for engaging with each one of the moving, creative texts that give life to this volume. We hope this book will be beneficial to you and to the communities that offer a special meaning to your life—our borderless intercultural communities. We hope these moving voices will help you nurture the core of your life purpose and explore ways to continue transforming pain and sorrow into passion and creative, life-changing social interventions.

Let's continue imagining and actively engaging in world-making feminist projects collectively as we learn to decipher together the current challenging and unpredictable times. May Gloria E. Anzaldúa's inspirational words—"May we do work that matters. Vale la pena, it's worth the pain"—help us nourish fear-free, wide-open hearts that are inspired, hopeful, and committed—always in community.

CONTRIBUTORS

Leisy J. Abrego (she/her) was born in El Salvador and is a Professor of Chicana/o and Central American Studies at UCLA. She is a law and society scholar who studies the intimate consequences of US foreign and immigration policies for Central American migrants and Latinx families in the United States. Her books include *Sacrificing Families: Navigating Laws, Labor, and Love Across Borders* (Stanford University Press, 2014), *Immigrant Families* (coauthored with Cecilia Menjívar and Leah Schmalzbauer, Polity, 2016), and *We Are Not Dreamers: Undocumented Scholars Theorize Undocumented Life in the United States* (coedited with Genevieve Negrón-Gonzales, Duke University Press, 2020).

Katie L. Acosta is a Professor and Director of Graduate Studies in the Department of Sociology at Georgia State University. She is the daughter of immigrants from the Dominican Republic and lived her earliest years on the island. Her research centers the intersections of gender, sexuality, Latinx studies, race/ethnicity, family, and immigration. She is the author of *Amigas y Amantes: Sexually Nonconforming Latinas Negotiate Family*. Her most recent research explores the experiences of Central American and Mexican asylum seekers and the ways asylum politics shape race and ethnic ties among various disadvantaged, racially minoritized groups in Atlanta.

María Luisa Amado (she/her/hers) is a Lincoln Financial Professor of Sociology at Guilford College. A Panamanian, she came to the United States as a Fulbright Scholar to pursue graduate studies in sociology. She has published two books, *Mexican Immigrants in the Labor Market: The Strength of Strong Ties* (2006) and *Neoliberalism and Labor Displacement in Panama: Contested Public Space and the Disenfranchisement of Street Vendors* (2024). In 2016, she coproduced a film, *Bien Cuidao: The Informal Economics of Survival in Panama*. As an amateur photographer, Amado has exhibited her photography at Guilford and on her website, Flickering Stories of the Road.

Briana Barner (she/her) is an Assistant Professor in the Department of Communication at the University of Maryland. Barner is an interdisciplinary critical and cultural communications scholar with research interests in Black podcasts and Black cultural production. Her work has appeared in academic publications such as *Radio Journal: International Studies in Broadcast & Audio Media*. She is currently working on a manuscript about the cultural production of Black podcasts.

reelaviolette botts-ward (she/her) is a UC President's Postdoctoral Fellow in Medical Anthropology at the University of California, San Francisco, where she brings radical Black feminist healing arts to medical science spaces. As founder of blackwomxnhealing, she curates courses, publications, and exhibitions with everyday Black women at the center. She is the 2024 poet in residence at the Museum of the African Diaspora, and a contributor in residence for Columbia University's *Synapsis: A Health Humanities Journal*. Her first book, *mourning my inner[blackgirl]child*, was published in 2021. botts-ward received a PhD from UC Berkeley, an MA from UCLA, and a BA from Spelman College.

Gema Cardona is a researcher, motherscholar, and educator; she holds a PhD in education from the University of California, Berkeley, and an EdM from Harvard Graduate School of Education. Cardona self-identifies as a first-generation PhD from a low-income immigrant family. Her research is situated at the intersection of community engagement, critical race theory, and critical methodologies. As an educator, she practices Freirean liberatory education principles to empower college students to be critical thinkers. In her free time, she enjoys cooking and baking. She is an avid sports fan and competed in track and cross country in high school and early college.

Judy Cervantes holds a bachelor of arts in American literature and culture from the University of California, Los Angeles, and a postbaccalaureate in Women, Gender, and Sexuality Studies from Cal State, Los Angeles. She remains highly interested in work and research related to the condition of girls and women in the United States. Cervantes is a mother, a Spanish-language educator, and a small business owner. She lives in Pasadena, California, with her daughter, Eloisa; her mother, Leticia; and her dog, Coco.

Alicia Chatterjee (she/her) is a doctoral candidate at the University of Pennsylvania School of Social Policy and Practice and a social work therapist invested in anti-colonial care. Broadly, her scholarship is concerned with critical studies of clinical practice in its past and present forms. Her current research brings together decolonial theory and historical methodology to investigate the development of clinical social work in the United States as it articulated alongside global histories of race.

Ada Cheng is an educator turned storyteller, solo performer, and curator/producer who has used storytelling to illustrate structural inequities, raise critical awareness, and build intimate communities. Committed to amplifying and uplifting marginalized voices, she has created numerous storytelling platforms for BIPOC and queer communities to tell difficult and vulnerable stories. Cheng has been a speaker for the Illinois Humanities Road Scholars Speakers Bureau since 2019. She is the 2023–2024 Lund-Gill Chair at Dominican University. She is also one of the recipients of the Public Humanities Award from Illinois Humanities in 2024. Her interests encompass academia, storytelling/performance, and advocacy.

Faith M. Deckard (she/her/hers) is an Assistant Professor of Sociology at the University of California, Los Angeles. Her research broadly explores how marginalized groups experience, navigate, and respond to social control institutions. Of particular interest is the US criminal legal system, with her current project examining how commercial bail entangles families in a complicated economic and social system of obligation, debt, and punishment. Her research and teaching are rooted in the conviction that our lived experiences can be a vehicle for producing, or a touchstone for understanding, knowledge and converting it into practice.

Cassandra Flores-Montaño, a regional recruitment manager at The Ohio State University, earned an MA in American Studies and Ethnicity from the University of Southern California in 2023. Her thesis explored the history of Connexxus/Centro de Mujeres, a lesbian-serving organization in West Hollywood and East Los Angeles. She examined how lesbians navigated demographic and social differences to build political social capital in the 1980s. Flores-Montaño's academic and professional focus aligns with her passion for advocacy, equity, and inclusion in higher education, where she strives to create opportunities for underrepresented communities to thrive.

Dominique Garrett-Scott (she/her) is a multi-hyphenate creative, researcher, and storyteller. She is a Black feminist sociologist whose work explores the interior lives of Black women and girls. With a background as a student, labor, and community organizer, she seamlessly blends her Southern roots and her activist past with her current role directing community research to empower Black and Brown youth across California. A storyteller at heart, Garrett-Scott brings complex issues like fatphobia and desirability into focus using her social platforms to uplift conversations about plus-size fashion, beauty, and misogynoir. You can find her on all socials at @domthefurious.

Andrea Gómez Cervantes (she/her) is an Assistant Professor in the Department of Sociology at Wake Forest University. Her research examines the experiences of Indigenous and mestizo Mexican and Central American migrants, including folks with undocumented, DACAmented, and semilegal statuses; asylum seekers; and mixed-status families in an increasingly unequal and anti-immigrant political context. As a Mexicana immigrant and first-gen scholar, she is especially interested in creating initiatives that address the well-being of immigrant families and communities in the US and abroad. Her book, *Illegality in the Heartland* (forthcoming), is currently under contract with the University of California Press.

Olivia González is a postdoctoral fellow in the University of Pennsylvania's Annenberg School for Communication. González received her PhD in communication from the University of Southern California. Her research examines the politics of race, class, and gender within contemporary structures of media production and media education. Her current work centers on screenwriters' fights for fair labor practices and climate justice.

Gloria González-López holds the C. B. Smith Sr. Centennial Chair #1 in US-Mexico Relations and is a Professor of Sociology at the University of Texas at Austin. She is the author of two books, *Family Secrets: Stories of Incest and Sexual Violence in Mexico* (New York University Press, 2015) and *Erotic Journeys: Mexican Immigrants and Their Sex Lives* (University of California Press, 2005). She is honored to have coedited *Bridging: How Gloria Anzaldúa's Life and Work Transformed Our Own* (University of Texas Press, 2011) in collaboration with AnaLouise Keating. She has published her academic work extensively in Spanish. Because of the kindness and generosity of students, colleagues, mentors, and supervisors, she received the 2021 Simon-Gagnon Lifetime Achievement Award and the 2022 Feminist

Scholar-Activist Award, both from the American Sociological Association, Sexualities Section and Sex & Gender Section, respectively. González-López teaches graduate and undergraduate courses examining feminist theory; sexuality and gender; sexual violence, trauma, and society; Mexican American and Mexican studies; and social inequality.

Nohely Guzmán is a ch'ixi feminist and anti-colonial PhD student in the Department of Geography at UCLA. She holds a master's degree in Latin American Studies from the University of Texas at Austin. With over a decade of activism and research in the Bolivian Amazon, her work focuses on Indigenous understandings of embodiment, intimacy, territoriality, and life-politics. Guzmán is the co-founder and current executive director of Jasy Renyhê, an anti-colonial feminist organization based in La Paz, Bolivia.

Jessennya Hernandez (she/her) is an Assistant Professor in the Department of Sociology at California State University, Northridge. Her research interests include race and racialization, gender and sexuality, liberatory practice and social justice, transnational and decolonial feminism, Black feminist thought and women of color feminisms, and queer theory and politics. Hernandez is the child of Mexican immigrants and was born and raised in the Inland Empire of Southern California. Along with teaching, researching, and publishing about the region, Hernandez also organizes with Black and Brown working-class folks in a grassroots mutual aid collective.

Mabel E. Hernandez is an Assistant Research Professor at the Center for Education, Identity and Social Justice at USC. She received a PhD from USC's Rossier School of Education. As a first-generation Latina scholar, her mixed-methods research focuses on college students' experience on campus, a sense of belonging, issues related to religion and diversity, and students' intersectional identities such as race, religion, and gender.

Theresa E. Hernandez (she/they) earned a PhD from the Urban Education Policy program at the University of Southern California with a Rossier Dissertation of Distinction award. Her research combines intersectionality and organizational theories to examine the design and implementation of diversity, equity, and inclusion (DEI) work in academia. In particular, Hernandez has explored how participation in grant-funded higher education DEI initiatives manifest or impede intersectional equity, institutional transformation, and social justice. Their work examines how systemic and organizational processes impact the day-to-day lived experiences of women of color and other marginalized populations in higher education.

Nathalia P. Hernández Ochoa (she/her/ella) is an Assistant Professor at Kean University in the Department of Political, Social and Cultural Sciences. A first-generation Salvadoran scholar, she is an interdisciplinary decolonial feminist researcher whose work explores visual ethnography, storytelling, and poetry. Her research focuses on Indigenous, mestiza, and Afro-descendant women's struggles and contributions to social change in Latin America. She investigates intersecting forms of violence based on gender, race, class, and sexuality in Central America and healing processes through ancestral knowledge. She believes in artivism (art + activism) as a powerful tool for social transformation and collective healing.

Briceida Hernandez-Toledo (she/they) is a doctoral student in Chicana/o and Central American Studies at the University of California, Los Angeles. Born and raised in Las Vegas, Nevada, they work at the intersections of ethnic studies, geography, and gender studies. Informed by their positionality, their research focuses on Latinx communities and space formation in Las Vegas. They want to uncover the rich experiences and meaning that local Latinx residents give to Las Vegas, a place that is understood solely as a site for reckless pleasure and leisure. Ultimately, Hernandez-Toledo hopes to advocate for activism, feminism, social justice, and self-care within and outside academia.

Leigh-Anna Hidalgo (she/her) is an Assistant Professor of Ethnicity, Race, and Migration at Yale University. Her research focuses on immigration, informal economies, urban space, and labor movements, drawing on seven years of ethnographic and digital humanities work with leaders of the Los Angeles Street Vendor Campaign. Her current book project, *Un Movimiento Caminando* (working title), is under contract with Duke University Press. Born in Los Angeles to a Salvadoran father and an American mother, she spent her childhood between Guatemala and El Salvador during the 1980s and 1990s. She currently lives in Connecticut with her husband and children.

Gizem N. Iscan (she/her/hers) is an adjunct lecturer in Women and Gender Studies at Hunter College and at Brooklyn College, CUNY. Iscan holds a BA in American culture and literature from Istanbul University and an MA in English from Brooklyn College, CUNY. She is a PhD candidate in the American Culture Studies program at Bowling Green State University, where she holds a dual advanced certificate in women's and gender studies and ethnic studies. Her research, peer-reviewed articles, and poetry focus on the intersections of gender, migration and immigration, identity construction, borderlands, and femicides.

Maissa Khatib is a Palestinian American research scholar at the College of Health Solutions, Arizona State University, and an adjunct research associate at Valleywise Health. Her research focuses on migration, health, gender, and health disparities. Khatib received a PhD in interdisciplinary health sciences at the University of Texas at El Paso, providing her with a solid foundation for designing interventions and conducting comprehensive research. Driven by a commitment to addressing complex issues affecting marginalized populations, particularly underrepresented women, Khatib continues to support the voices and rights of these communities, striving for a more equitable and inclusive world.

Lucia P. Leon (she/her) is an Assistant Professor of Latin American and Latina/o Studies and Social Justice at Dominican University of California. She is a scholar of migration, trained in the fields of ethnic studies, sociology, and gender studies. Inspired by her personal and political commitments to immigrant communities, Leon's research focuses on US immigration law, Latina/o/x immigrants and families, and sociolegal inequalities that shape immigrants' everyday lives. She earned a PhD from the University of California, Los Angeles, where her scholarship analyzed legal consciousness and legalization among undocumented and recently legalized Latino young adults.

Ana López Hurtado (she/they) is a Colombian poet and doctoral candidate in Latin American Studies at the University of Texas at Austin. She holds a master's degree in European, Latin American, and comparative literatures from the University of Cambridge, a graduate certificate in Epistomologies of the South from CLACSO, and a BA in Literary Studies from Pontificia Universidad Javeriana. Her research explores the affective dimensions of paid domestic work in Colombia from a decolonial feminist perspective. Her poetry book *Aquí donde tiemblo* (2021) was published by Sincronía Casa Editorial. Her work has appeared in *Rio Grande Review*, *Círculo de Poesía*, *Hipogrifo*, and *Portal*.

Michaela A. Machicote is a scholar, poet, and visual artist whose work explores Black feminist thought, state violence, and community resistance. She has coauthored research on state violence in the US and Brazil, and contributed writing on Black Brazilian trans feminisms and knowledge production. Her book-in-progress, *Jezebel by Another Name*, examines how Black women in Chicago resist carceral systems through everyday acts of care, refusal, and survival. Her work is grounded in lived experience, Black motherhood, and the politics of identity and power.

Paola Cossermelli Messina is a PhD candidate in Ethnomusicology at Columbia University. Her research explores Arab music in Brazil alongside questions of memory and belonging. Previous works include an oral history of Iranian musicians in exile and an experimental ethnography of a jukebox in a lesbian bar. A fellow for Columbia's Heyman Center for the Humanities and Center for Palestine Studies (2021–2022), she edited *No Place / لا مكان*, a series of radio plays by Palestinian playwrights. Beyond academia, she is the senior producer of the Arab Studies Institute's podcast *Status / الوضع*.

Kiana T. Murphy is a scholar-artist and Assistant Professor of American Studies at Brown University. Her creative and scholarly work centers Black speculative aesthetics, Black and queer feminisms, visual culture, and Black women's archives. Murphy is currently working on a book manuscript that bridges the speculative methods of Black girlhood studies and the archives of twentieth- and twenty-first-century Black women writers and theorists. Her work is published or forthcoming in *The Black Scholar*, *American Quarterly*, *MELUS*, and elsewhere, and has been supported by the Huntington Library, the National Endowment for the Humanities (NEH) Institutes, and the Institute for Citizens & Scholars.

Nnenna Odim (she/her) is Igbo from Biafra, Arawakan from the Bahamas, and Black American from Chicago. With experiences as a multiage early childhood teacher in the Caribbean, South America, and Turtle Island (United States), Odim studies community expertise and storytelling by examining early learning environments and their related power dynamics. Drawing on the intersections across Black geographies, Indigenous and place-based studies, ethnography, and early childhood education, she is interested in child brilliance. She has published work about inequity in early childhood studies, action-based research, storytelling in communities, and futuristic visions in early childhood.

Divana Olivas is an Inclusive Excellence Postdoctoral Fellow in Chicana/o/x Studies at the University of New Mexico. Olivas's research is situated at the intersections of Chicana/o/x studies, critical food studies, New Mexico regional history, and social movements in the twentieth and twenty-first centuries. Her work is interdisciplinary, using archival research, oral histories, and visual and cultural analysis to explore the individual and collective expressions racialized communities express through food. Originally from New Mexico, she was raised by Mexican-immigrant parents in El Cerro and also considers Namiquipa, Chihuahua, home.

Joanna B. Perez (she/her) is a Professor of Sociology at California State University, Dominguez Hills. As a proud daughter of Guatemalan immigrants and a first-generation scholar, she is committed to engaging in social justice work. Her research lies at the intersection of immigration, family, education, and social movements. Her work examines how systems of power and inequality shape the social conditions of immigrant communities. She holds a BA in sociology with a double minor in labor and workplace studies and civic engagement from the University of California, Los Angeles, and an MA and PhD in sociology from the University of Illinois Urbana-Champaign.

Jyoti Puri is a Professor of Sociology at Boston University. She has written widely on sexuality, state, nation, and gender, and she is currently working on a Guggenheim-funded project, Migrant Death: Race, Religion and National Belonging. She has coedited a special issue, "Feminist Mournings" for the journal *Meridians: Feminism, Race, Transnationalism* and has published a critical genealogy of the sociology of death, "The Forgotten Lives of the Sociology of Death," in *The American Sociologist*.

Blanca A. Ramirez is an Assistant Professor in the Department of Sociology at the University of Texas at Austin. Her primary goal as a researcher is to theorize how state structures like law and policing shape group understandings of the legal system, perceptions of agency, and the larger consequences of these dynamics. Her multiple award-winning works have been featured in *Social Problems* and the *Journal of Ethnic and Migration Studies*. This work has been supported by the National Science Foundation Graduate Research Fellowship, the Ford Foundation Predoctoral Fellowship program, and the Haynes Foundation Fellowship.

Iris M. Ramirez is a Salvadoran scholar and recent PhD graduate from UCLA's Department of Chicana/o and Central American Studies. An incoming ethnic studies instructor at Butte College, she does research focusing on Central American history, migration, and labor in Los Angeles, with a particular emphasis on the experiences of Latina/o garment workers. Her dissertation, grounded in firsthand narratives, honors her mother's journey as a garment worker and amplifies the sacrifices and voices of those confronting systemic inequality to build better futures for their families.

Jingqiu Ren received a PhD in sociology from Texas A&M University in 2023. She has professional experience in both the private and public sectors. Her research interests focus on social demography, spatial analysis and applications, population health and healthcare organizations, and labor and workforce analysis.

Sara Rezvi (she/they) is an Assistant Professor at Dominican University and a former middle and high school mathematics teacher. Their research explores the intersections of teachers who work from a critical mathematics orientation. Working in community with other critical and activist scholars, Rezvi has published in research journals including the *Journal of Urban Mathematics Education* (JUME). She is a first-generation, disabled, queer, and Muslim American immigrant born in Karachi, Pakistan, and raised in Chicago.

Liliana V Rodriguez is an Assistant Professor of Chicanx/Latinx Studies in the Department of Ethnic Studies at the University of California, Berkeley. Rodriguez earned undergraduate and master's degrees from the University of Texas at Austin and a doctoral degree from the University of California, Santa Barbara. Her areas of interest include Latina/o sociology, international migration, immigrant youth, ethnographic research methods, and studies of race and ethnicity. Her current work centers the experiences of adolescent arrivals as they navigate life in the United States during contested political times.

Meztli Yoalli Rodríguez Aguilera (she/they) is an Assistant Professor of Latin American and Latino Studies at DePaul University. They earned their PhD in Latin American Studies at the University of Texas at Austin and specializes in environmental racism, ecological grief, mestizaje, state violence, and anti/decolonial feminism in Latin America, with their work intersecting race, gender, environment, and affect. They were awarded the 2021 National Women Studies Association and University of Illinois Press (NWSA/UIP) First Book Prize. Their book manuscript (forthcoming from University of Illinois Press) is tentatively titled *Grieving Geographies, Mourning Waters: Race, Gender, and Environment on the Coast of Oaxaca, Mexico*.

Sharmila Rudrappa is a Professor of Sociology and department head at the University of Illinois, Chicago. She has written widely on South Asian immigration into the United States, high-wage labor migrations, domestic violence, and markets in assisted reproductive services. She is author of two award-winning monographs, *Ethnic Routes to Becoming American: Indian Immigrants and the Cultures of Citizenship* (Rutgers University Press, 2004) and *Discounted Life: The Price of Global Surrogacy in India* (New York University Press, 2015). Currently, she is working on three research projects on high-wage workers in India and fertility decision-making, global markets in human hair, and the social ecologies of viral tropical diseases. Rudrappa teaches graduate and undergraduate seminars in feminist theory, labor, migration, and reproductive justice.

Jessica L. Sánchez Flores (she/her/ella) is a Nahua-descent scholar from Guerrero, Mexico. She is an Assistant Professor in the Department of Spanish and Portuguese at Colorado College. Her research centers primarily on the cultural production by Indigenous artists and creators from Mexico and the diaspora. This research is in dialogue with methodologies and theories from cultural and literary studies, critical Indigenous studies, and women and gender studies. In sum, the work of Sánchez Flores showcases and brings forward the voices and presence of Indigenous artists as weavers of their own stories who are thriving.

Karina Santellano (she/her/ella) is an Assistant Professor of Sociology at the T. Denny Sanford School of Social and Family Dynamics at Arizona State University. She studies and teaches the sociology of race and ethnicity, immigration, class, work/occupations/entrepreneurship, and urban sociology. Santellano's book project examines Latino/a/x entrepreneurship pathways, experiences, and meaning making, particularly via the site of Latino/a/x-owned and -inspired coffee shops in Southern California. Her research and writing appear in academic journals and public outlets and have received support from the Society for the Study of Social Problems (SSSP), the American Sociological Association (ASA), Sociologists for Women in Society (SWS), and other entities.

Shenée L. Simon is a fierce feminist and founder of S.H.E. Collective, Inc., an organization advancing women's peace and security (WPS) for BIPOC girls and women, centering spirituality, wellness, and environment. She is a 2024 Art of Wellbeing Fellow, 2022 Women's Earth Alliance Accelerator Fellow, and 2020 WCAPS Fellow. Simon chairs the Texas chapters of the Truman National Security Project and WCAPS. She is pursuing theological studies at Brite Divinity School and holds degrees in women and gender studies, human resources, and nonprofit management. She is a proud army spouse and homeschooling mama of four.

Christen A. Smith is a Professor of Anthropology and Black Studies at Yale University. She is the author of the book *Afro-Paradise: Blackness, Violence, and Performance in Brazil* (University of Illinois Press, 2016), coeditor of the book *The Dialectic Is in the Sea: The Black Radical Thought of Beatriz Nascimento* (Princeton University Press, 2023), and co-editor of Black *Feminist Constellations: Dialogue and Translation across the Americas* (University of Texas Press, 2023). In 2017, she started Cite Black Women, a transnational initiative that brings awareness to society's gross tendency to ignore Black women's intellectual contributions and not to cite Black women inside and outside of the academy. Smith teaches courses on African diaspora anthropology; gender, race, violence, and embodiment; global Black feminisms; and violence, trauma, and memory.

Wesley Stevens is an Assistant Professor in the School of Journalism and Mass Communications at the University of South Carolina. Her research explores the regulation of Black identity and its commodification through neoliberal discourses and consumer subjectivities. Much of her work examines how Black creators navigate digital platforms and how discriminatory algorithms shape discourses about racial identity. When she needs to take a break and regroup, she turns to her favorite cartoons, enjoys experimenting in the kitchen, and practices creative writing to sharpen her focus and refresh her spirit.

Fatima Suarez is an Assistant Professor of Sociology at the University of Nevada, Las Vegas. Her areas of specialization include gender and masculinities, intersectionality, families, and Latina/o sociology. Her forthcoming book, *Latino Fathers: What Shapes and Sustains Their Parenting* (NYU Press), explores the social factors that shape, sustain, and undermine Latino men's parenting. She is a first-generation scholar.

Joseph Emil Tibiru (he/they) is an immigrant from Ghana. His time at the University of Texas at Austin began in 2017 and ended in 2022. He graduated with a bachelor's degree in African and African Diaspora Studies as well as Women's and Gender Studies. Moreover, he earned a master's degree the following year in Women's and Gender Studies. With great thanks to his professors and mentors, he was able to construct his thesis, titled "Vision of Love: Envisioning the possibilities of a Black TRANSformation." This work explored the theory and praxis of abolition and placed it as a contender for the liberation of our most subjected in society: Black transgender women. He is currently a sixth-grade English language arts teacher with Harmony Public Schools in Houston.

Amira Yaem Trevino (she/her) is a PhD candidate in Counseling Psychology at the University of Utah. Trevino holds an MEd and is passionate about equitable access to quality education and trauma healing practices. She aims to elevate oppressed voices to inform services through research, therapy, and writing. Her research interests include impacts of relational trauma (e.g., childhood sexual abuse) on cultural identity development and cultural conversations in psychotherapy. In 2022 she contributed to the book *Children and Trauma: Critical Perspectives for Meeting the Needs of Diverse Educational Communities*. Her hope is to use her lived experiences and education to empower others in their healing.

Mercedes Valadez is an Associate Professor in the Division of Criminal Justice at California State University, Sacramento. Valadez earned a BA in criminal justice from California State University, Bakersfield; an MS in criminology and certificate of advanced studies in homeland security from California State University, Fresno; and a PhD in criminology and criminal justice from Arizona State University. Her work investigates disparities and discrimination in criminal justice outcomes based on race/ethnicity, nationality, and immigration status. Her work is published in *The Sociological Quarterly* and *Journal of Latinos and Education*.

Pavithra Vasudevan (she/they) is an Assistant Professor of African and African Diaspora Studies and Women's, Gender, and Sexuality Studies at the University of Texas at Austin and a cofounder of the UT Austin Faculty and Staff for Justice in Palestine. Vasudevan's book in progress, *A Toxic Alchemy: Race and Waste in Industrial Capitalism*, is a geopoetic catalyst testifying to the fragmentation of life under racial-colonial capitalism. Vasudevan employs performance, film, poetry, and creative writing methods to reimagine scholarship as storytelling. She is a practitioner of move-ment forms including Bharatanatyam, Odissi, Aikido, and Yoga; a student of Qawwali and Hindusthani music and poetry; and a mama to a rainbow unicorn. https://pavithravasudevan.com.

Michelle Velasquez-Potts is an Assistant Professor of Gender and Sexu-ality Studies at Santa Clara University. Her research areas include feminist and queer theory, science and technology studies, critical prison stud-ies, and disability studies. Her monograph *Suspended Animation: The Rise of Force-Feeding in Carceral Times*, under contract with the University of North Carolina Press, examines how state power makes specific use of the feeding tube and the practice of force-feeding to control both bodily life and death among incarcerated people. Disability justice and abolitionist praxis guide her work inside and outside the classroom.

Anahí Viladrich, a native of Argentina, is an interdisciplinary social science scholar and public health specialist whose work focuses on international migration, gender, and culture. The author of more than sixty peer-reviewed publications, her book *More Than Two to Tango: Argentine Tango Immigrants in New York City* received an award from the Association of Latina/o and Latinx Anthropologists of the American Anthropological Association. A full professor at Queens College (sociology and anthropol-ogy), she is also affiliated with the Graduate Center of the City University of New York (CUNY). Viladrich serves as academic director of the CUNY Faculty Fellowship Publication Program.

Cynthia D. Villarreal is an Assistant Professor of Educational Leader-ship at Northern Arizona University. Her scholarship interrogates issues of racial equity for racially minoritized faculty and students in higher educa-tion. She uses interdisciplinary theories to interrogate policies, structures, and cultures that are rooted in complicated racial histories and deeply held assumptions. She holds a PhD in urban education policy from the Univer-sity of Southern California. During her time at USC, she was the founding president of the Latina PhDs at USC student organization.

Rachel Yim received a PhD from the University of Washington and most recently was a visiting Assistant Professor of Asian American Studies at Scripps College. Her dissertation, "Speculating on the Terms of 'Small, Foreign, and Female': Reimagining the Temporality of Technology Through Asian American Cultural Production," examines how technology is understood through progress, using a speculative framework to instead imagine a future that centers the materiality of an economy that is predicated on racialized and gendered labor. She is currently working on a novel about love and motherhood.